eMarketing

Seth Godin

D1418248

A PERIGEE BOOK

Dedicated to my friends Julie Maner, Megan O'Connor, Lisa DiMona, Carol Markowitz, Karen Watts, Jen Gniady, Amy Winger, Bruce Cota, Robin Dellabough, and Anthony Schneider.

Thank you for sharing the vision.

Perigee Books
are published by
The Berkley Publishing Group
200 Madison Avenue
New York, NY 10016

Copyright © 1995 by Seth Godin Productions
All rights reserved. This book, or parts thereof,
may not be reproduced in any form without permission.
Published simultaneously in Canada

First edition: March 1995

Library of Congress Cataloging-in-Publication Data

Godin, Seth.
    eMarketing / Seth Godin. — 1st ed.
        p.   cm.
    "A Perigee book."
    ISBN 0-399-51904-1
    1. Marketing—Data processing.   2. Database marketing.
3. Teleshopping   4. Internet Advertising   I. Title
HF5415. 125.G63   1995
    658.8'4—dc20   94-23733
                                                        CIP

Book design by Karen Engelmann
Cover Design: Darrin Ehardt

Printed in the United States of America
1 2 3 4 5 6 7 8 9 10

Acknowledgments

This book couldn't have been written without the help, insight and contributions of many people. We were fortunate to have enthusiastic support from individuals and organizations in every industry we profiled. Special thanks are due to: Don Peppers and Martha Rogers, the consultants and writers who first described database marketing in *The One to One Future*; Jim Rosenfield, President of Rosenfield and Associates and a widely known expert in the database marketing field; Mary Cronin, author of *Doing Business on the Internet*; Michael Strangelove, publisher of the *Internet Buisiness Journal* and author of *How to Advertise on the Internet*.

Thanks also go to: Maury Kauffman, Managing Partner, The Kauffman Group; Tom Barrett, President, Touch Tone Services; Sarah Stambler, Editor, *Marketing with Technology News*; Brian Cavoli, Instant Information; Edward Liss, President, MarketFax; Chris Moon, President of Techno Marketing; Jill Thomas, Ion Development; William Carlson, RTC Industries; Steve Dworman, author of the *Infomercial Marketing Report*, Tim Hawthorne, President of Hawthorne Communications, and Bill Thompson, author of *Inside Infomercials*. Chris Locke gave us help along the way, as did Sam Decker.

Special thanks to Regis McKenna, President of Regis McKenna International. Regis has been a visionary and a role model of mine for years. Jay Levinson, the original guerrilla marketer, our guru and occasional co-author was the godfather of this book. It would never have been written without Jay's insight, encouragement and enthusiasm.

Thanks to Karen Engelmann for another great book design, and to the extraordinary staff at Seth Godin Productions who contributed to this book: Julie Maner, Carol Markowitz, Megan O'Connor, Karen Watts, Lisa DiMona, Jen Gniady, Amy Winger, Bruce Cota, Robin Dellabough and Anthony Schneider. Thanks also to Geoffrey Klein.

Behind every good book is a great editor, and this one is no exception. Without the vision and determination of our editor, Julie Merberg, it's unlikely you'd be holding this in your hand today. Julie is a whirlwind, filled with positive energy and a sense of mission. She's also great to work with. We're also indebted to Aileen Boyle, John Duff, Liz Perl, Robert Welsh, Susan Petersen, Corinda Carford, Sabra Elliott, and Donna Gould for their help and enthusiasm. Sabrina Farber at Barnes & Noble helped give us perspective on the real world as well.

Contents

Foreword

"The future is not what it used to be."
Paul Valéry

Paradigm shifts don't come along very often. But when they do occur, they change all the rules. Because they're so rare, most of us don't recognize a paradigm shift while it's happening. And then by the time we recognize it, it's too late.

The invention of the supermarket led to a paradigm shift. So did the success of the car and the creation of the suburbs. Think of how your parents could have profited if they had seen these seismic shifts coming.

eMarketing is about the greatest paradigm shift of this century. It revolves around two critical issues:

1. *Companies can have dialogues with large numbers of individuals at very little cost.*

2. *Companies can keep track of individual habits, estimate individual desires, and work to satisfy them.*

Over the next few years, there will be countless bumps on the Information Superhighway. Companies will fold, billions of dollars will be lost. The naysayers will call it all a fad, and turn back to their traditional businesses.

The naysayers are wrong. The changes occurring as you read this are profound, and they will fundamentally change the way business is conducted. Consumers will find it far easier to spend money, and astute companies will find it far easier to generate a profit.

Some of the technologies described in this book are crude at best. They're the equivalent of silent movies in the evolution of the motion picture. But they work, they generate profits, and businesses are using them to great effect.

You can't profit from this revolution until you get yourself involved. The learning curves are steep, there are risks, and the payback may not occur for months or even years. But the entrepreneurs who take advantage of the changes happening today will establish beachheads in the markets of tomorrow.

Let us know what you find on the Information Superhighway. Maybe we'll see you along the way.

Seth Godin
seth@sgp.com

INTRODUCTION

WELCOME TO THE THIRD MARKETING EPOCH

We're at the dawn of a new age of marketing — the Third Marketing Epoch. It's an age in which smaller businesses can easily outmaneuver large ones. Where once large companies will falter and die. An age in which astute entrepreneurs can make astounding profits.

The paradigm of business is changing for the first time in more than a hundred years. This irrevocable change will affect the way we buy and sell goods and services. It will alter the structure of business forever, and companies that ignore the shift do so at their own risk.

Like all true paradigm shifts, this change will create mammoth opportunities for those who see it in time. When the rules change, the companies that dominated the old markets will have little advantage. These large companies will be hindered by inertia and blinded by their previous success — most of them won't survive the transition. Just as the railroads were decimated by the shift to air travel fifty years ago, and typewriter and word processor manufacturers never recovered from the birth of the personal computer (remember Wang, Olivetti, and Lanier?), this paradigm shift will create countless winners and losers.

The First Epoch

During the First Epoch, which lasted more than 4,000 years, people bought products and services from their neighbors. Anyone who could grow corn, shoe a horse, or make a candle could open a business, and it was easy to succeed. Society was local, and commerce was needs-based. Virtually everyone was a small businessperson, and each person lived and died by his reputation.

While it was easy to go into "business," it was difficult to make much money unless you were a banker or a king. John the corner barber built his reputation on the quality of his haircuts and his conversation. He never aspired to be rich. One can only cut so many heads of hair in a day. This limit on the number of hours in the day meant that few farmers, butchers, or tailors were rich.

In this First Epoch, the consumer was king. If a few villagers took their business elsewhere, the blacksmith couldn't feed his family. If a wealthy customer wanted a particular type of shawl or a certain spice, the small businessman would do everything he could to fill the request. Shopkeepers and craftsmen knew each customer by name, and relationships lasted for generations.

The Second Epoch

The Second Epoch began with the Industrial Revolution, and came into its own at the beginning of this century. With the birth of the chain store and the Sears catalog, the same product could be sold not just in one store, but in hundreds of stores nationwide. Society became non-local, and commerce became wants-based. Incomes rose, and the desires of consumers rose with them. A successful product could generate millions of dollars in profit. Naturally, manufacturers were ecstatic.

Several critical shifts in power took place during this epoch. Merchants gained power, because they could decide what products were carried in their stores. Producers gained power, because their brand names and their advertising drew consumers into the store. The individual consumer, however, lost power. Suddenly, his particular needs mattered a lot less.

The years immediately after World War II were the glory days of the Second Epoch. Supermarkets, shopping malls, and television advertising created a culture that could be addressed en masse, rather than individually. It was difficult for a small businessperson to break into the rich world of mass marketing. Companies such as General Motors, General Foods, and Radio Shack spent enormous amounts on mass consumer advertising. By capturing market share, these companies generated profits and prevented new competitors from entering the marketplace.

When small businesses occasionally did this — Apple, Nike, and Volkswagen come to mind — they made headlines. They were the exception to the rule.

Breaking into the market wasn't easy, or cheap. Steve Jobs and Steve Wozniak started Apple Computer in a garage on a shoestring. But they didn't capture America's attention until they spent $750,000 to air a commercial during the Super Bowl. They had to get their product into 4,000 stores nationwide, and onto the cover of 17 magazines in one month, before they could turn an interesting hobby into a truly profitable company.

When we think of marketing, the activities of the Second Epoch usually come to mind: gray-flanneled men on Madison Avenue, mysterious food-testing labs run by fictional people like Betty Crocker, and huge assembly lines churning out slightly inferior products. The much-maligned mass-marketer was a target for critics, as intellectuals yearned for the personal touch and high quality of the nearby craftsmen.

The Third Epoch

In the 1990s, computer networks, fax machines, sophisticated telephony, and cable television have transformed the marketing landscape. The Third Epoch has arrived.

For the first time since the invention of money, we can deliver products and services directly to millions of people — without countless middlemen, huge advertising budgets, and the tremendous risks of mass marketing.

In many ways, it's a lot like the First Epoch. Once again, it's vital to reach individual consumers and satisfy their desires. Companies succeed by providing personal service and high-quality products to very specific markets. But today, those markets aren't local. They're global.

Consider the way we buy flowers. In 1800, during the First Epoch, you bought tulips from the merchant on the corner, who had purchased them from a local hothouse. The hothouse didn't have very many customers, since there was no efficient way to ship the flowers across the country.

By 1970, at the height of the Second Epoch, FTD had cornered the flower market. You could pick a bouquet out of a catalog at a local florist shop. The florist sent the order by wire to another florist closer to your friend. FTD took a cut on the transaction, which it used for its multi-million-dollar national ad campaign. FTD chose a limited number of bouquets that would appeal to the maximum number of people — ensuring a level of quality, but also guaranteeing a level of mediocrity.

In 1994, at the dawn of the Third Epoch, PC Flowers sells more than $10 million worth of flowers a year, generating well over a million dollars in annual profit for its founder. PC Flowers has no store, no catalog, and only eight employees. It sells bouquets over the Prodigy computer network. The company uses the FTD network to deliver flowers efficiently, but has done away with expensive overhead. Prodigy offers PC Flowers a market of two million potential shoppers. Having become FTD's largest single outlet, they're now in a position to change the way FTD does business.

Even better, look at Calyx & Corrolla. Call their toll-free number and order an exquisite bouquet of orchids or lilies. The order is transmitted by computer directly to an appropriate grower, who ships the flowers the next day, by Federal Express, directly to the recipient. Calyx keeps detailed records of each customer, and uses this data to expand its offerings and the sales it makes to each customer.

Not only are traditional businesses succeeding in this new era, technology has opened up all kinds of new business opportunities for savvy entrepreneurs.

Neil Shapiro, for instance, serves more than 150,000 people every day from his spare bedroom. His job didn't even exist 20 years ago. He moderates twenty forums, or discussion areas, on an online computer network called CompuServe. He makes sure members have easy access to files, advice, and companionship. In exchange for his services, CompuServe pays Neil a handsome commission. To earn his living, Neil doesn't even have to leave home.

Barriers Are Falling, Yet Others Are Being Built

The barriers that prevented competitors from entering the marketplace during the Second Epoch are rapidly falling. Calyx & Corrolla doesn't compete with FTD or the local florist. Real estate isn't nearly as important as it once was. The size of your marketing budget isn't the factor it used to be.

At the same time, other competitive barriers are rising, and quickly. Relationships with customers are precious, and marketers who have the foresight to establish them aren't going to surrender them easily. Once a consumer has established a bulletin board account, or a database at the local grocery store, or a preference list at the local record store, it will take more than a 20%-off sale to entice that customer to switch.

Astute marketers have realized this and begun the race to establish customer relationships. The companies that build mutually beneficial relationships with consumers will profit mightily, and will build barriers that will last for decades.

This book discusses the technology that makes the Third Epoch possible. More important, it tells you how you can use these tools to your advantage.

The Third Epoch is still young, and excellent opportunities are still available. Now is the time to build this era's version of IBM, Ford, or American Express — before another entrepreneur rushes in to serve your niche.

REGIS MCKENNA ON THE FUTURE OF MARKETING

Regis McKenna is the founder and president of Regis McKenna, Inc., one of the country's leading technology marketing and public relations firms. Best known for its work with Apple, RMI has been on the cutting edge of the marketing revolution for years. These comments are excerpts from a speech McKenna gave at the Advanstar conference in Chicago in 1994.

There are three changes raging through our environment that are going to radically alter the way we do business.

The first change is diversity. In 1982, there were about 80 television stations in all of Europe. Today, there are almost 900. There are more automobile companies today than there were 25 years ago. There are more cookie companies; more ice cream companies. You name it, there's more of it. The average grocery store in America has gone from 10,000 items on the shelf to about 25,000 items in the last decade alone. There's diversity of products, goods, and services, which means more competition, but also diversity in our society. By the end of this decade, a majority of Californians will be minorities. There are about 250 different languages spoken in California right now.

Choice. We have more choice in our lives. If you went out to buy a personal computer, you have a choice of 1,000 brands. If you went out to buy an automobile, you have 650 different brands. If you went out to buy mustard, you have 1,000 different brands of mustard on the American marketplace.

Speed is the next change. The pace of life is faster. We don't seem to have much time much anymore. I remember several years ago talking about the 4-day work week and the 4-hour work day. And we all looked forward to that day, that somehow or other we would get to a stage where we would have this 4-day work week. It would be wonderful. And instead we find ourselves on call 24 hours a day. We have fax machines in our hotel rooms, cellular phones in our automobiles and briefcases. And so the day is now filled with communication.

And the next thing is mobility. We are more mobile as a society. One hundred years ago when the immigrants came to this country, they never expected to go back to the old country, to the land of their birth. Today, people come to this country, and even people of low income go back and forth constantly. We are finding ourselves more mobile as a society. And people are more willing today, because of job situations, to pull up stakes and move anywhere where there's a job.

Finally, through all of this, we're full of information, we're more aware, we have instantaneous access to almost anything around the globe, yet we're more discontented as a people. And this is not just the discontent of us in this country. There are over 50 ethnic conflicts on the European continent, and in fact we may see that all of the individualization that information and awareness creates may not just create this homogenous world that we all thought was going to happen, but indeed a more conflicted world.

It's my thesis that society's institutions — business, government, education, and so forth — are built on the models of the technology of the era. The technology of the Industrial Revolution was mass production. That also happened to be the way we designed our education systems. We put children into rows, we give them all the same textbooks, we give them the same tests, IQ tests, move them up at the same levels, grade everybody the same way, and any deviation you expel, which turns out to be a manufacturing term.

In our organizations we did the same thing; we divided management and labor. It's not efficient to have people thinking and doing, so we divided thinking and doing. We created a design box, a manufacturing box, a marketing box, a sales box, a quality box, and a customer box. Each person in those boxes was given a job description and levels within those. You passed things off. It wasn't your job to design the process. You worried about your box. Recently we found out, in the last decade, that quality belonged in every box, and it shook everybody up. This is a revolution, to think that everybody's job was quality. That used to be the guy in the quality box's job, and if you had a problem with quality, you fired that person.

So we are different today because the technology models are different. In the

Industrial Revolution, the model of mass production was largely controlled by collaboration between large institutions and government. If you look at the telegraph, and television, radio, the automobile — you had to get a license to operate all those things. And you had to have government involvement in the early stages of these activities to allow that technology to move progressively through society. The automobile, which was invented in the 1890s and mass-produced in about 1914, didn't really change us as people until the 1950s or 60s when the superhighways were created by government agencies.

So technology was very highly controlled by these large institutions and by government involvement. We had regulated institutions, and then eventually we saw social change. But the world is changing fast. The average home in America 25 years ago had 25 fractional horsepower motors. Today, the average home has well over 100 microchips. My car has 56 in it. Take a look at the impact of technology. Twenty-five years ago, there weren't 25,000 computers installed anywhere in the world. Today, we sell about 50,000 computers a day. And now you have 60 million homes in America that have computers in them. And you see the growth of technology to the extent that we now have about 150 million computers installed around the world.

So the technology moves rapidly and diffuses into society almost instantaneously. Do any of you have a license to operate your computer? There are 25 million people on the Internet, adding a million people every month. You don't have to have a license to operate it. There are millions of fax machines out there. You don't have to have a license. You can hook up and talk to anyone, anywhere, without any interruption.

There are three factors that I see that are most important that are occurring because of technology. One is diversity — not only as people, but there are more places, things, services, and so forth, and if you look at the underlying cause of this, it has to do with programmability. Seventy-five percent of the machine tools that are produced in the United States produce 50 items or less at any one run. Fifty items or less at any one run! We've created the capability for an infinite variety of short runs, for programmability. If you have a computer processor in a product, you have a programmable system; it allows you to create an unlimited number of applications. So programmability underlies diversity, which gives the consumer more options. That means segmentation. We can now segment people into smaller groups, because we can program everything. We couldn't segment without programmability. We couldn't create these refinements without programmability.

The second thing is that we are now in a real-time world. It used to take maybe a week or two to confirm a transaction between London and Singapore. Now it takes less than a second. By the end of this decade, we will be able to move all of the information in all of the libraries of the world from point to point in under one second. So things happen instantaneously. We live in a real-time world. We have cut design cycles down from years to weeks and months. We have created programmable manufacturing that says you can now manufacture in shorter cycles, shorter runs. You don't want to have inventories anymore because the diversity around the globe will eat away at you. And so you can't afford the cost structure you used to have, so all organizations are downsizing in order to compete, to be faster on their feet. Let's have less inventory, so we're now saying, let's get that customer and the design people closer together.

The real-time world is upon us and coming even faster, and putting great demands on marketing, because your marketing is either enhanced by or limited by your design and production systems. If you can only mass-produce a particular product, then your marketing is already defined for you. If everything is customizable, if you have shorter product runs and you can customize things or program things, or you can provide variations, now we're talking about service. Because service means adding value, means working with customers to put feedback into the loop. We didn't need service 25 or 30 years ago because you just put the goods out there and there was less competition, in a mass-production environment.

Finally, the connections. In a highly diverse world that's real-time, you can't deal with it unless you're connected. You know, you've probably recently read about Ford Motor Company saying it was going to reorganize worldwide. Why do that? Well, you can't have 25 different locations buying parts, because you're in a competitive world today. You've got to have one region or two regions and they've got to be connected so you don't have 25 different inventories all duplicating efforts. With telecommunications and satellite technology, we can now connect the world and provide more efficiency.

Let me get back to diversity for a second. Here's a question for you: Who owns the largest market share of the personal computer business? The answer is "other." And who owns the largest market share of beer in the United States? It's not Budweiser, it's other. And cookies? It's not Nabisco. And fast foods? It's not McDonald's.

So think about what it does to the consumer. Forget about the manufacturer for a second. Think what happens to the consumer when the consumer has lots of choice. What happens when you have lots of choice is you can be fickle. When you have that many goods, you have diverse products on the shelves. When you have diverse products on the shelves, you have customer choice. Which means the decline of the megabrand.

So the major brands have been declining, and what brands are growing? Other. And they're growing because they can be produced cheaper, and we are more aware as a society, and we know that all soaps have phosphates in them, and they're all the same anyway. It's demanding more of us in terms of service, of understanding the consumer.

The Conference Board, a nationwide research organization, did a survey of about 300 senior executives from major corporations around the world a few years ago. And one of the conclusions was that they believed that the marketplace would continue to be full of surprises, that extrapolation of past business trends into the future is no longer possible. All business is based upon looking at the history and extrapolating the future. But the future has very little to do with the past these days.

Porsche lost 80% of its U.S. market share in the last five years. It wasn't because they have a bad product; they have a fairly good product. But what changed? The economic environment changed. The value of the deutschmark relative to the dollar. Gas guzzler tax and luxury tax added thousands of dollars to the cost. Social changes. The yuppies of the 80s now have kids and are buying minivans in less than a few years. The whole world around us, economic, political, social, and technological changes occurred so fast that the old institutions couldn't keep up. They weren't in touch.

That's why I think that what we're talking about is real-time marketing, the ability to create a dialogue with the marketplace on a real-time basis. And that means moving from a monologue to a dialogue. Most promotion today is a monologue. We sit down and we design advertising to tell our customers what it is that we want them to think. The language of advertising is, how many impressions did you make today? Again, that's the old industrial model, as if people are sitting there waiting for you to go ka-chung, ka-chung, ka-chung, ka-chung, and all of a sudden, a pattern is established in the brain that says this is brand, and therefore I buy it.

Madison Avenue says awareness leads to behavior change, but it isn't true. We're aware of a lot of things we never buy. If awareness led to behavior change, we wouldn't have any problems in anything. And the companies that advertised the most would be the most successful. In 1992, the largest advertisers in the computer industry were IBM and DEC. The largest advertiser in 1973 in personal computers was Texas Instruments. Where are they now?

IBM spent $100 million on PC Junior, and it failed. The average individual is exposed to 2500 commercials a day. If you watch television, as a normal human being, each year you are exposed to 200 hours of commercials. Awareness doesn't lead to behavior change. What leads to behavior change is a dialogue, is experience. We change through experiences.

I once heard George Burns giving a little talk, and the commentator was praising him and Gracie on their successes over the years, and George Burns very modestly said, "No, it wasn't us, it was our audience that made us successful over the years." And the commentator wanted to ignore him. But he said, "No, no, no, it was our audience that made us successful." And he went on to explain that what he did was that each night they would come up with different routines and play them to the audience, and they would watch for reactions. And when they got positive reactions, they would start building on those routines. And when they got a negative reaction, they'd drop them. That was real-time. They would sense, they would see, they would watch, they would feel, and then they would build. And that's what real-time marketing is all about. It's a dialogue of reaching the marketplace, sensing what's going on. It is not about trying to make a large number of impressions.

Marketing is a learning process. It is not something that you do, it is not simply a transaction in which you're doing all the action, you're not marketing at people, it becomes a learning process so that everything you do, you're gaining knowledge, in order to enhance, to build, to change, and to incrementally improve what you do. And everything in the future is going to be integrated with a service. Everything. Every product is going to become more servicelike. Because again, the way to differentiate yourself is no longer through the technology itself, but in the use of the technology to create a tool for improving service.

NEW RULES FOR NEW MEDIA

Redgate Communications Corporation, founded in 1985, builds revenue-generating interactive new media environments and manages multimedia content databases, delivering the content via custom publications, CD-ROM, cable, broadband, demand fax, private satellite networks, online services and digital shopping clubs.

Redgate publishes the Macintosh Product Registry, is an equity partner in the En Passant digital shopping venture, and created Interactive Information Networks. The company was recently acquired by America Online, Inc., and is headquartered in Vero Beach, Florida.

1. Market digitally.

Everything required to move from the industrial age solidly into the knowledge age has been invented and will soon be put into place. It's all digital. It's all for the purposes of storing, retrieving, and making personal use of vast amounts of information. Think digitally. Breathe digitally. Execute digitally. A new media basic.

2. Tell. Don't sell.

Marketing and advertising communications previously aimed for people's emotions. Now the target is your customer's savvy brain. Knowledge-age customers want to be well informed, not sold. They know what they're looking for. They're looking to see if you have it. If you do, tell them. Inform without hype, in depth and with utter accuracy.

3. Own the data.

Don't just gather it. It's your surefire route to that targeted customer. Among other things, owning the data means you own the right to receive data changes and updates as they happen, not weeks or months later, when it may be too late. And that same data, so long as it's focused and current and coincident with a sound strategy, enables you to hold the media accountable for marketing successes or failures. In fact, accountability is a prerequisite for anything that calls itself "new media."

4. Forget mindshare.

"Mindshare" was the coveted goal of industrial-age marketers who practiced one-way communication. New media, even at its most basic levels, is two-way communication. It's interactive. If you've done your homework, the customer ends up getting into your mind...into the heart and soul of your company. You aren't buying mindshare anymore. You're buying timeshare. You want your customer to want to spend time with you...as much time as possible.

5. Hide nothing.

In the industrial age, you told customers what you wanted them to hear when you wanted them to hear it. In the knowledge age, you have to tell them everything they want to know when they want to know it. New media like infomercials, CD-ROM, fax on demand, telephony, and online computer services give you all the time in the world to do just that. Use that time well. Hide nothing. Show everything.

6. Create for buyers.

Your customers are turning to new media because they're ready to buy and they're ready to buy now. Create accordingly. Create for buyers who want every ounce of information at their disposal. Create as if the purchase is imminent.

7. Create electronically.

Use the world of digital electronics as your layout pad. Realize that creativity today must often embrace text, graphics, video, audio and animation all at the same time, and will most often be an interactive creative product, with your customers having final say over how the information will be received and fed back to you. Make the shift now from the world of magic markers to the magic of computers.

8. Know your customer's nickname.

There's no such thing as the masses anymore. Targeting and segmenting is crucial. So recognize the uniqueness of each and every one of your customers.

Know ages, incomes, lifestyles, and habits, as usual. But also know how each customer is distinctly different from the next. Know their very special needs. Know them by their nicknames and the sizes of their socks if you have to. Then customize your message (and your product or service) to suit each one.

9. Forget your customer's fax number.

Not right away, though. The fax machine is still with us, but it won't be for long. Get ready for enhanced, sophisticated electronic mail — e-mail that can transmit not only text, but also graphics, audio, and video. It's coming.

10. Generate reality, not image.

Say good-bye to selling status. Stop thinking of your customers as people who buy just to have more and more possessions or the latest version. Now they're buying for the best reasons: to make life easier, safer, or more fun. They're buying because they have a genuine need, and that's because they've become more genuine as people. Get real. Nothing less will do.

11. Make acquiring knowledge fun.

New media is about satisfying your customer's hunger for knowledge. If you really want your customer to learn about everything you do and about everything you have to offer, take a lesson from the world's best teachers: make it fun. Make the process an enjoyable, rewarding experience. Your customer will reward you in return.

12. Make accessing knowledge easy.

Point. Click. Touch. Retrieve. If you make it any harder than that for your customers or associates to access knowledge, they won't. You have to think digitally and you have to function electronically in order to survive in the Knowledge Age, but your customers want the electronic aspects to be invisible. Make sure they are.

13. Be ready to transact.

New media is about having relationships with customers, even entire markets. Get ready to have millions of transactions each and every minute. The transactions can last but a few minutes or a few months, depending on the size and complexity of the need and the offering. A cable TV home shopping channel can respond to 20,000 calls a minute. Is your business up to handling that?

14. The customer is still right.

And the customer is still king. But in the age of knowledge and new media, the customer is also prime minister, president, chief information officer, and controller. Respect customers as you've never respected them before. Satisfy their very real need for quality, timely and accurate information, and value. Make your customers as central to your company's success as your employees.

15. Respect the earth.

New media connects us all in ways that save mountains of wear and tear on the planet as well as our nervous systems. Working and shopping from home, video conferencing and other telecommunications will save energy, reduce pollution, reduce highway accidents, and increase productivity to the tune of $37 billion in annual benefits by the year 2010. New media is a path to good citizenship.

16. New media is new revenue.

Information is valuable. And knowledge age customers want to know what your company knows. So the sooner you can turn your content and information into digital matter, the sooner it will earn you money. A number of digital content delivery vehicles now available make this possible, including 900 numbers, fax on demand, and CD-ROMs. You'll also want to consider owning a cable channel (or two) in the soon-to-be-delivered universe of 500-channel television. New media is costs turned into profits.

DATABASE MARKETING

USING TECHNOLOGY TO IMPROVE SERVICE IS THE HEART OF EVERY CONCEPT DISCUSSED IN THIS BOOK.

A recent Bain & Co. study confirms a commonsense hunch: increase customer loyalty and you'll increase profits. This theory doesn't surprise many people, but the sheer power of customer loyalty did. The study showed that a 5 percent increase in loyalty can translate into a 60 percent increase in profitability.

In this book, you'll learn about all kinds of technology-based tools that will increase the effectiveness of your marketing. But all of them are virtually useless without a brand-new attitude. Unless you sign on to the element of eMarketing that's the crux of it all — the basis for all of the other eMarketing concepts — you'll remain stuck in the mass-marketing 1950s.

e

What is this revolutionary concept? Database marketing. To succeed and grow in the 1990s and beyond, you have to use database marketing to identify your customers precisely, market to them efficiently, and keep them as loyal customers forever.

Database marketing focuses on gaining customer share rather than market share — that is, using information about the customer to sell more to that customer rather than selling to more customers. By shifting your focus to customer share, you can expand your profitability by increasing revenues from each repeat-buying customer.

Harlequin publishes romance novels that sell millions of copies a year. Yet a tiny fraction of the population actually buys these books — far less than 10 percent of all women account for 90 percent of the company's sales.

So why should Harlequin market to everyone? Ninety cents out of every dollar it spends on mass marketing is wasted.

This 90/10 rule is true for almost every business. In fact, many businesses are closer to 99/1 — one percent of the population accounts for 99 percent of their sales. Yet businesses continue to market to huge populations, constantly trying to acquire new customers when their old customers are more than willing to buy more from them.

Database marketing isn't just a game for the big guys with massive computer capabilities. The principles American Airlines uses to make certain air travelers "customers for life" are the same ones that can help the tiny pharmacy on Main Street stay alive in the shadow of Payless and Wal-Mart. New information technology puts the smallest database marketer on equal footing with the giants, helping her strengthen her position in the face of the fiercest competition.

The Death of the Mass Market

Although it's been around for years, database marketing is now vitally important because the mass market is collapsing. It's getting harder and harder to sell one standardized product to everybody. For the first time since the end of World War II, the individual customer is king. Early in this century, Henry Ford was able to build millions of cars (in any color — so long as it's black) and take advantage of mass production. With the consumer boom that extended into the 1970s, manufacturers were worried far more about meeting exploding consumer demand than about customizing their products for niche markets.

The boom sagged in the 1980s. The number of new products began to exceed the number of people clamoring to buy them. Store shelves are groaning from the enormous variety of products being offered. The choices are mind-boggling: the number of products in the average supermarket exceeds 30,000. In 1993 alone, a staggering 17,000 new products were introduced.

Years ago there were four or five beers to choose from at the corner store. Now there are dozens. Stores sell hot sauces from 40 countries. Shoes come in a rainbow of colors, at every price point from $3 to $3,000.

The variety of products is not the only factor at work. The fragmentation of the media has made conventional mass marketing obsolete as well. Consider magazines: *Life, Look, The Saturday Evening Post,* and other mass-market giants have been replaced by *Victorian Decorating* and *Lifestyle* and *Doll House Builder* magazines. Marketers used to rely on TV advertising that ran on one of the three networks. Now you can no longer guarantee that you'll even reach a majority of TV viewers with an ad schedule that narrow.

The death of the truly mass media has a marvelous upside: you can reach virtually any category of consumer you'd like. Why waste your time reaching everyone?

Think about the products or services you offer. Are they equally attractive to every consumer? Probably not. Virtually every product, no matter how popular, has niches of consumers that find it irresistible. Identifying those niches and capitalizing on them is the strategy for this generation of marketers.

The Cost of Acquiring a New Consumer

Last year, the average consumer was bombarded by more than 5,000 commercial messages. Obviously, he ignores and forgets most of them. Think about the last TV show you watched. What was advertised? If you're like most people, you have no idea. More then ever, it makes sense for companies to cater to existing customers instead of paying the significant costs of acquiring new ones.

This strategy is anathema to any old-school mass marketers. The watchword at the giant food companies was to grab market share. Market share translates into efficient media buys, efficient factories, economies of scale in everything from packaging to coupons.

But without the reliance on mass media, many of these economies of scale aren't as important. Creating a shorter run of a product that will be embraced by its target audience is far cheaper than producing a huge run for a disinterested consumer.

In addition to ad clutter, marketers are facing a new skepticism. Years of scams, lousy products, inferior service, and advertising overkill have led many consumers to be leery of almost any new product. More and more, we're relying on the people and the businesses we trust to deliver the products we need.

Share of consumer is now much more important than share of market. How much business you can generate from each hard-won customer is a more important question today. If the local drugstore can persuade you to buy groceries, milk, videotapes, and film from it, the store can increase profitability without significant media expenses.

Reaching the Individual

Database marketing takes two concepts — segmenting the audience and relying on existing customers — and turns them into a science. With database marketing, you take the information you gather about your customers and use it to reach them on a one-to-one basis.

If you know things about your customers, you can offer them products and services they want. Doing the work for the time-stressed consumer helps both of you. Database marketing gives you the tools you need to gain information about consumers and satisfy their needs.

Don Peppers and Martha Rogers, authors of a database marketer's bible called *One-to-One (1:1) Marketing*, put it this way: "As good products are offered by lots of competitors, the best sales go to those who develop good relationships with individual customers."

There are grand strategies and small ones, and both work. For example, in its "Friends and Family" program, MCI collaborated with one customer at a time to create a vast network of calling circles. The strategy brought new customers into the fold and solidified MCI's relationship with existing customers. Few people would switch from MCI after working so hard to convince their friends and family to sign up for the discount. Everyone was talking (and joking a little) about Friends and Family, and the long-distance wars were nationwide news.

Note that MCI did not engage in a mass-marketing strategy. Instead, it relied on its existing customer base, and discovered what those people really wanted — the opportunity to save money on their most-called friends. By offering their existing customers a better service, they were able to keep those customers and, not coincidentally, have those customers bring new ones to MCI.

The more subtle strategies are equally effective. For instance, the Ritz-Carlton hotel chain quietly maintains a customer database that records every preference or habit a guest displays. Which hotel services — dry cleaning, fitness club, concierge — does she use? What dishes and beverages does he order through room service? If a customer goes to the Ritz in New York and orders a glass of white wine and a glass of ice on the side, that order is recorded in the database. A few months later, when she goes to the Ritz in, say, Laguna Niguel, and orders a glass of white wine from room service, the wine is delivered with a glass of ice on the side, because the Ritz knows that's the way she likes it.

This is not just a stunt. The Ritz-Carlton uses the information it gets about an individual customer to strengthen its relationship with that customer. This approach is the opposite of mass marketing, which uses the data about an individual to project his habits on the whole market. In effect, a mass marketer creates a prototype of a customer and aims broadly at that hypothetical target. If he's lucky, he hits a few customers who want his product or service. As Peppers and Rogers assert, "Traditional mass marketers find customers for their products. One-to-one (1:1) marketers find products for their customers. The most valuable thing any company produces is customers."

Take the Ritz. It could poll its customers to discover which cities they usually visit. If a surprising number of Ritz regulars are visiting Mexico City on business, it may make sense for the company to build a hotel there. Doesn't this make more sense than building the hotel first, then trying to find customers for it?

At Tower Records and other record stores, a customer can take a compact disc he's interested in to the kiosk at the center of the store. If he has previously registered, he can swipe his "i•Card" through the kiosk scanner, then hold the sealed CD up to the machine.

The kiosk will read the UPC code on the back of the CD, look up the album in its database, and play him an excerpt! Even better, it keeps track of everything he listens to and everything he buys.

When he registered for the i•Card, the system got his name, address, and basic demographic data. As time goes by, it learns what he likes and what he doesn't.

Soon, overall trends start to develop among customers. The machine learns, for example, that Billy Joel fans often like Elton John too.

Instead of just acting as a passive preview service for sealed CDs, the i•Station can become a superintelligent salesperson. When the new Bonnie Raitt CD comes out, it knows which customers bought the last three Bonnie Raitt CDs and could send them postcards letting them know the new album is in the store. Or perhaps the next time a customer scans a Billy Joel album, it could suggest that she might like the new album from Elton John — and play an excerpt for her.

The value of the i•Station to a record store should be obvious. It changes the company's business: now Tower Records is more concerned with *finding products for customers* than with *finding customers for products*. The kiosk shifts a lot of power from record companies to record stores, and guarantees that the satisfied i•Station customer isn't going to spend a lot of time bargain hunting at Musicland or Sam Goody.

But what about the customer? He wins too. For the first time, there's an effective way for him to find the music he really likes. The discount coupons that come in the mail as a result of his having used the i•Station are nice, but even better is the fact that the store is trying to make him happy. He's got a full-time music expert worrying about what album he should buy next. That's worth something.

Rental cars are a lot less sexy than CDs, but National has managed to generate a significant relationship with its best customers as well. A few years ago, it introduced the Emerald Club. Geared toward frequent travelers, the club issues an Emerald Card to club members, who pay $50 a year for the privilege.

When she arrives at the airport, the Emerald Club member goes straight to a clearly marked island that is surrounded by the cream of the National fleet. She can pick a car immediately, get in, and drive away. All she has to do is stop at the security gate and swipe her card through a card reader. The scanner records all the necessary information from her card and awards her frequent-traveler points, which she can accumulate for benefits such as airline and hotel discounts.

The relationship here is quite strong. Emerald Club members never need a reservation, never wait in line, never fill out a form. The more they travel, the more frequent-renter bonuses they get. And since it's a business expense, members don't even notice the small service fee. Why would anyone switch?

National identified all the needs of its very best customers and met them. The electronic card lets National identify its biggest and best customers, and the times of the year they travel most. The company can determine which cities need enhanced facilities. It's also in an excellent position to create co-promotions. For example, it could offer discounts on hotels in cities it expects its best customers to visit.

Recognize that National could never have set up the Emerald Club unless it knew a lot about its customers. It had to know who the frequent renters were, what cities they visited, what they wanted in a rental car. This customer knowledge, and the desire to increase the share of consumer among its best customers, led to a profitable increase in business.

Also note that National is able to charge for the privilege of belonging. This is not just a marketing gimmick. Instead, National is offering something of real value to its customers, and they're willing to pay for it.

Acquiring Data and Using It

T he easy part of establishing a database marketing strategy is collecting the data. New technologies make it easy and cheap to discover your customers' habits. You can use UPC scanner data, membership cards — even a simple pen and paper — to discover exactly who's buying what. The Database Marketing Resources section at the end of this chapter lists a number of companies that can create database systems for almost any company.

The hard part of database marketing is figuring out what to do with all that data. For years, companies collected warranty cards for refrigerators, software, automobiles, and more — and boxed them up, unused, in dusty warehouses. The biggest danger of database marketing is that you'll collect too much data, overwhelming your systems and leading to paralysis.

The corner grocer never had this problem. He saw all the facts firsthand, and knew, for example, that if a lot of his customers had babies in December, he'd better make sure there was plenty of baby food on the shelves in March. However, predicting the future desires of large groups of people using their current habits is a trickier task. Collecting lots of data can raise the chance of success — if the data is used properly.

The most successful database marketers are constantly testing. A restauranteur can collect the names and addresses of 1,000 people who had lunch in his restaurant last week, for example. Instead of announcing a special dinner menu to all of them, he can mail information to 50 or 100. Of course, the more customers you work with, the more important it is to test. It's not unusual for a marketer to have as many as 1,000,000 names in a database.

The cost of testing is dirt cheap compared to the benefits. A company with 10,000 customers in its files can reach groups of 50 with regular mailings on new pricing strategies, colors, hours, and more. The cost of these mailings is low, but the information gathered is priceless. For the first time, the company will know what people *really* want.

Don't underestimate the value of a conversation. General Electric has hundreds of engineers standing by to talk with any appliance customer who takes the time to call. (Try it. Their number is (800) 626-2000). While these problem-solvers have increased GE's loyal customer base, the information GE gains is perhaps even more valuable. Their engineers know which products are easy to use and which aren't, and they learn what other features and devices their customers need.

Using Database Marketing in the Real World

L et's say you're the local dry cleaner. Your database file on your customers includes some vital stuff — name, address, telephone number, the services the customer regularly uses. Your customer base is small enough that a stack of index cards is probably all the technology you need.

Mr. Utopi has been a customer for years. You know he brings his shirts in every Saturday, likes them with a touch of starch, and needs them folded and in boxes for traveling. Twice a month he brings in a suit, and maybe a sports jacket and slacks. He's a customer with the most regular behavior. So how can you do more for him, based on the information you've gathered on him over the years?

He's a single guy, regular habits, loyal customer. Send him (and a passel of others like him) a promotional appeal, inviting him, as a valued customer, to your "Let Us Do Your Sheets" service launch. He gets his sheets done for free as an introduction, a 10-percent-off discount on his next three uses of the service, and before you know it, your loyal customer is a loyal customer in a whole new category — even better than a new customer, who might just be trying you out to take advantage of the sheets promotion.

On a larger scale, Waldenbooks, a national bookstore chain, is working hard to keep track of what its customers buy. The store issues a discount card to frequent buyers. Every time a customer buys a book, the store's computers record the purchase. The potential uses for that type of information are numerous. Walden has already started mailing coupons to frequent buyers when new books (in categories they've previously shown interest in) come into the store.

Waldenbooks is also using its database to market more efficiently through catalogs. In 1992, it divided its customer database into 100 distinct groups and mailed out 12 specialized catalogs. With further testing, the chain will be able to fragment its catalogs even further, coming closer and closer to a one-to-one relationship with each customer.

Imagine taking it to the next level. Fans of Stephen King might receive a postcard heralding a new novelist that *The New York Times* called "the next Stephen King." Or a customer who regularly bought several hundred dollars in books every Christmas could be invited to a special gift-buying session at the store, when there would be extra gift-wrappers on hand to help out.

Coca-Cola has built a database of information about its 300,000 fountain customers (stores where the stuff comes in a cup, not a can). The database identifies the attitudes and requirements of each fountain customer, from convenience stores to fast-food restaurants to theme parks.

The system constantly measures the customer's satisfaction level, and every marketing communications or sales call directly addresses the customer's concerns and interests. The best part is that Coca-Cola gets a record of the customer's merchandising history, allowing the company to anticipate situations and help customers increase sales. For example, if a number of stores showed an increase in Sprite sales due to regional advertising, the sales rep could alert accounts in the region that they ought to keep extra stock on hand. Even more personal, a promotional technique that worked in one amusement park could easily be transferred to a customer at another, noncompeting park.

Lowe's home improvement chain is determined to act as the customer's best ally when it comes to building something at home. About a quarter of the company's customers use a Lowe's charge card, so its computers know who's buying what.

Lowe's can use information on purchasing behavior to determine the lifestyle of its best customers. The company uses this data to send newsletters to customers, encouraging them to take on new projects, such as building a deck. Armed with instructions and a materials list, the customer is far more likely to take on the project. And, of course, they're more likely to buy from Lowe's — even if they could get the stuff cheaper down the street at Home Depot. The customer is satisfied, and Lowe's makes more money.

Note the common theme. In each case, the savvy marketer is working to cement his relationship to the customer by saving the customer time and money, or by making selections and recommendations that the customer appreciates. By focusing on share of consumer, these visionaries are making it nearly impossible for a competitor to steal market share.

United Artists Theatres, one of the largest chains of movie houses in the country, is testing a database technique. It gives moviegoers membership cards. Each time a member attends a movie, the card is swiped through a scanner, recording the movie, date, and time. The company then mails special promotions to people they know are interested in certain types of movies. For example, someone who went to see *Terminator 2* would probably be interested in seeing *Speed*.

United Artists now has dramatic leverage over its competitors, and a valuable tool to offer to movie studios. Movie marketers' biggest challenge is generating the first one million ticket sales — creating word of mouth and buzz. United Artists is in an excellent position to bring those million people into its theatres with sneak-preview marketing targeted directly at individual consumers.

Database marketing is an effective tool for reaching your competitor's customers as well. Catalina Marketing offers direct distribution of food coupons at 80,000 cash registers around the country. For a fee, Catalina will deliver a coupon for your product to any person buying your competitor's product instead. This precise targeting has had extraordinary results. It costs a brand marketer $7.50 for every traditional coupon redeemed by someone who isn't currently using their product (there's a huge amount of wasted printing). With Catalina, it costs about $2.42.

Sharing Data

Once you know something about your customers, you have something of value. Use this information carefully, and you can benefit your customers and your bottom line. If you sell your customer data to every Tom, Dick, and superstore, you may generate short-term profits, but you won't develop customer loyalty. Limited trades and co-promotion make much more long-term sense.

Some analysts predict that innovative companies will increase their data sharing. If you want to share data with another company, ensure that:

• *company principals know and trust each other*

• *databases are of comparable size*

- *there are strong market affinities between the databases*

- *you get an agreement in writing*

- *a third party does the data processing*

- *all parties have agreed about what they will and won't share (confidentiality is key)*

At the simplest level, the stores in a strip mall (a dry cleaner, an optician, and a florist, say) can exchange their customer lists. They know that these customers are willing and able to come to this mall. Offering the customers of one store a valuable coupon to try the other store is a win-win promotion. When the florist shares her mailing list, she doesn't have to worry that her customers will suddenly start buying bouquets at the optician. But if they come to the mall to take advantage of the optician's special on contact lenses, they may spot the florist's display of roses and buy a dozen on impulse. At no risk, the florist has increased her profitability. So, of course, has the optician.

Rodale Press and the Meredith Corporation exchange data to increase sales for their book divisions. The typical reader of Meredith's magazine *Better Homes and Gardens* is a generalist, but Meredith can determine which readers have specific interests, such as gardening, cooking, or decorating. This affinity information is of great interest to Rodale, a publisher of books on such topics. In exchange, Rodale gives Meredith its mailing list, which Meredith uses for subscription promotions. Both companies have databases of similar sizes, so one isn't getting more out of the arrangement than the other. And although technically they are competitors for readers' dollars, they each have a slightly different position in the market, so the information they share enhances and strengthens each other's presence.

Ten Core Concepts of Database Marketing

- *Frequent purchaser prizes*

  American Airlines invented this incredibly powerful technique. By giving customers an additional reason to stay loyal, you increase their investment in your company every time they buy your product or service.

- *Reminders*

  Calyx & Corrolla Florists will call customers eleven months after they sent a bouquet for a special occasion, reminding them what they did last year and asking them if they want to do it again.

- *New products*

The best way to perform research and development in most industries is to ask your customers what they want. Then make it. Hard Manufacturing asked pediatric nurses how it could improve its line of hospital cribs. Nurses asked for a built-in scale. Even though the new crib cost more than double the standard model, hundreds flew out of the factory, generating significant profits.

- *Predict future habits*

People who buy houses eventually buy furniture. Families with babies will need strollers pretty soon. Track this behavior, predict it, then offer a shortcut.

- *Segment your audience*

Don't send a perfume sample to someone who's allergic. People who like science fiction want to hear about new David Brin and Star Trek books. Save your money and your customers' time by sending promotions to interested customers only.

- *Be a smart friend*

You have access to a huge amount of product information. Your customer is too busy to gain your knowledge. So share what you know and save the customer time and money. Chemical Bank has a huge, accurate database of corporate clients. Its bankers can identify programs that will generate profits for these customers and then let the customers know about them.

- *Offer discounts*

It costs much less to market to an existing customer than to obtain a new one. So keep existing ones happy and reward their loyalty by offering them special frequent-buyer discounts. Egghead Software offers customers a CUE card which generates an instant rebate at the cash register.

- *Identify the stars*

Most businesses have a small core of regulars who pay the bills. Identify these people and don't let them go. Give them the best seat in the restaurant, a special line at the checkout, or advance notice of your end-of-season sale. In Step, a Manhattan shoe store, sends a postcard out two weeks before a big sale, offering regulars a special day before the public gets the discount.

- *Co-market*

  Acquire new customers by leveraging a noncompetitor's relationship with his customers. The trust is often transferable, so you can frequently acquire a new customer at a fraction of the cost of persuading a stranger to spend his money.

- *Identify new markets, locations, and delivery mechanisms*

  Find out where your best customers like to shop, what they like to buy, and whether they want home delivery or a subscription service. Then give it to them. Green Mountain Coffee Roasters polled its customers to discover that a subscription-based coffee delivery service was at the top of its customers' wish lists.

INTERVIEW WITH
JAMES R. ROSENFIELD

In his 25-year career, James R. Rosenfield has become one of the world's most respected marketing and direct/database/relationship marketing authorities. His major area of expertise involves the application of direct/database marketing techniques to nontraditional environments, such as consumer products, financial services, and travel.

He writes regularly for publications worldwide, and has published over 200 articles and monographs. He is also the chairman of Rosenfield & Associates.

Q: What are the problems marketers face in the 1990s that database marketing might solve?

A: One of the reasons for the fashionability of database marketing is that the mass market has conspicuously collapsed — that's pretty old news by now. Combine that with the fragmentation of media, and it makes the conventional means of delivering mass messages in fixed forms to large audiences obsolete. It raises the question, "How do I communicate on a more individual basis with people?" and that leads to the idea of databases and database marketing.

Q: When building a database, what kind of information should a company be trying to obtain?

A: You need to know who your customers are and what they do, and everything else is secondary. A lot of companies don't know who their customers are. Does Procter & Gamble know who its customers are? No. It knows its trade customers but not its end users.

Once you know who your customers are and what they do, you can begin adding demographic, psychographic, and geodemographic data. You then use this information to draw up profiles of your customers. Patterns start to emerge. You begin to see similarities between certain types of customers. Profitable customers will tend to have some commonalities, as will unprofitable customers. Most customers in most businesses, though, will cluster in a middle region of marginal profitability or unprofitability. When you compare the profiles of your most profitable customers against this large middle group, you'll find that lots of marginal customers look exactly like your profitable customers, except for one thing: their behavior. Implication: these customers are giving most of their business to your competitors. By aggressively trying to stimulate them, you can maximize your share of customer, which is probably the single most promising short-term profitability tactic of the 1990s, at least in mature categories.

It's also a way of refining new customer acquisition, by looking for new customers who match the profiles of your profitable existing customers.

Q: **Suppose you were talking to a large company that has run countless sweepstakes and promotions where they have asked for names and addresses, so they probably do know who some of their end users are, but they haven't used that information or expanded on it. What would you tell them to request on their next sweepstakes or promotion?**

A: If I were talking to any packaged goods company, I would suggest that they make an investment in data capture. For example, they should try to find out what competitive brands people use, because they are fighting for share of customer in the 1990s. It's no longer just share of market. Brand loyalty has fragmented. People tend to be loyal to a circle of brands these days rather than to just one brand. Then, without being obtuse or invasive about it — people are quite rightly concerned about protecting their privacy — I would suggest they try to find out life-cycle and lifestyle information. That's the kind of thing that facilitates relevant, individualized communications.

Q: **What could the company do with that information?**

A: Let's use Procter & Gamble and Tide detergent as an example. Suppose they find out that three million heavy users of Tide also play tennis, a lifestyle detail. That would enable Procter & Gamble to do a targeted promotion based on tennis to these three million people. If people are interested in tennis, tennis has a kind of iconic power for them; they relate to tennis messages and tennis imagery. They would obviously pay a lot more attention to that particular Tide promotion if it were tied into tennis than if it were a mass message.

Q: Is that the goal that the database marketer should have in mind? In other words, should database marketers be building relationships with customers one by one?

A: It depends. You can't literally build relationships one by one if you are Procter & Gamble. You do it cluster by cluster. Tennis players are a large cluster. Huge companies can get into trouble if they take the one-to-one concept too literally. A friend of mine, who works for Ralston-Purina, sells more dog food than anyone else in the world. He said, "I don't care about this one-on-one stuff. I don't care what color eyes people have. Just make sure they have dogs." From a mass-packaged-goods standpoint, what database marketing comes down to is "make sure they have dogs." Because if they don't have dogs, you waste 72 cents of every advertising/promotional dollar, since only 28 percent of American households have dogs. Speaking of packaged goods, it's clear that products that lend themselves best to database marketing tend to be psychology- and emotion-intensive — health and beauty aids, baby products, and pet products, for example.

Q: What companies or products are most suited to making use of database marketing?

A: Companies who have extended contacts with customers are well suited to database marketing. The length of the contact allows more time to gather information. When you sit in an airplane, the airline potentially has your attention for as long as you're a passenger. When you deal with a bank, you're usually a customer over a long period of time. It's not surprising, then, that airlines and banks are among the leaders and pioneers in this kind of work.

   The kind of contact optimal for database marketing usually has an emotional or psychological dimension, as I mentioned before. Businesses that are information- or transaction-intensive also have an edge. If your business doesn't have these traits, you have to invent them. The problem with most packaged goods is that they don't have any of these traits, with the exceptions I just listed. Packaged-goods businesses have to synthesize these other characteristics. It can be done, but it takes some inventiveness.

Q: Suppose another type of business, a retail clothing store, for example, wanted to set up a database. What type of information should they be gathering? What special services could they offer based on this information?

A: First of all, you capture information at the point of sale. You find out name, address, phone number. Obviously, if you are a retail clothing store, you're already finding the sizes customers wear and the kind of items they buy. Find out birthdays. Get life-cycle and lifestyle data. Then, when you have a slow season, you can target promotions aimed at your best customers. That is precisely how a retail store would do it.

Q: Who are some of the movers and shakers in the world of database marketing right now?

A: The categories are financial services, telecommunications, travel, mail order, and tobacco.

Q: What is the best example of database marketing you have seen?

A: I would say American Airlines AAdvantage program comes pretty close, but there aren't any perfect systems yet.

Q: Why do you think American Airlines has been successful?

A: American Airlines has succeeded in detaching its database from the conventional idea of marketing, and distributing it as the central nervous system of the organization worldwide. A database should be used in all sorts of ways to link more closely with the customer. I think that marketing in the past, to quote consultant Regis McKenna, has pretty much just been selling stuff and collecting money. Marketing right now is pretty much still that way. Marketing in the future — and the future is now if you want to be smart andsuccessful — is the tissue that connects products and people, companies and customers. American Airlines has its database distributed throughout its systems worldwide, so that any American Airlines terminal, anywhere in the world, can call up my record right away. I have about three million miles on American Airlines, making me one of the most frequent flyers. Every time I have a transaction with the airline in South America, or in Europe, or here in the U.S., a flag pops up that says, "This guy is important, treat him nicely," and they do. That helps cement the relationship and bond me further with American Airlines. I think they have taken database marketing to the next plateau, which is not just conventional marketing, but the actual tissue that bonds me to them on a day-to-day basis.

Q: **Where does the potential for database marketing lie? A lot of companies are engaging in promotions and campaigns to build their databases. That's obviously the first step. What should step two be, and where should the companies expect to be five years from now?**

A: Well, step one really is to have a strategic purpose. Just jumping in without knowing what you are doing isn't going to get you very far. You also have to come to terms with the changes in culture and technology. And you need to realize that if your competitors have a customer database and you don't, they have a sustainable competitive advantage over you. Remember: most companies are forced to share their customers with competitors. If your competition knows who their customers are and you don't, you could be in trouble. One more thing: you must take database marketing seriously, and not just dabble. Database marketing does not lend itself to dabbling. You have to plunge into it all the way, or it's not going to work. A few years ago, I thought that you could experiment with it. I was wrong; you can't.

Step two is to allocate a budget based on the impact of customer retention on profitability. In the last couple of years, figures have shown that a small increase in customer retention can account for a huge increase in profitability. That starts to cost-justify the investment.

Step three is to get into a cultural mode where you love your products less and your customers more. A database is literally an investment in customers.

The use of the marketing database five years in the future will be a progression from using it for site selection, direct-mail targeting, and telemarketing, to using it more as an infrastructural central nervous system in the way that American Airlines does. Database marketing will also influence the way companies purchase media for general advertising. It will influence the way advertising messages are created both for direct marketing purposes and for general advertising purposes. The various terms that people use — direct marketing, general advertising, above the line, below the line — are already starting to blur, and in a few years, we will not be talking about direct marketing, advertising, sales promotion, PR, or any of those things. I think we'll just call it marketing, and within 10 to 15 years, anyone who is doing marketing will be doing some kind of database marketing simply by definition.

52 Ways to Use Database Marketing

1. *Track the use of office supplies and automatically deliver refills*

If you notice that a particular customer buys 10 packages of copy paper every month, deliver 10 more packages three weeks after the last order. Your customer will be pleased she doesn't have to take the trouble to reorder. If you include a replacement toner cartridge for the photocopier and a catalog of specialty copy papers, you'll increase your sales.

2. *Send supporters of the local orchestra notice of a new CD*

A record store can get access to a finely targeted list of potential customers by sharing its mailing list with the local orchestra. Couples with season tickets to the Baroque series will want to know about the new Vivaldi album. The orchestra benefits too — it can use the shop's list to send brochures to record buyers. By working together to promote interest in classical music, both parties increase their business.

3. *Offer a formula and diaper delivery service to new parents*

Hospitals, pediatricians, or parenting magazines may sell mailing lists of new parents. What better way to build customer loyalty than to offer a convenient delivery service at the very time exhausted new parents are looking for ways to save time?

4. *Offer discounted tire rotation to customers who purchase new tires*

Don't settle for one-time business. When a customer buys tires from you, you know he's going to need to rotate those tires eventually. Use your knowledge to build your business. Offer him a reason to return, like a discount coupon for a service he needs, and chances are he will.

5. *Sponsor a nationwide picnic and reunion for loyal customers*

Everyone likes to feel valued. What do people do for their good friends? They invite them over for dinner. Invite all your customers to a picnic and you increase their goodwill toward you. If your company operates nationwide, hold regional events to make sure as many people as possible can come.

6. *Sell souvenirs, T-shirts, and other doodads to rabid fans of a rock group*

Fans of the Grateful Dead are notorious for their devotion. Many "Deadheads" spend their vacations (or their lives) following the group from concert to concert. Build on the loyalty all fans feel for their favorite bands. Ticket-sale records provide finely targeted marketing lists. Why waste your time and money trying to sell heavy-metal t-shirts to possible Barry Manilow fans when you can sell directly to 10,000 people who have already spent $30 each on Metallica tickets?

7. *Offer free dessert to regular restaurant customers*

Remember when your mom used to reward you for finishing your brussels sprouts by letting you have an extra piece of cake? It made you think twice before leaving your vegetables on your plate next time, didn't it? Reward your best customers for their loyalty to your restaurant with a treat. They'll remember your generosity next time they have to book a family celebration or office party.

8. *Sell sprinkler systems to clients of a lawn maintenance company*

A lawn maintenance company wants its clients to keep up their lawns between visits. It makes the maintenance company look good, and more important, increases the likelihood that the customer will be satisfied with his lawn. Sprinkler companies want to find people who have already proven their interest in lawn care. It keeps them from wasting time on people who don't really care. A joint sprinkler/maintenance promotion benefits everyone.

9. *Offer gutter cleaning to regular chimney cleaning clients*

If you have a set of customers who hire you to clean their chimneys every spring, why not use that loyalty to generate new business in the fall? Point out that clogged gutters are as much a hazard as clogged chimneys. If you offer a discount to customers who use both services, you can just about guarantee client loyalty and satisfaction.

10. *Regularly poll supermarket customers on new products they liked*

A manufacturer introduces a new brand of triple chocolate fudge cookies with a flashy ad campaign and in-store samples. But three months later, the company doesn't know who actually bought and liked the cookies. By conducting a customer survey in supermarkets, the company can get this information and offer satisfied customers a coupon for the largest package, reinforcing their loyalty.

11. *Offer a Diet Coke coupon to anyone buying non-fat yogurt*

Weight-conscious shoppers tend to buy more than one type of low-calorie food. It doesn't make much sense to buy both low-fat yogurt and extra-rich rocky road ice cream. Build on certain customers' proven interest in low-calorie products by offering them discounts on other diet products, or a free sample. New technology allows you to deliver the coupon automatically, at the checkout.

12. *Sell wedding services (flowers, bands, etc.) to brides ordering a dress*

When they're planning a wedding, many brides think about their dresses first. These big-ticket items are hard to select and take months to make. This early stage of the planning process is the perfect time to draw the bride's attention to your wedding-related services. With the escalating prices of a full-scale wedding, many brides will value a discount for customers who buy more than one product or service.

13. *Invite season ticket holders to a meet-the-players party*

Reinforce your season ticket holders' loyalty to your theatre by making them feel part of the production. At a meet-the-players party, they can chat informally with actors, argue with the director about the interpretation of the play, and find out how the set designer achieved a certain effect. They become participants, not merely observers, and their commitment to your theatre increases.

14. *Offer free personal banking services to corporate officers with company bank accounts*

Corporate banking officers already spend a lot of time in your bank. As executives, they are busy people with many commitments. If you give them a good reason to move their personal accounts to your bank, you'll make it possible for them to combine two trips — the nightly business bank deposit and a run to their personal bank for grocery money — into one. They'll appreciate your effort to make their lives easier, and you'll get grateful new customers.

15. *Sponsor a monthly barbecue with new car purchasers to get new user feedback*

Everybody loves free food. Play on that attraction by inviting all your new car buyers to a free barbecue. They'll appreciate the free event, and you can ask them for informal feedback on the cars' performance. They'll be more likely to respond to a personal question at a social event than on an impersonal paper survey that arrives in the mail.

16. *Insert an offer for a free newsletter in a product to gather names and addresses*

A software company can offer a newsletter to users of its desktop publishing package. Users can trade information and shortcuts, and the company can promote new ways to use the software. Better understanding of the product leads to greater customer satisfaction. Of course, the company can also use the list of newsletter subscribers to market related products.

17. *Pay your customers for improvement suggestions*

Ask your restaurant customers to fill out suggestion forms, including their name and address, and offer a cash prize or free meal for the best suggestion received each month. You'll get a list of customers who care enough about your restaurant to suggest improvements. You can send these people notices of promotions, discount coupons, and samples of your new menu. And you'll get useful feedback and ideas for change.

18. *Watch customer purchases and offer economy-sized alternatives to frequent purchasers of the more expensive small size*

If you give customers at your pet food store frequent-shopper cards, you can track their purchases. If the database shows that one customer buys four tins of cat food every second day, send her a coupon for a bulk package of 12 cans. Anticipate her needs. Perhaps she buys small quantities frequently because she doesn't have a car to transport larger orders. Offer her a free delivery service.

19. *Call ten customers every day just to ask them how they like your product*

Most customers figure that once they buy your product, you'll have no further interest in them. Surprise them, and they'll remember you. Phone random customers and ask them what they think of the product. You'll get valuable feedback, and your customers will be flattered that you asked their opinion.

20. *Offer free rental of expensive tools to your best hardware customers*

Keep track of your customers' purchases. Let them know that when they've purchased $400 worth of supplies, you'll give them free rental of a floor sander or a jigsaw for the weekend. Once they've "invested" some money in a future "purchase," why would they spend their money at another hardware store?

21. *Track pizza delivery orders and offer subscriptions at dramatically decreased prices*

Does a family order a pizza every Sunday during football season? Eliminate their hassle and increase your planning capability by offering a subscription discount. Bring them the pizza automatically (unless they cancel it) at a great discount.

22. *Create a service that will maintain the houseplants your greenhouse sells to businesses*

Again, don't settle for one-time business. Why should another company profit from the hard work you did to secure the initial sale? Office managers are often hesitant to buy live plants because they fear no one in the office will take care of them. By offering the managers a low-cost maintenance service, you'll overcome this reluctance.

23. *Distribute easy-to-use, pre-printed order forms for fax paper or other frequently ordered consumables*

Produce specific order forms for products your customers order often. Make it easy for them to reorder by printing product codes right on the form, saving them the trouble of looking up each product in your catalog every time. Add your fax number so they don't have to pay postage.

24. *Track customer ordering habits*

If your most loyal restaurant customers order your fettuccine over and over but rarely order your hamburger, expand your menu based on their demonstrated preferences. Offer other pasta dishes such as linguine and lasagne. Organize an Italian Week promotion, with a strolling accordion player and special prices on Italian wines.

25. *Keep a record of the houses you've painted*

Many homeowners won't remember to do house maintenance until some problem — a leaky roof, a dripping tap — reminds them. By that point, damage will have added to the maintenance costs. The homeowner will feel foolish for leaving the task so long, and resent the extra expense. If you notify past customers that they need repainting before expensive rotting sets in, they'll be grateful. You'll create goodwill along with repeat business.

26. *Offer customers "express ordering"*

Poll customers to see if they'll pay for the convenience of having their regular order ready and paid for when they walk into the store. If you have a record of a customer's usual order — three boxes of blue pens, eight packages of legal pads, and five boxes of double-sided diskettes, for instance — you can package it in a box and charge it to the customer's account, saving her the tedium of running around the store to pick up the items and standing in line to pay for them.

27. *Run a contest, requiring customers to give their name and address to enter*

If your business doesn't usually collect information from consumers, run a contest. Nike, for example, has little data on who is using their sneakers. They could start a newsletter or club for people who enter the contest. By creating opportunities to interact with customers, you can gather data and build a relationship.

28. *Keep the name, address, and charge card data for every customer of your Chinese restaurant on file*

There's no need to ask for every piece of information each time an order comes in. Because the customer knows he'll save time when he orders from your restaurant, he will be more inclined to call you when he gets a craving for egg rolls and less inclined to call your competitor — even if that restaurant is having a special on egg rolls this week.

29. *Keep a chart of your busiest periods and account for them*

When you opened your diner, you figured lunchtime would be your busiest period. But you soon realized you were perpetually short-staffed in the late afternoon. By looking at your records and using a little deductive reasoning, you'll realize that your most loyal customers are seniors from the nearby high school, who stop in on their way home to order fries and Cokes. Build on that loyalty by running a discount coupon in the high school paper. And add more staff in the afternoon to keep your customers happy.

30. *Track purchases and offer discounts*

Many book and magazine buyers are fiercely loyal to their favorite book-shops. Does one of your regular customers purchase the same three home decorating magazines every month? Give her 10 percent off her entire purchase, and send her notices of new decorating and architecture books with a discount coupon.

31. *Send visitors to your last trade show a free pass*

If you run a trade or consumer show, most of your profits probably come from your exhibitors, not visitor entrance fees. If the show doesn't have lots of visitors, exhibitors won't pay for the privilege of exhibiting. By giving last year's visitors an incentive to return, you foster goodwill among both groups of clients — visitors and exhibitors.

32. *Run specialized supermarket promotions*

Encourage customers at your grocery store to apply for a check-cashing card. On the application, ask for basic information such as name, address, family status, and occupation. You'll create a perfect database for targeted promotions. Send all your bachelor shoppers discount coupons for gourmet frozen dinners. Promote your free babysitting service to busy parents. Tell nurses, security guards, and other night-shift workers about your new round-the-clock hours.

33. *Register gift purchases*

Everyone's familiar with the bridal gift registries at china stores. But there's no reason why a shop selling children's clothes and toys couldn't offer a similar service for doting relatives. The "Grandma Club" could keep records of previous purchases and updated information on children's sizes, and offer members frequent-buyer discounts.

34. *Sell home-security services to frequent flyers*

If an executive is registered with an airline's frequent-flyer club, he's probably already worried about leaving his home unguarded for long periods of time. Purchase the airline's mailing list and promote your home burglar alarms, smoke alarms, and deadbolt locks to these people.

35. *Market to college seniors*

If you sell cars, business suits, or credit cards, obtain a list of senior students at the local college. Send them a direct mail package about your product in January or February, and follow up just as they're finishing up their final exams. If they've been hired by an on-campus recruiter, they'll be realizing that they're going to need a vehicle to get to their new job, clothes to wear when they get there, and some way to pay for it all.

36. *Send a fitness newsletter to customers of your sports shop*

Create a newsletter that gives readers tips on starting an aerobics program, information on local hiking routes, and details of upcoming cycling marathons. You may pique their interest in a sport they haven't previously participated in. If you include a discount coupon for exercise wear, hiking boots, or cycling shorts, they'll buy from you if they decide to take up the sport. Even better, consider running novice hiking trips or bike tours for loyal customers.

37. *Market your craft supplies to knitting magazine subscribers*

If you run a wool shop, share mailing lists with a knitting magazine. Find out the magazine's editorial schedule. If it plans to run an article about baby sweaters, order extra baby patterns and wool, then send subscribers discount coupons for the products. Customers will think you read their minds.

38. *Market to couples considering retirement*

Do you own a retirement resort? Get together with noncompeting firms that also sell products aimed at retirees. Hire a financial planner to give a free seminar on budgeting for retirement. Use the mailing list of people who attended the seminar to launch a co-marketing promotion with the other firms. For instance, you can offer prospects a free video of your retirement resort, while an airline offers a discount on flights to Florida.

39. *Offer frequent customers an incentive to purchase more*

Cosmetics makers have been using this tactic for years. They send customers who regularly buy their facial soaps or moisturizing lotions notice of a special promotion. If the customer buys $30 worth of the company's products, she'll get a free makeup bag with trial-size samples of lipstick and perfume. Not only does this promotion give the customer incentive to buy products she already uses, it introduces her to new ones she may not have known about.

40. *Sell golf-related merchandise to members of a country club*

Use a country club's mailing list to market your line of golf-themed prints, ceramic figurines, and greeting cards.

41. *Run a cooking class*

Do you own a cookware shop? Run low-cost, one-day cooking classes on exotic cuisine: Indian curries, phyllo pastry, French bread. Show students how to use unfamiliar appliances and cookware. At the end of the class, give them a package of discount coupons for the products they used. You could share the cost of the class with a gourmet food store, which could offer the students discounts on hard-to-find spices and specialty flours.

42. *Give frequent romantic movie watchers a romantic reward*

A video store can track who rents romantic movies, and offer these renters a frequent-buyer reward: a free video of *Casablanca,* a discount coupon for dinner at a candlelit French restaurant, or a box of Belgian chocolates.

The more they know about the customer's habits, the more they can help improve her leisure time.

43. *Market to harried parents*

A chain of day-care centers can use its mailing list to market services aimed at busy families: housecleaning services, pizza delivery, laundry service, lawn care, even a dog-walking service.

44. *Ask your customers what they need*

Do you sell clothing by mail? Offer your customers a $5 discount on their next order if they complete a mail-in survey. Ask them what kinds of clothing they'd like to buy but can't find. Customers may ask for pieces that don't wrinkle when packed or resist stains. They may be looking for colors that suit them but aren't necessarily "hot" this year. Or maybe they can't find decent business suits in half-sizes. Offer these items, and you'll increase customer loyalty — and sales.

45. *Make your premium stand out from your competitors'*

Many video stores offer customers a free video after they rent 10. Give your customers the choice of a book of movie reviews, a tin of gourmet popping corn, or a bottle of wine.

46. *Promote services to college students*

Colleges are strapped for cash, and students frequently spend money like water. A college can team up with car dealerships, travel agents, bakeries, or even the local pizzeria to offer a wide variety of services to students. Students save time and don't have to worry about being taken advantage of. The college benefits because students are happier, and businesses contribute to the college's coffers in exchange for access.

47. *Offer incentives to infrequent customers*

If a man comes into your jewelery store to buy an engagement ring, it may be the first time he's ever set foot in such an establishment. Give him a reason to return by sending him discount coupons for pocket watches or engraved cufflinks. Remind him of his anniversary every year.

48. *Make frequent customers feel special*

Give your best customers a client card that entitles them to services less frequent customers don't receive: free skate sharpening or ski waxing, same-day delivery service, at-home shopping, or free gift wrapping.

49. *Offer discounts on computer software upgrades*

Microsoft is a master at using database marketing to satisfy customers and enrich itself. Each new software version solves problems that customers have reported (note the relationship) and allows Microsoft to sell another product to a satisfied customer.

50. *Keep in touch*

Joe Girard, the most successful car salesman of all time, got that way by sending greeting cards. By sending every customer he'd ever had a greeting card every month, Joe kept his name at the top of the heap. By the time the old car died, Joe was practically a member of the family.

51. *Beat the back-to-school rush*

In August, parents are bombarded with back-to-school advertising. Beat the crowd by mailing details of your store's specials on pencils, crayons, knapsacks, children's clothing, or computers to parents who bought from you last year. Mail the package in July, and include special offers on popular products. Even better, offer regular customers the chance to fax their order in advance or to automatically receive exactly what they bought last year.

52. *Offer free advice*

A large hardware chain runs a toll-free number that provides customers with detailed advice on how to perform various projects. By interacting with the consumer, they can discover which products are difficult to use, and can work to make sure that every project is a successful one.

Database Marketing Resources

Specialists and Marketing Consultants

1:1 Marketing
411 Soundview Ave.
Stamford CT 06902
(203) 348-6252

1:1 Marketing is a marketing and management consulting organization that develops individualized, interactive relationships between a company and each one of its customers. The firm helps its clients harness new information technologies and interactive communication vehicles to effect long-term increases in customer share, one customer at a time.

The firm's services include workshops and seminars on the strategies and tactics of 1:1 Marketing; opportunity assessments, which help companies make the transition to 1:1 Marketing; and consulting support on program strategies and implementation.

DiMark
2050 Cabot Blvd.
West Langhorne PA 19047
(800) 543-2212

DiMark is a database marketing consulting firm specializing in the health, financial, telecommunications, and insurance industries. It refers to itself as a "vertically integrated direct marketing outsource company," meaning that it has all the services necessary for database marketing under one roof. It can take your database, integrate transactional data on a daily basis, analyze and manipulate the information, and develop marketing tools and techniques to help you reach your market.

The company specializes in event-driven and milestone marketing programs. In 1992 and 1993, *Forbes* magazine recognized DiMark as one of the "200 Best Small Companies in America."

Direct Marketing Resource Services, Inc.

333 Seventh Ave., 20th Floor
New York NY 10001
(212) 465-0814

Direct Marketing Resource Services, Inc., was founded in 1983. DMRS is a full-service, independent marketing database consulting organization. It develops long-term strategies and campaigns that help clients make the best use of their database information.

DMRS provides marketing database consulting to business-to-business, consumer, telecommunications, finance and insurance, arts and entertainment, publishing, and fund-raising companies. It also works with direct, sales promotion, and general advertising agencies. The company's clients include Avis, Coca-Cola Fountain Services, and General Foods.

MarketPulse

Four Cambridge Center
Cambridge MA 02142
(617) 868-6220

MarketPulse designs database marketing systems for large-scale marketing needs. It uses its patented MarketPulse database software to help marketers capture and manipulate consumer information in order to conduct market analysis and target a profitable customer base.

The technical staff at MarketPulse offers to help you fine-tune your database and tailor it to your specific needs. They can also help you develop a long-term strategic direction for your database marketing efforts. They have set up systems for many large companies including book publishers, catalogers, business-to-business marketers, and entertainment and travel companies.

Raab Associates

19 Price's Lane
Rose Valley PA 19063
(215) 565-8188

Raab Associates has provided database marketing consulting since 1987. It has set up database marketing systems for many clients, including Bell Atlantic, General Mills, and Lenox Collections. Raab Associates can make recommendations about software vendors, database management, and market research and analysis.

Company president David M. Raab writes software review columns in *DMNews*, published the *Guide to Database Marketing Systems*, and frequently speaks on the subject of database marketing.

Database Marketing Software and Systems Developers

Customer Insight Company

6855 South Havana
Englewood CO 80112
(303) 932-2680

Founded in 1986, Customer Insight Company (CIC), a Metromail/ R.R. Donnelley & Sons Company, provides desktop database marketing solutions. CIC's newest product, the AnalytiX System, lets companies perform sophisticated analyses of large volumes of customer, prospect, and/or transactional data. AnalytiX facilitates customer segmentation, promotion tracking, profitability analysis, customer retention, and cross-selling. It also offers in-depth, customized reporting capability through a graphical user interface.

With more than 600 software installations in the United States, Canada, and Mexico, Customer Insight Company supports clients in various industries including financial services, telecommunications, cable, publishing, and direct marketing. Through its relationship with Metromail Corporation, CIC also offers companies a wide variety of direct marketing services and products.

D.A. Lewis

PO Box 815
Doylestown PA 18901
(215) 340-6860

D.A. Lewis is a technical development company that specializes in creating databases and in consulting clients about the best way to maintain customer information in the most meaningful way. It can recommend software programs and platforms that help marketers organize and manipulate database information.

May & Speh
1501 Opus Place
Downers Grove IL 60515
(708) 964-1501

In business since 1947, May & Speh uses proprietary software technologies to develop customized database marketing systems for inquiries, updates, promotional tracking, statistical analysis, and management reports. It works with clients to organize and analyze internal and external list information. It then enhances that information with geodemographic and census information to create scoring models that identify the best customers and prospects. Finally, after each promotion based on that information, May & Speh performs a response analysis and adds the results to the database system.

OKRA Marketing Corporation
6301 Benjamin Road, Suite 103
Tampa FL 33634
(800) 275-6572

OKRA Marketing Corporation, a research-and-development-driven company, creates and implements database marketing systems. It serves more than 300 clients in many industries.

OKRA's PC-based customer information systems allow users to better target their direct marketing efforts, maximize cross-selling, improve customer retention, measure profitability, and track performance. Additionally, OKRA produces DOS-based products for business-to-business marketing, mail-management systems, and profitability measurement.

Database Marketing Publications

Direct
911 Hope Street, Box 4949
Stamford CT 06907
(203) 358-9900

The Cowles Report on Database Marketing
470 Park Ave. South, 7th Floor
New York NY 10016
(212) 683-3986
For subscriptions, call (800) 775-3777.

Database Marketing Glossary

Customer share: how much of any individual customer's business has one company acquired.

Database: a compilation of related data organized for ease of retrieval and use.

Database management system: the software used to create and maintain a database.

Database marketing: a system of analysis of customer data used to build and strengthen customer relationships.

Market share: the percentage of all sales made in one market by one company.

Market segmentation: breaking a large heterogeneous market into small homogeneous segments, for which individual marketing programs are developed.

Micromarketing: the use of marketing programs aimed at precisely defined market segments.

Overlay: the addition of new database fields to existing records (such as demographics) that help the user craft target marketing programs.

Relationship marketing: a marketing approach that calls for special attention to the individual customer, as a way of building long-term loyalty.

MARKETING BY FAX

*It's 3 a.m. and a programmer is cursing his
hard disk — it just crashed and he has a
deadline to meet tomorrow.*

*Five hundred people who took a cruise
a year ago are wondering if they should
take another one.*

*A stock investor wants to get expert
advice and up-to-the-moment quotes
on his portfolio.*

*A woman sees an ad for a Ford Taurus
and wants more information before
she goes to a dealer.*

*How can these people get the information they need?
For a long time, companies could only reach them
with 24-hour operators and mass mailings.
These methods were imperfect. The
programmer would get a busy signal, or
he would be put on hold or transferred.*

Five hundred letters would go out to the potential vacationers, but one day later, the rates would change and there would be no way to notify them.

The investor would want something written down, rather than verbal advice that was easily forgotten. The woman looking for a car would have no choice but to ask the dealer her routine questions, taking valuable time only to find that the car was not what she was looking for.

Now these people are getting satisfactory answers. Businesses have discovered that they can build relationships with potential customers, and provide improved customer service to current clients, around the clock. One machine can do this for them. The fax machine.

Virtually every business and over two million American homes have a fax machine. For important business deals, the fax machine has rendered ordinary mail nearly useless. Negotiations between a company in England and its subsidiary in Australia used to take weeks using the postal system. Even the quickest courier services take at least a day. But the fax machine provides instant written communication. You can easily use the fax machine's speed and cost efficiency to boost your marketing efforts.

There are three main ways to use fax technology for marketing:

- *Fax on demand. Customers call a number and request specific documents, which they receive right away in their fax machine.*

- *Database to fax. A computer extracts information from a database to respond to a caller's inquiry, and faxes that information to the caller.*

- *Fax broadcasting. A business sends a personalized document by fax to a number of contacts.*

Use fax technology to give your customers information or assistance as soon as they ask for it — or even before they know they need it. Catch prospective customers right at the moment they are thinking of buying. If you provide answers to frequently asked questions by fax, you improve your customers' satisfaction with your products, and they are more likely to purchase these products again. Surprisingly, you can accomplish all these feats and save money at the same time. Everyone benefits.

When the California Cable Television Association runs its annual conference and trade show, the organization's small office is swamped with calls for registration and exhibition information. Recently, the association set up a fax-on-demand system to handle these requests. The result? The system dealt with 4,000 callers quickly and automatically, and the association's employees didn't go crazy.

Still unconvinced? Perhaps we should clear up three common mis-
conceptions about marketing by fax: 1) it's complicated; 2) it's expensive; and 3) faxed materials are poor quality.

None of these is true.

First, a basic system is simple for your customers to comprehend.
Unlike more technical solutions, the concepts behind fax on demand are
simple and easy to describe.

Second, for less than $2,000 a year, a service bureau can set up a sim-
ple fax-on-demand system for you that gives toll callers access to 125
documents. Just a few sales from this setup can cover the cost of the system. The cost per customer can be less than postal fees — and you don't
have to lick a single stamp. You won't be wasting money trying to sell
to people who aren't remotely interested in your product. Fax marketing also saves money on printing, and allows you to make modifications
up to the moment of transmission. If you've ever had to modify and
reprint a newsletter, you know this feature alone can save you thousands
of dollars.

Third, it is possible to send high-quality fax documents. The quality
of the fax depends on the quality of the original and the resolution of the
receiving machine. A desktop-published item that is sent to a fax machine
with a resolution of 200 dots per inch (dpi) is almost laser-perfect.
Obviously, pictures don't appear in full color, but a data-intensive document can be delivered with élan and impact.

Fax on demand, database to fax, and fax broadcasting each have
advantages, depending on your type of company and the information
you want to transmit.

Fax on Demand

Most people think of fax machines as magic devices that somehow
spirit a letter from one place to another. Actually, the technology
is pretty simple. Once an image is fed into a fax machine, it exists
in electronic form. Instead of sending the image right away, the machine
can save that electronic file until it's needed. Fax on demand revolves
around this concept.

Thousands of faxes can be stored in a computer until a caller requests
one. Then the machine sends the appropriate fax image to the caller automatically. No one has to feed the sheets into the fax.

Here's how a sample interaction might sound:

Welcome to the 1994 Export Hotline. To receive instructions in English, press 1.

Enter the country from which you are calling by pressing,
1 for the United States
2 for Canada
3 for Mexico
or 4 for any other country.

If you are unregistered for 1994 and need the 1994 registration form, press 1 now.
For market information,
press 2 now.

Please enter your ten-digit account number, which is your registered fax number, beginning with the area code.

I'm sorry, but the number you have entered is not a valid account number. You may complete your document selection. However, please note that the Export Hotline will attach a one-page registration form to your document request. To register for 1994, please complete the attached registration form and fax it back to the number indicated. Once you register, you may call as often as you like.

Please enter your five-digit document code now.
You have entered document code number 9-5-0-0-0.
If this is correct,
press 1 now.
To re-enter your document code,
press 2 now.
If you would like to obtain another document,
please press 1 now.
If you have completed your selection,
please press 2 now.
One moment, please.
Once you press the start button on your fax machine, the document you requested will be faxed to you immediately. Please call as often as you like. Please press the start button now.

Computer companies have found fax on demand particularly useful. Their technical support people have to deal with a huge volume of calls. As a result, customers often have to wait as long as half an hour before reaching a technician.

Microsoft Corporation realized that most users calling its technical support line were looking for answers to just a few common, basic questions. Microsoft prepared comprehensive answers to several hundred of these questions and made them available as fax-on-demand items. Now users can get the information they need instantly, and technicians have more time to address more complex problems.

Fax on demand can also increase the value of your advertising dollar. Place a magazine ad promoting numerous products. You have no room to describe each product in detail; the purpose of the ad is simply to make potential customers aware of the products themselves. If customers could easily find out more about individual items, the ad's value would increase tenfold.

It's easy to send them this information instantly. Just print a code number next to each product in your ad. At the bottom of the ad, ask customers: "Do you want to find out more about our products? Receive detailed information instantly by fax! Call (800) 555-5555 and follow the instructions you hear. When you are asked for the code number of the product you are interested in, enter the number you see on the ad next to that product."

Fax on demand is an astonishingly simple marketing tool with nearly unlimited possibilities. In effect, you are setting up a 24-hour operator who answers your customers' questions immediately, never takes a vacation, and never asks for overtime. Customers can get information, technical support, or advice when their interest is at its peak — even on Sunday afternoon or at 3 a.m.

The result is increased customer satisfaction, which leads to better relationships between customer and company, better sales, more revenue, and long-term customer loyalty. This low-cost venture has high reward potential.

Don't forget that fax on demand saves you and your employees time and money. Sales reps are especially receptive to these systems. Suddenly, sales calls will be shorter and more to the point because customers will know the answers to their basic questions before the sales rep even walks in the door.

What sort of documents should you store? It's completely up to you. You can create a slick, well-designed document with the visual impact of a magazine ad. You can include a coupon, to give callers even more of an incentive to buy your product. You can request the customer's name and address and send him a free sample.

DON PEPPERS AND MARTHA ROGERS ON USING FAX ON DEMAND TO DISSEMINATE INFORMATION

Don Peppers and Martha Rogers, Ph.D. are authors of The One to One Future, *the groundbreaking book on database marketing that Tom Peters called "Book of the Year." Don Peppers runs 1:1, a marketing consulting firm in Weston, Connecticut, and Martha Rogers is associate professor of telecommunications at Bowling Green State University in Ohio. They were the first to outline the specifics of the paradigm shift that is forever changing the face of marketing in the 90s.*

Nearly any business has a need to disseminate information to its customers and prospective customers. Occasionally, disseminating highly specialized information to a relatively narrow audience can be one of the most significant activities a business has.

Consider the business of selling computer peripherals. People who are in the market for tape backups, modems, printers, cables, and so forth have a diverse set of highly specific needs. In most cases, a person will want to understand as much as possible about the exact specifications of a piece of equipment before purchasing it.

Often the customer looking for such information will find it necessary to go into a computer store — CompUSA or EggHead, for instance — in order to talk with a knowledgeable sales person. But if your business is selling this kind of device you don't necessarily have to rely on physical retail establishments and human experts simply to distribute specification sheets and diagrams.

MacWarehouse, a catalog service that sells computer peripherals to Macintosh users, has a fax-on-demand system for disseminating complex specifications and other information. Find the product you are considering in their catalog, and chances are it will have a fax-box number associated with it. So you go to your own fax machine, dial the number for MacWarehouse's fax-response service (the area code is 203, so you pay the toll on the call), and at the voice prompt you enter the fax-box number for the item. Then you'll be told to push the start button on your fax machine, hang up the handset and, on the call you just made, the specifications for the item will be printed out on your fax machine.

Thus, if I'm particularly interested in a new CD-ROM drive that's fully compatible with my existing Macintosh system software, I can find out what I need to know quickly and easily, and MacWarehouse doesn't have to pay for a staff of computer experts to be available on the phone just to answer my detailed — but fairly routine — questions.

The MacWarehouse example illustrates a single-call fax-on-demand application. But there is also a two-call fax-on-demand application, and it works like this: to get information you call not from your fax machine, but from your home or office phone. Then, following the voice prompts, enter the number of your fax machine, as well as the fax-box number of the item or topic you want information about. Within seconds after you complete the call, the marketer's computer dials your fax machine and faxes the information requested.

Fax-on-demand information dissemination not only eliminates the need for operators standing by to answer routine questions — it also reduces the need for printed brochures, and dramatically shrinks the lead time necessary to update rapidly changing information. The information you get when you access a fax-on-demand service is coming directly from a computer. This information doesn't have to be printed in hard copy prior to your fax machine printing it, based on the digital stream of data coming directly from the computer.

- As a stockbroker, you could use fax on demand to provide a completely updated portfolio summary to your clients, whenever they want.

- As a realtor, use fax on demand to disseminate detailed information about the houses you have listed for sale, along with pictures, floor plans, and maybe even the last offer.

One of the biggest marketing advantages of fax on demand is that it represents a 1:1 connection with an individual customer or prospective customer. To the extent that you can track this interaction, you will be able to follow up the connection with products, services, offers, and communications that are increasingly tailored to the individual needs of individual customers.

Therefore, if you set up a fax-on-demand service for your current customers, be sure to require the use of PIN codes to access the system. That way, you can know which customers asked for which information and when.

And if you plan on setting up a fax-on-demand system for prospective customers, you may want to consider paying the extra telephone charges involved in a two-call system, so that you can at least capture every prospect's fax number automatically.

Fax on Demand Success Stories

Computer Hardware and Software

Computer hardware and software companies are constantly producing new products and upgrades. They use fax on demand to give potential buyers basic, easy-to-understand information on these products as soon as they come on the market.

IBM, for instance, has a library of fact sheets organized by product types, such as networking systems, application software, and education information. Each type has a code. Callers enter the code on their keypad to get information on all the new products of this type. You can try out the system by calling (800) IBM-4FAX.

Symantec Corporation was deluged with calls in late 1991 after it released upgrades of two popular products. Many callers wanted a product description. It took a service representative five minutes to respond to each one of these requests, costing the company about $65,000 annually. When Symantec set up a fax-on-demand system, the company improved its customer service, got positive feedback, and increased sales. The system includes a fax survey feature (to generate feedback from customers) and transmits an automatic acknowledgment after an order is received. Call Ibex Technologies' fax line at (800) 289-9998, ext. 196 for a sample document, the new version of the Norton Desktop for Windows. It combines easy-to-read text, pictures of the computer screen, and labels explaining the different aspects of the Norton Desktop.

Hewlett-Packard's fax-on-demand system combines product information and technical support. Individuals can use both, if necessary. Call (800) 333-1917, ext. 1 for a sample. You can request prerecorded troubleshooting tips, installation tips for HP LaserJet products, information on the DeskJet or DeskWriter printers, a list of service parts, and other documents.

Travel and Tourism

Does your company encourage people to travel? Provide specific facts about locations or points of interest to prospective clients via fax.

The California Division of Tourism ran an ad on national television that invited viewers to call an 800 number for free information by fax or mail. The information was divided into categories such as "Family Fun" and "Romantic Getaways." The fax-on-demand system sent three-page faxes of information on each category that included discount coupons for local attractions. Ninety thousand people called the service, and 15 percent of them requested materials by fax.

Travel Agent Magazine ran an ad promoting a system giving travel agents immediate access to information about cruise packages, prices, and promotions. The ad brought in 25,000 responses and increased cruise sales by 40 percent.

Cruise companies have had tremendous success with fax on demand. MarketFax, a service bureau, reports that cruise companies are the largest category of business it handles.

Periodicals

The Wall Street Journal, seeking to draw high-tech advertisers, ran an ad in *Advertising Age* promoting a toll-free number that readers could call to find out how high-tech companies could benefit by advertising in the *Journal.* The paper also makes articles from its European and Asian editions available for free by fax, in a service sponsored by AT&T.

Inc. magazine sells previously published articles through fax on demand (see "Small Business Support" later in this section). *National Business Employment Weekly* offers employment information on 60 to 70 cities by fax, for a small fee. Readers can receive the information they need almost as soon as they get the original publication.

Sports

Everyone involved with a recent ad in *Golf* magazine benefited. Several country clubs were featured in the ad. Each club had its own extension from the main fax-on-demand number. The clubs made use of the magazine's strength — the ability to reproduce vivid photos of their facilities — and used fax on demand to supply much more detailed textual information than the ad could hold. Readers felt much better informed, the advertisers could trace the effectiveness of the ad, and the magazine could see which advertisers had the highest volume of calls. The magazine and advertisers will use this information to plan future ventures.

Publishing

Publishers use fax on demand to distribute advance samples of their publications, or to provide additional material for existing publications. Doubleday set up a system that offers samples of its current business books, including *The Republic of Tea: How an Idea Became a Business* and *The Currency Connection*. Houghton Mifflin's *Information Please Business Almanac* has additional articles and data available by fax. Call (815) 229-4911 from your fax machine and enter 999 when you are asked for a code to receive a sample document.

Small Business Support

Fax on demand is an ideal method to make fast-breaking news available to the growing number of small businesses. *Inc.* magazine offers small-business management information through a fax-on-demand system. For a small fee, individuals can obtain articles on topics ranging from advertising to finance to personnel problems. In the first three months of operation, the system handled 10,000 requests. To get an index of article topics, call (800) 995-4455, and enter 16101 when prompted.

Need information on exporting? Call the Export Hotline at (800) USA-XPORT. Established by International Strategies, Inc., and sponsored by large corporations like AT&T, this free service for small businesses provides fax-on-demand documents on all aspects of exporting. Documents include How to Export, How to Import, Trade Shows, Multilateral Organizations, and documents on more than 40 countries that include information on agricultural products, construction materials and equipment, telecommunications equipment and services, and more.

Many divisions of the government provide support for small businesses. The U.S. Department of Treasury and the U.S. Department of Agriculture both have fax-on-demand systems to distribute this information. Call (202) 622-1133 for the Department of Treasury and (202) 690-3944 for the Department of Agriculture. Both of these are one-call systems, so you have to call from a fax machine.

Tax Forms

With the sponsorship of several newspapers, a fax service bureau called Instant Information, Inc., offered federal and state tax forms by fax, for a small fee. Someone in California, for instance, could get a Massachusetts tax form within seconds — and avoid a long, expensive call to the Massachusetts Department of Revenue. The service was tremendously popular, particularly for state tax forms and unusual federal forms. The biggest demand came on April 12 and 13, when requests came in for extension forms.

Education

Anyone who has ever registered at an educational institution knows the amount of paper involved in the process: registration forms, course calendars, and more. Boston University, New York University, and Northeastern University have used fax-on-demand systems to provide course information, syllabi, and other documents. Students can even register by fax. The service, in effect, gives students a 24-hour registrar and financial advisor.

Hotels and Resorts

ITT Sheraton, the Gramercy Park Hotel, and Vail Ski Resort, among other hotels and resorts, have made information on meeting facilities, accommodations, business services, sports facilities, neighboring attractions, and transportation available by fax.

Marketing

Marketing firms such as Carl Rodia Associates and Globemark Wholesalers provide product sheets, brochures, specifications, order forms, price lists, and schedules to clients by fax. Some firms also use fax on demand to deliver information on product availability and shipping dates to their field sales forces.

Real Estate

Fax on demand suits the needs of real estate agents and their clients perfectly. Because houses are big-ticket items and thousands are for sale at any one time, agents need to reach many buyers, and buyers crave detailed information. Agents can provide prospects with up-to-date information on mortgage rates, fees, and available houses and apartments — including floor plans, photographs, plot plans, and terms — even while they're out showing other homes. Better Homes and Gardens Real Estate, Century 21, and ERA Real Estate are only a few of the companies who have benefitted from this system.

Oil and Gas

Exxon makes more than 2,000 documents available through fax on demand, including Material Safety Data Sheets (health, hazard, storage, fire-fighting procedures, and other safety-related information), which are required by OSHA law for chemical industry products. The system also provides status updates on Department of Transportation shipping information to distribution locations, product order confirmations, and other current information.

Bingo Card Fulfillment

Typically, when magazine readers fill out "bingo cards" — perforated cards that allow them to request more information about advertisers by mail — they have to wait several weeks for the material to arrive. But if a magazine uses a fax-on-demand system to fulfill these requests, it reduces the time factor drastically. The customer receives the information while it's fresh in his mind, not when he's already forgotten about it. The system also reduces advertisers' costs to fulfill requests. Because readers get information instantly, advertisers' sales increase, and the magazine itself enhances its position.

Forbes and *Fortune* have both used fax on demand for their bingo card fulfillment. They report excellent response. *Enterprise Communications* magazine uses a modified version of the technology. Instead of requesting faxes, subscribers give their subscriber ID number to the automated system. Advertisers receive a fax of that subscriber's information immediately, and they can contact that caller directly. They also report great response.

Fax on demand works best for business-to-business publications, because the recipient must have access to a fax machine. However, more and more people are buying fax machines for their homes, so there is a growing consumer market as well.

British Airways, TWA, and other airlines have bingo cards in their in-flight magazines and have reported a good response to their fax-on-demand systems.

Database to Fax

D atabase to fax is a highly specialized form of fax on demand. When customers call, they get access to a computer. The computer extracts information the customer requests from a database, assembles it into a document, and faxes the document to the customer. Such a system is useful in situations where information changes frequently or is stored in many pieces. A standard fax-on-demand system holds a finite number of documents, but a database-to-fax system lets users create customized documents based on hundreds of pieces of information.

This system works well for reporting stock quotes, for example. An investor can call up and get information on individual stocks from the database. The system then faxes her a printed record of the information, so she doesn't have to rely on her own memory or handwriting. In such cases, a hard copy is much more helpful than a voice message.

The database can be changed at any time. Stock prices change all the time, so the new quotes have to be entered, as often as every hour. Some investors or brokers might call several times a day, and receive new data every time.

The phone essentially becomes a remote computer terminal, issuing commands and sending the output to the fax "printer." Almost anything that now needs a human and a computer screen can be automated. A caller could find out the nearest branch of a particular store by calling a database-to-fax service and entering his ZIP code or area code. Any business whose prices or specifications change often, or that needs to inform field agents about a product's availability, could use a database-to-fax system. Firms could limit access to employees or preferred customers by requiring callers to key in a PIN code. These systems also let businesses include additional information, press releases, coupons, and other information on their faxes.

Database to fax is not yet widely used. Touch Tone, a service bureau, is one firm that sees great potential in the concept, and their clients report high satisfaction with it. Ibex Technologies, a software provider, is also involved in database-to-fax marketing, using Windows software to allow businesses to enter their information quickly and easily.

A QUESTION AND ANSWER SESSION WITH MAURY KAUFFMAN

Maury Kauffman is managing partner of The Kauffman Group, an enhanced facsimile services consulting firm, focused on the sales, marketing, and communications benefits of fax technology.

Q: What companies or products are best suited to fax on demand or fax broadcasting?

Let's take fax broadcasting first.

Information that is best suited for fax broadcasting is anything that's timely or time-sensitive, dynamic information, information that is changing on a daily, weekly, or hourly basis, that needs to be transmitted or received by hundreds or thousands of people geographically spread out. The ease of use of fax broadcasting allows anyone to transmit dozens, hundreds, or thousands of pages practically simultaneously to a list of people who need to receive their information. That list could be changing on a regular basis, as often as need be.

Some examples of industries and companies that do very heavy fax broadcasting: number one, the travel industry. Cruise lines, for example, were very early adopters of fax broadcasting. Once the cruise ship sails, any berths that are not full are lost revenue for the cruise lines. So cruise lines, as they get closer to their cruise date, will fax broadcast the information about available berths to thousands of travel agents nationwide. The travel agents, in turn, see that there is a special offer on ABC Cruise Line for a ship leaving to a destination next week and they can get 50% off on that particular berth. The travel agency is quite excited about that because they can call their best customers to try to sell that space to them. The customers are quite happy because they can get a quick vacation at a greatly reduced rate. The cruise line is also happy because they can fill a berth quickly and inexpensively.

Another industry that was quick to appreciate fax broadcasting, and probably has the largest number of pages broadcast on a daily basis, is the mortgage lending and banking industry. Every business day mortgage rates change, and there are dozens if not hundreds of mortgage initiators (companies that provide mortgages), who fax out their rates to mortgage brokers and agents telling them what the latest rates are. Many times these rates can change during the day. They listen to what the Chairman of the Federal Reserve says, and if he hints that interest rates will go up, every rate will change in the whole industry and tens of thousands of pages need to be tranmitted immediately. These are rate sheets that list adjustable rate mortgages, fixed rate mortgages, with different points, closing fees, and so on. There are pages upon pages of rates that are constantly changing. When a consumer goes for a mortgage, the mortgage or loan agent will look at the faxes that he or she receives from the mortgage lenders telling them what the most up-to-date rates are. The mortgage lending industry used to do everything via phone, and you could wait on hold for hours trying to get the rates. By the time you got the rates, they had changed.

Other organizations that should use fax broadcasting are companies that do business-to-business marketing. If you're currently selling a product or service and using direct mail, business to business, an excellent suggestion is to add fax broadcasting to your marketing mix. Take 10%, for example, of your direct-mail budget and allocate it to fax broadcasting. Do several tests. If you're used to dropping mail pieces to 50,000, test a fax broadcast to 5,000. Remember, with broadcasting you want to make the point clear, succinct, and easy for people to respond to, just as you would for direct-mail copywriting. A well-designed fax broadcast should have space for, "Yes, I like the information, let me sign and place the order." If it is designed well, the fax out can also be the order form faxed back in.

I'll give you an example: a bicycle manufacturer may have an overstock of a particular bike, so they fax broadcast every bike dealer in the United States that they are overstocked on model 123. If you would like 10 bikes or 20 bikes of model 123 at a reduced rate, sign your name here at the bottom of the page, give us the quantity you want, and fax it back. That's a quick and neat marketing campaign that could be pulled off for a fraction of what direct mail would cost, plus the fact that the turnaround time is absolutely minuscule.

That in a nutshell is an example of where fax broadcasting is successful. Anybody who is doing any business-to-business direct mail should give it a shot. However, you want to make it succinct, you want to make the message clear, you want to make it easy for them to respond. And you don't want to do this every single day. You have to be careful about what's becoming known as "junk" fax, which is much like junk mail. All of us in marketing don't like those terms, but nonetheless, they're here to stay. You want to make sure that what you're fax broadcasting is a message that you know the recipients are really going to want to receive. This way, when they get your fax, they will like it and respond to it. If it's a special offer, you can put a deadline on it. I would never send them anything if they may not think, "Wow, I would like to get this," because you'll defeat the message and after a while they will throw away your faxes whether it's real news or not. So don't inundate them. Use it sparingly and you will get much higher rates of return.

What companies or products are best suited for fax on demand? Any company or organization that does any literature fulfillment whatsoever. This can range from the smallest manufacturer's rep who is sending out price lists of what he/she is selling, all the way up to the largest manufacturers like IBM and AMP. Their fax-on-demand services have literally thousands of pages of spec sheets, price lists, press releases, and practially every piece of literature they've ever printed is put into their system. Any company that ever receives a call from a prospect or a lead or a current account or a customer, just asking for more information, is absolutely suited for fax on demand. This is because fax-on-demand literature fulfillment is much less expensive than conventional means of literature fulfillment.

It is certainly less expensive than putting an item through the mail. It's much more timely and less labor-intensive than someone who is answering a phone, looking for the literature, and hand faxing it. On top of all that, the bonus is that you're putting your information out "live" to the people who want it 24 hours a day, seven days a week. Many of us work longer hours or don't work 9 to 5, and others may want your literature on the weekends, when they are reading a magazine, or when they are following up on their direct mail, or looking at your catalogs. Putting fax on demand live 24 hours a day is the most cost-effective, cost-efficient way of fulfilling literature.

More and more manufacturers are adding this just for specification sheets. Every major software company in the country, not just the Lotuses and Microsofts, Symantecs and the Adobes, offers a fax-on-demand service. Even the smaller companies are putting in fax on demand for basic technical support.

Companies that staff inbound call centers with highly trained professionals to answer customer service questions especially need fax on demand. These are highly paid professionals, and it is not very cost-effective to have them fulfilling literature requests. In the computer field, when someone has a basic question like, "How do I write a macro?" or, "How do I cut and paste?" it is very simple for the representative to say, "If you pull up document 123 from my fax-on-demand system you can get step-by-step instructions. If you have a problem then, call me back."

Another organization that is perfect for fax on demand is the association. There is an association for everything. Every single association has the same concern and the same department: membership. Every time somebody wants new membership information they call up and get the person in charge of membership and that person mails or faxes. All membership information can be put on fax on demand. All the information about the upcoming conferences or conventions the organization has, the dates, the place, the speakers, the format, the registration forms, the housing forms, can quite easily be put up on fax on demand. So could all the copies of the magazines or newsletters that they publish and lists of the books or periodicals, audio tapes, videotapes, and everything else that the association sells. These are all member benefits that are basically the reason the organization exists. And they can be put up live 24 hours a day, seven days a week for their members.

One last industry that is really ideal for fax on demand is the publishing industry. Magazines such as *Forbes, Fortune, Inc., Consumer Reports, Travel Weekly*, all have fax-on-demand applications. One basic use for periodicals like these is bingo card fulfillment. Magazines using fax on demand automate the entire process.

Instead of circling a number and mailing it in, you call an 800 number, you punch in a code for the advertiser you're looking for, and out comes the information instantly, 24 hours a day. It is instant gratification for the magazine or newspaper reader. Also the advertiser is quite happy about it because it puts their information in the hands of the lead when they want it, when they are thinking about it, and that certainly is when a lead is the hottest. Publishers are also selling information via fax on demand. They are selling article reprints from articles that have been published in the magazine in the past. They are putting together bundles of magazine articles, everything we wrote within the last five years on this particular topic, you can get now for $9.95.

In essence, anyone sending out any type of information on a regular basis should take a serious look at fax on demand. Let me add that in terms of the market research end of fax on demand, when an individual retrieves a document (let's go back to the magazine for example), when they receive a document you know that document 123 was requested on January 1, 1999, at 2:00 in the afternoon and you know the fax number of the person who retrieved it. In its most raw sense, that's all you know. But that in itself is information because it can tell you which documents on your system are being requested the most and which ones aren't, and which ones should be updated most often. Take this a step further, if you're a magazine publisher and you want more market research than that. Every magazine has a subscriber code, an ID number, generally printed on top of the mailing label. So as a magazine publisher, you can have your readers call the fax-on-demand application, punch in the code for the advertiser they want, then punch in a subscriber ID number. You as the publisher now have instant information in terms of all the demographic information on that particular reader that you've collected over the years. You know who they are, what they are, what they retrieved, and when they retrieved it. That information can be forwarded directly to the advertiser immediately, letting them know that this particular person has retrieved their information.

Q: **In setting up the menu for the fax-on-demand system, businesses have the option of requesting additional information such as the name and phone number. What kind of information do you recommend businesses request?**

That depends on a couple of factors. If you don't feel you actually require the market research information, don't ask for anything, because as soon as you ask for the name or the phone number, or the address or even the customer ID number, your response rate and call volumes will drop. Customers are not stupid. They know that Big Brother is watching, that someone is collecting that information. So if you're not as concerned about receiving hard sales leads, let that information go. Just provide the service. You can get feedback from your customers. They'll tell you if they like the fax on demand. If you don't feel like you need to follow up on every lead, if that's not the nature of your business, don't request the information.

However, if you feel that you do want to request the information, then generally the way it works is one of the voice prompts will say, "At the end of the tone, please leave your name, phone number, and address and your fax will be sent promptly." Callers generally don't consider the fact that the whole process is automated and their name is not actually going to appear on the cover page of the fax.

However, it is more expensive and much more cumbersome for your business, because that information has to be transcribed, and transcription is expensive and not always reliable. People will not spell their name, they will not talk phonetically or slowly, so that you can understand exactly what they have said. If your service is national, there will be different dialects. It's going to be very difficult. Expect that somewhere between 30 and 60 percent of the people will respond and leave their information. Don't ever think that everybody is going to leave their name and address and phone number for you. You may also find that some people will hang up when they are asked for this extra information because they do not want to be identified. So you will lose calls by asking people to do this. As an alternative, the voice prompt can simply say, "If you would like, please leave your name and phone number at the tone." This way, you give them a choice, and they know that they will receive their fax either way.

If market research and marketing is the absolute key to this service, and your number one goal is to build a database, then I highly suggest you offer some sort of inducement. For example, "At the tone, please leave your name and phone number. After you do so, a discount coupon will be included with the information that you've requested." Now you don't have to tell them what discount coupon it is, and it could simply be a generic discount for 5% off any order over $1,000. However, you're giving them something for them giving you their name. Every company in the world does some sort of couponing or discounting. Consider doing something like that as an inducement to raise response rates, and to also raise the number of people who will leave that information on their application.

Q: Do you have examples of creative ways businesses can use fax technology?

I'll use a manufacturing company as an example, called ABC. ABC sells 5,000 items and they are all commodity items. You can get them from a hundred different suppliers, all over the world. Each competes on price and service. Let's say they're baseballs and you can buy them anywhere in bulk. Manufacturer ABC has decided to put up a fax-on-demand application describing all the different types of baseballs and sporting goods and products they manufacture. So the first thing they do is put up a very basic application with 20 documents in it, one on baseballs, one on bats, one on gloves, one on helmets, each product they have in their line.

ABC then tells its customers that when they call, they must enter their customer ID number. Then they punch in their requests and receive the documents. Phase two: at the end of the month, management receives a report on the fax-on-demand application and sees every single customer and what documents they received. They track their sales volume for the last month to see if those customers actually purchased the products for which they requested information. Phase three is where we get a bit more sophisticated. As soon as the customer pulls up the document they want, they receive the literature. Simultaneously, a fax is sent to ABC headquarters telling ABC's director of sales and marketing that this particular customer, with this customer number, just pulled up the document for gloves. He now has instant information in his hands saying customer 123 just pulled up information on gloves. That's a sales lead. He can now pass that lead to one of his sales reps to follow up. Ten minutes after the customer receives the information on gloves, he or she should get a call from the ABC sales rep asking him if he wants to buy those gloves. Phase four: ABC Manufacturing is a big company. They have offices in nine states nationwide. When that customer enters their customer ID number, we know who they are. We're going to look at that ID number and instead of just sending a fax to headquarters to the director of sales and marketing; we're simultaneously going to send the same fax to the regional office of ABC Corporation that is closest to the customer. So if that customer is in Omaha, the Omaha office is also going to get a fax saying customer 123 just retrieved documents on gloves. The local sales rep in Omaha should contact that customer. Now, not only does headquarters know, but the regional office knows. The next phase: headquarters gets reports at the end of the month. They can check their regional offices and see if Omaha is actually following up on their leads because they can look at the end of the month and see how Omaha is doing as compared to the other regions with their customers using the fax-on-demand application. It's almost a bit "big brotherish" but if you're in the headquarters of the corporation, you want to make sure your satellite offices are following up on leads, and this is a wonderful, cost-effective way of doing it.

Q: What do you think has been the most successful use of fax technology?

The most successful use of fax technology has probably been the ability to fax right from your PC. Nothing is easier or more user-friendly or more efficient than hitting a function key or flash key and being able to fax exactly what's on your screen to an individual or as many people as you want. That has been the most successful use of basic fax technology. The more successful use of enhanced fax technology in terms of the most successful fax-on-demand application I've ever seen are business-to-business niche-oriented applications.

An extremely successful fax-on-demand application is a state newsletter to attorneys. There is a publication called *Lawyer's Weekly Publications* which puts out a newspaper every single week in six or seven different states. And each state is completely independent. So *Massachusetts Lawyer's Weekly* is a newspaper that comes out every week and in there are headlines and summaries of every single court case that is handed down in that particular state through every level of court in the one-week period. In that state in that week, there could be 3,000 pages of decisions handed down. They could never completely be reproduced in the newspaper, and no lawyer needs every single decision ever handed down. Instead, this company provides the headlines and one or two sentences about each case, and then if you're an attorney and you want information on that particular case or you want the whole opinion, you call the fax-on-demand application. It is a revenue-generating application, so you are invoiced for the information you retrieve.

The information is highly specific to attorneys. No one else would use the service. It is updated on a weekly basis. It is extremely timely and it is extremely effective. It would never work for the general public. It wouldn't make any sense because consumers or businessmen don't need to pull up court opinions handed down every single week. But something highly targeted like that is always the most successful application.

Q: Where do you think fax technology will be five years from now?

The real question in my mind is whether or not we can assume that sometime within the next five years, virtually every consumer in the United States will have a fax machine in their home. Currently there are three things stopping consumers from putting fax machines in the home and all three of these barriers are falling. The first one is the price of the machine. We've now seen thermal fax machines fall under the $200 mark, where you can walk into a Staples, Office Warehouse, or Office Depot, and purchase a full-featured thermal fax machine for $179. This is at the same price point that VCRs have fallen to. Years ago, VCRs were much more money than that. Now you get a full-functioned, fully programmable with remote control VCR for about $175. You will see that fax machines will hover around the $150-$175 range. But you will add more and more functionality at that range. It is a reasonable price for consumers to put the fax machines in their homes.

The second barrier to putting a fax machine in the home is what's known as "line arbitration." Line arbitration is the problem of having to install a second phone line into your home to handle the fax machine. Consumers are not going to want to install second phone lines into their homes. It is difficult, it is costly, and basically it is a pain in the neck. However, line arbitration is not much more than a switch that will reside inside the fax machine that will allow the fax board inside the machine to listen to and understand the incoming call, and to differentiate phone calls from fax calls. The technology is available now. It is not that inexpensive and it is not yet 100%, but we are moving very rapidly toward it being highly successful and more cost-effective.

The third barrier to fax machines in the home in five years is basically a compelling reason. There have to be compelling reasons for consumers to put the fax machine in their home. I guarantee you when the price comes down and the line arbitration issue is solved, marketers across the country will give individuals hundreds, if not thousands, of reasons to put fax machines in the home. I envision it something much like what I call the "Polaroid strategy." That's basically, "We will give you the camera, so buy the film." My interpretation of that is that long-distance carriers, Regional Bell Operating Companies, and local exchange carriers will basically give fax machines to consumers. All they want them to do is use the lines.

Take the combination of these three issues: inexpensive machines, line arbitration problem solved, and applications available. Put it together with the fact that the RBOCs are going to be trying to convince consumers to purchase machines, and you're going to see everyone having a machine within five years.

Just think about it. Teachers could fax home extra credit or even homework assignments to parents to make sure they are completed correctly, and make sure younger children don't lose or forget them. In fact, every teacher in the company could leave all of their long-term or even extra-credit assignments in fax-on-demand systems. So parents could pull down extra information via fax-on-demand systems any time they want. Whenever a child is sick, for example, a parent could pull down the entire lesson plans for that day via fax on demand and make sure the sick child is still kept up to date, thereby not missing anything from staying home from school.

Q: Suppose every business utilized fax technology to market its products so that every commercial and every advertisement was accompanied by a phone number to receive more information via fax. Is this an area within the realm of possibility? If it were to happen, do you think consumers would be dulled by the capabilities and stop responding or would it add to the enthusiasm?

First of all, this is absolutely available and in the realm of possibility. In fact, I think it's going to happen. Every single company that offers an 800 number because they want consumers to call them for free will be offering a fax-on-demand number. Instead of having to staff these 800 numbers, the inbound call centers, around the clock, 24 hours a day, 365 days a year, they will be able to staff down because much of the information that they're providing you'll be able to get via fax on demand. Once consumers have fax machines in their home, it could be a Sunday afternoon, they could be watching a ball game or an infomercial or anything, see something on television that they like and respond to it to retrieve the information, any time they want. Anybody in marketing will tell you, and certainly anybody in marketing already knows, that a lead or a prospect is hottest when in their minds suddenly they decide they want more information on a particular product or service. At that second, they are the hottest lead money can buy. If they have to wait one week, two weeks, three weeks, even a couple of days, for information to be mailed to them or faxed to them they become cold. They may even forget why they requested the information in the first place, which is why fax on demand is so wonderful. It provides instant gratification. If you see a gizmo on television and you want to get more information on that gizmo, you can get it instantly. Not only will you get that information, but you can get an order form for that information, too, which basically means all you have to do is sign your name, fill in your credit card number, and fax it back.

Think of the economies of scale from a marketing point of view. The most expensive part of what I just described, using conventional methods, is having an operator stand by and take those calls. If consumers will accept information via fax, and then order it via fax, that's like simply filling out a form and faxing it back, which they can do from the comfort of their own home. The cost saving to the manufacturer, to the company providing the product, will be astounding. Furthermore, I think that after an initial learning period, consumers will like this much better. Because many times consumers don't like to dial an 800 number and talk to a salesperson on the other end. They know it's a salesperson. They know they're going to be upsold. They know they're going to have to repeat all the information they give them, spell out their names, spell out their address, give them their phone number. Consumers don't like to repeat their name and address 300,000 times over and over and over again. With the fax, they can simply fill out the fax whenever they have a moment and fax it back. It may take a little bit of a learning curve in the beginning, but I think you will find they will like it much better.

On top of that, because they filled out the order form and faxed it back, they will automatically have a written record for their files that they have placed this order. This will save marketers in the long run countless amounts of money and hours from callbacks and chargebacks. Consumers will have the order form in their hands. It will be an instant reminder when the credit card bill comes. Yes, they did order this. Yes, they want it and here's the information that came along with it. So I really think it will solve more than one problem.

In terms of whether it will add to consumers' enthusiasm or they will stop responding because it will be dull, I absolutely believe it will add to consumers' enthusiasm. When a consumer can have his wishes fulfilled instantly via fax on demand or via any method, they like it. They respond well and they will continue to respond. Once consumers become accustomed to fax-on-demand applications, they will use them over and over again. The motto I like to use is, "Don't ever forget, repeaters repeat," and that's a very important saying. If you know the law of sales that 80% of your sales comes from 20% of your customers, that's the same thing — repeaters repeat. Once a customer understands fax on demand, realizes how easy it is to use, he or she will use it over and over again. That has been proven many times by many current ongoing fax-on-demand services that are out there. They know what people call for repeatedly and they know that certain groups of people do call constantly. In it are people they have been marketing the service to for years. Once they become accustomed to it, they will use it. They will look for it, and they will look for new information on it.

Q: Do you think that fax technology is or will be eclipsed by electronic mail and online capabilities?

There is no easy answer to this question. In the next ten years, I don't think so. The reason is this: people reading this book are sophisticated marketers. Many understand the benefits of being online, and electronic mail and the Internet and other online services. You and I are sophisticated marketers. We are looking for new technologies. We are considered early adopters. I'd like you to think to yourself about your next-door neighbor. I'd also like you to think about your parents, or your brother and sister. You may be very sophisticated. You may be online. You may love electronic mail and you may think it's absolutely the future. But what do your parents think? What do your next-door neighbors think? What about your brother and sister? Are you online with them? How long do you think it will be until you are online with them? You'll be online very quickly with your colleagues, not only in your office but in other offices because you're early adopters, because you may love technology. But I want to wait and see how long it takes for everybody to be online.

In my opinion, it is going to take much longer than ten years. First of all, compare e-mail to sending a fax. There is nothing easier than picking up the telephone, punching in a number and sending a fax. Literally, a child could do it. There isn't a machine in any office that is as user-friendly as a fax machine. With e-mail you still have to log on a computer. You have to turn on a modem. You have to make sure it's all connected properly. You have to dial into a communications software package. Put in the correct protocols. You have none of those difficulties whatsoever when you're sending a simple fax. From the sales and marketing point of view, look at the large online services that are out there, the Prodigys, the America Onlines, the CompuServes. America Online is a public company but some of the other companies are owned and managed, for example, by Sears and IBM and H&R Block, that have spent hundreds of millions of dollars on these online services and in over ten years they have yet to break even. They have yet to make money. They are way ahead of the curve and in my opinion, it is going to take at least one generation before every person in this country is online.

Second, when it comes to transfer of files, the technology is difficult to understand. Currently there are five different common modem speeds. That's the first question. What modem speed are you on? Then you have to worry about bits and parities and handshaking and all of the other concerns and questions that need to be answered before you can actually log on with someone else. If you've never done it before, it's not as simple as it sounds. And even people who have done it, and do it every single day many times, have to spend 10 or 15 minutes talking to someone first before they can connect with them and transfer files. At this point, it's more convenient to send a fax.

Here's an analogy I would like to make. AT&T introduced the 800 number approximately 27 years ago. At that point, they were the only long-distance carrier, and 800 was a new type of billing service, where consumers or any individual that dialed an 800 number did not have to pay the toll call. The toll call and the toll charges were to be paid by the company providing the 800 line. It seems kind of silly for me to say that to you today. However, 27 years ago no one understood that. It was quite revolutionary. It took AT&T more than 10 years to convince consumers that the prefix 800 equaled toll free and that when a consumer dialed an 800 number they were not going to pay for that charge. That's why years ago, when 800 was advertised, it was also always advertised, "dial the toll-free number 1-800." It took more than ten years before consumers felt comfortable dialing 1-800 numbers and before they fully appreciated the fact that 800 meant that they did not have to pay for that particular call. And that was with all of the marketing muscle of AT&T thrown behind it to let consumers know that this service was free to them.

Now, it's been ten years since a number of the larger online services have come around, and their penetration rate in the homes is absolutely minuscule. Worse than that, they are losing more subscribers every year than they are gaining. And worse than that, even when these online services can keep new subscribers coming online, the usage level of subscribers peaks very, very early and then levels off.

It's a bell curve. It goes back down. And yes, there are early adopters and people who love online services and use them every day, but the percentage of those are quite low. Generally, there is a curve in the beginning, in the first couple of months where they ramp up and from that point on they drop off. Many of them pay for the services for a while and then almost never use them.

Twenty years down the road do I think that fax will be taken over completely by e-mail? It's hard to say. I think there will be a great deal more e-mailing going on because there are some advantages to e-mail once the whole world has it. Do I think that fax will completely go away? No. There were people who thought that television would replace radio, and radio would be history. Well, radio is not history. Do we listen to it nearly as much as we watch television? No, absolutely not, but radio has its niches. There are times like in the car and at home that we listen to radio more than other times. Fax will find its niche, perhaps anything that needs a signature because there are yet to be really good signature-verification methods online. I'm not sure there will ever be good signature-verification methods online. It's just too easy to fake that. So perhaps whenever a document needs to be signed and then verified, fax technology will take care of that. So yes, I think fax will be around for quite a long time and yes, e-mail will eat into that in the long run, but you're talking 20 years plus until you get to that stage.

Q: Please talk about the advantages and disadvantages of in-house fax systems versus fax service bureaus.

When a client comes to me and wants to put up an enhanced fax application, whether it's fax broadcasting, fax on demand, fax mailboxes, whatever, there's a series of questions I ask to determine what I think is best for this particular client. The first question is: what is the nature of the application? What problem do you want to solve? Once I have a clear understanding of the application, there are basically four different ways to go using enhanced fax technology. The first way is to purchase a small system, a two- or four-line system that will do everything you need for a small investment. The second way is to purchase quite a large system. Instead of two or four ports, we are now talking about 12, 24, 48 ports, something that would be used in an inbound call center for a very large operation. The third way is to purchase software and to configure your own system. We're not talking about off-the-shelf software. We're talking about software that starts at about $10,000 and goes up from there. The fourth way is to hire an enhanced fax service bureau.

In terms of configuring your own system, purchasing software, purchasing the fax and voice board, purchasing the computers to run it and the telephony lines and putting the whole system together, it's wonderful if you're a technology company. If you're a high-tech Silicon Valley company, if you're already in the software business or the computer business or the telephony business, you've got computer programmers, and telephony engineers on staff, who know how to put these systems together, then purchasing the software and building your own system is for you. However, very few companies know how to do this. Don't think if you know how to have a network of PCs that you know something about telephone engineering. If you don't have telephone engineers on staff, then this is not something you want to do. This is not something that should be handed over to an MIS department. They don't know anything generally about telephones and if they don't know anything about telephones, this is not something they are going to get involved with. It is much more involved than simply computers. However, for a certain segment of the business-to-business community, purchasing software and building a system does make complete sense. It really depends upon the nature of your organization.

The second way to do it is purchase a very small system. When I say very small, these systems are about the size of a VCR and cost around $5,000. They can store up to 1,000 pages of documents and they'll typically have two or four phone lines connected to them. These plug-in-and-play systems (as they are called), are excellent if you have a very small organization and you handle anywhere from 20 to 50 calls a week. If you want to have the appearance of providing a service like many larger companies do, and if the information you want to provide doesn't change much from day to day, then a small system like this makes a lot of sense. However, that's not usually the case for many of the companies that are reading this book right now.

The third and fourth way to get an enhanced fax is to use a large system. We're talking about 12, 24, or 48 ports that start easily in the $10,000 — $15,000 range and can certainly approach $100,000 very quickly. Or you can hire an enhanced fax service bureau. An enhanced fax service bureau operates much like other conventional types of service bureaus, like a telemarketing service bureau, for example. When you may not want to have a bank of phones in-house and hire people who do nothing but do your outbound telephone marketing, you would hire a telemarketing bureau. For the same reason that if you do direct mail, you don't have the printing in-house, you go out of house and you hire a printer. It's the same with fulfillment. If you are doing a lot of mail fulfillment or sample fulfillment, you probably do not do the fulfillment in-house. You've probably hired a company that specializes in fulfillment and does nothing else, and that way they can do a better job than you can do yourself. For those same reasons, you would consider hiring an enhanced fax services bureau. A sophisticated, better enhanced fax services bureau will have several hundred phone lines attached to a UNIX-based operating system. They will have computer programmers and technicians on staff full time who can engineer an application, and keep it up and running all the time. They will have customer service representatives on staff who understand enhanced fax technology and can help, not only you, but help your customers if they are having problems using your service or using your application. They will also maintain and upgrade their equipment on a regular basis to make sure that it's the fastest, most sophisticated equipment on the marketplace and ensure that your application never goes down.

Another advantage of hiring a fax service bureau is that there is no large capital outlay. You are not buying equipment. You are simply hiring someone and using their equipment already in place. A large service bureau will have many clients, and those clients will all use the same equipment, just as a printer uses the same press for many different press runs and for many different clients. Therefore, a service bureau is able to offer you rates much in line with what you would expect to pay if you had tried to do this in-house without the standard capital outlay. It shouldn't cost you more than several thousand dollars for even a very sophisticated application. Ongoing fees will not be much when compared to conventional forms of direct marketing and direct mail.

The disadvantage of using a service bureau is the lack of control. You will never have 100% control over your application. Many people don't want 100% control over their application because that's not the business they're in. You have to decide, and again you look at the nature of your organization, the nature of your company, what type of business you want to be in. That depends on what you're already doing. Most magazine publishers, in fact every magazine publisher that I know of and that I referred to in the past, all hire fax service bureaus. Magazine publishers know how to put out a magazine. They know how to write. They know how to sell advertising. They know how to find subscribers. What they don't know is how to engineer and program a fax-on-demand application. So they go out of house to hire people to do it for them. Larger companies that do know how to do it, for example, IBM and Hewlett-Packard, have in-house systems because they have the expertise on staff to know how to engineer and program an application. They know how to purchase the equipment. They know what equipment to purchase. They know how to maintain it, how to upgrade it, and how to keep it active and keep it live. It wouldn't make much sense for IBM, which has close to 100 phone lines, 1,100 documents, and tens of thousands of pages of information on their system, to take all of that information over to a service bureau. It wouldn't make much sense for IBM to take all of the information that they have, and the fact that they need to update it on a daily basis, and move it over to a service bureau. Their information is updated regularly. Their database of customers is updated on an ongoing basis and they want to be able to track it much more closely and print out reports on a regular basis so they know who is retrieving what and when on a much more timely basis than a service bureau would be prepared to offer them. Furthermore, due to the nature of their company, their corporate culture, their philosophy, and the fact that they know what they're doing with enhanced fax, it just simply makes sense for them to purchase a large piece of equipment. The same is true for Hewlett-Packard. The same is true for many of the computer companies, Lotus and Microsoft, Adobe, Autodesk. Since the capital is not that great for a very large company and they may already have the computers, fax boards, voice boards, and other equipment in-house, it makes sense for them to set up their own system. However, that is the nature of their company.

Finally, if you're going to be setting up a fax-on-demand application that ties into a database of individuals or subscribers, it may make sense to install a system in-house. Let's go back to the ABC Manufacturer example of baseballs and gloves and hats. If ABC is going to force you to punch in your ABC account number, and then ABC is going to track very closely who you are and that you've retrieved a document, it may make sense to have an in-house system. It would depend pretty much upon how large ABC Manufacturer is and who they have on staff and what they know how to do. If they get thousands of calls a week, then it probably makes sense for them to purchase equipment rather than go to a service bureau. It simply is one of the first questions that needs to be addressed and it's not an easy answer. There are the four ways to go. There are the two main ways to go, purchase a piece of equipment or hire a service bureau. You really have to look at your question. You have to look at what you want to do now. You have to look at what you want to do in the future, what your long-term goals are with fax on demand and what other applications you may want to put up once you have the basic application live.

I will say that approximately 80% of all enhanced fax applications nationwide are run at service bureaus. Even large corporations that know they want to purchase a system and bring it in-house often go to a service bureau first because they can try it before they buy it. As I've said, you can engineer an application and put it up live for several thousand dollars, or even less. It is much less expensive to try it that way and then purchase equipment when you know the application is successful, rather than purchasing the equipment and then hoping that the application will be successful. Because not every application succeeds. I call this line the "Field of Dreams." "If you build it, will they call?" Just because you build an application, or you put up a fax-on-demand service, it does not guarantee that people are going to call the service. That's why I suggest if you are putting up anything more than a basic service or especially a revenue-generating service, something where you are going to try to make money, I suggest you test it quite carefully and get outside help to make sure that you're not putting up something that is doomed to fail. Certainly half to 75% of all complimentary fax-on-demand applications are successful. But for revenue-generating applications, more than half of them fail, which is why you want to be careful. If you're looking to put up a straight literature-fulfillment application, like a magazine bingo card or more information about your particular company or product, then you probably have a sure-fire winner. I wish you the best of luck.

Fax Broadcasting

A fax broadcasting system sends one or more personalized documents to multiple locations, automatically. If you need to transmit information to a large number of people quickly, fax broadcasting can make your life easier.

You might want to send product updates to your best customers. If you send them by fax, they will get there nearly instantly, and you won't have to stuff a single envelope. The fee for the fax service is lower per document than postal costs. You'll save on printing fees, which can be high, particularly for multi-page documents. You can make modifications to your document almost up to the moment of transmission, ensuring that your customers get the most current information. Furthermore, the documents can go out after hours, when fax machines are idle, and the system requires no supervision.

Following are some examples of ways in which businesses have customized fax broadcast technology to suit their needs.

Newsletters

This is probably the most popular use for fax broadcasting. Newsletter publishers can cut their costs drastically by sending the newsletters entirely by fax, or by using a combination of fax and print. Sarah Stambler's *Marketing with Technology News* is a newsletter published by TechProse, Inc., an electronic publishing firm that specializes in the creative use of electronic alternative media in customer-driven marketing and research. It is distributed, appropriately enough, by fax.

The Boycott Law Bulletin, a newsletter that covers enforcement of U.S. federal anti-boycott laws that prohibit U.S. corporate compliance with certain aspects of the Arab boycott of Israel, used to come out once a month. Now, a shorter version is released twice a month by fax, which saves the publisher money and allows for more timely reporting.

The Tindall Report, a bimonthly newsletter published by ADT Research, analyzes the nightly newscasts of the three main television networks. The newsletter is printed and sent by mail. In addition, a weekly, one-page supplement to this newsletter, called The Tindall Weekly, is distributed by fax. Subscribers can order the newsletter alone, or the newsletter and the update.

Random Lengths, the most widely circulated market report in the forest products industry, comes out in print each week. In addition, the publisher offers frequent updates via fax or e-mail. Fifteen percent of the report's 13,000 subscribers have ordered both the newsletter and the updates, with 98 percent of these opting for fax transmission.

Political Issues

Businesses and organizations involved in political issues have found fax broadcasting to be an invaluable method of disseminating fast-breaking news. When a decision is made in the White House, or when an incident occurs anywhere in the world, these groups want their constituents to know about it immediately. The National Wildlife Federation has 450 state leaders as members. Its fax-broadcast system sends relevant news to each of these leaders minutes after it happens.

Restaurants

Even the smallest businesses may find fax broadcasting useful. The owner of the Hudson Deli in Westchester County, New York, used to fax menus to about 50 people every morning. The task took up to two hours at the busiest time of the day, just before lunch. The deli's simple fax-broadcasting system now sends the menus automatically, keeping customers happy and allowing the owner to spend those two hours in more productive ways. And when the deli has a special offer, the owner sends a fax about it to those same customers.

News Releases/Public Relations

Companies who promote a product by sending news releases to the media benefit greatly from fax broadcasting. Media professionals prefer to receive personalized news releases, and editors do not want to receive calls to verify receipt of the information. Fax broadcasting allows a marketer to send faxes with personalized cover pages, and the verification receipt confirms that the fax has arrived.

Periodicals

A number of publications have found that fax broadcasting complements their regular print run. Each day, Dow Jones & Co. sends a

JournalFax to paid subscribers. This two-page update of world and national news includes the Dow Jones Industrial Average. Call (800) 759-9966 to get a free sample. Dow Jones subscribers can also get real-time news on selected companies through a service called CustomClips.

For a small fee, *Home Office Computing* provides further information on some of its articles.

Magazines also use fax broadcast to reach their advertisers with updates on editorial calendars, rates, and special offers.

Recreation

To help it sell darts, Valley Recreation Products promotes regional darts and pool leagues in bars nationwide. Because the leagues have grown, the company needed a system that let teams exchange scores quickly. Now, teams fax their scores to an operator, who processes them and returns standings by fax within 24 hours. The system combines optical character recognition software with a database program.

Fax Broadcasting/Fax on Demand Combination

U sed in combination with a fax-on-demand system, fax broadcasting becomes even more powerful. Once a potential customer has called your fax-on-demand number, you have that person's fax number, phone number, company name, and other information you have requested. You can create a database with this data, and build on potential clients' demonstrated interest. For example, Adobe alerts its fax-on-demand customers whenever it offers a special deal on a new typeface.

Once you have a database of names and addresses, you can set up a system to fax documents automatically. You can even personalize these documents with the recipient's name and other information.

You can also use fax broadcasting to promote your fax-on-demand system. If you already have a database of contacts, you can send a document by fax broadcast and include a list of additional documents that are available by fax on demand.

The Central Dallas Association's newsletter, *Downtown This Week*, focuses on improving Dallas's downtown area. It is faxed to CDA's members at no charge. Included in the three-page newsletter is a menu of various documents available by fax, such as a schedule for the Dallas Education Center and an update of downtown construction projects.

Advertising in the newsletter covers the publication's costs. About 80 percent of the recipients distribute the newsletter to others in their offices, and less than 1/2 percent have asked to be taken off the distribution list. In the first month of operation, 144 people called the fax-on-demand system and made 216 requests for documents.

DFW GolfFAX, produced by a service bureau called Fax Resources, is a two-page document containing listings and ads. Readers can get more information on companies and clubs mentioned in listings and ads by calling a fax-on-demand number. The newsletter is distributed free of charge to golfers whose business cards were gathered at golf shows and country club directories. In its first two weeks, the fax-on-demand system handled 183 calls and 271 document requests.

The Economics Press in Fairfield, N.J., publishers of business training materials, announced its new fax-on-demand system in its newsletters. Callers could order articles on topics such as business writing and personal success strategies, for $6 or $7 per article. The company mailed the newsletters to 70,000 people. In just two weeks, 90 people called the service and purchased a total of 187 documents. While the magnitude of the project isn't large, it establishes an interactive relationship where none had existed.

Setting Up a System

You can set up an enhanced fax system in-house, or work with a service bureau. Because the cost of buying equipment isn't small, service bureaus currently handle 80 percent of all applications. Look for this number to drop as equipment prices decrease.

Callers make a toll call, dial an 800 number, or dial a 900 number. It's your choice. You can also choose a one-call or a call-back system. In a one-call, the customer dials the number using the handset on his fax machine, follows the instructions, and then presses the "start" key on his machine to receive the requested information. In a call-back, the customer enters a fax number, and the information is faxed to him a few moments later.

You can store your documents in the system's electronic library in several ways. The simplest method is to fax or scan the documents in. Some service bureaus let you transmit information from any fax machine. These methods are the simplest, but the images produced are not as clear as those sent directly from a computer. SprintFax, Ibex Technologies, and other companies offer software that allows you to upload high-quality images directly from your computer.

What if the customer's machine is out of paper, or she is receiving another fax? Some systems have an automatic retry feature. If the fax does not go through the first time, the machine will keep trying until it succeeds.

You can easily track transmissions. Many service bureaus provide a management report, a fax that records each completed broadcast immediately.

Application Tips

Before setting up a fax on demand or fax-broadcasting system, ask yourself the following questions:

- *What do my clients request most often?*

- *What kind of information is important to them, and can I provide it easily?*

- *Can I prepare special reports suitable for fax distribution?*

- *Can I use the system to provide hard-to-find forms to customers?*

52 Ways to Use Fax Technology

1. *Transmit weather info to farmers, and include an ad for your business*

If you sell farm implements, seed, financial services, or other goods and services of interest to local farmers, you want to build community goodwill. Offering localized weather information by fax — either through broadcast fax when emergencies strike, or on a daily basis — is a low-cost, high-impact goodwill generator. You can include an ad for your company with each fax sent.

2. *Distribute ticket availability information*

Ticketmaster and the local box office spend tens of thousands of dollars on phone lines and extra operators — even though more than half the callers ring off without buying a ticket. Each and every ticket-selling transaction requires a long discussion about available seats. By offering a listing of available seats through fax on demand, ticket sellers could dramatically decrease time spent on the phone while increasing customer satisfaction.

3. *Promote last-minute vacation deals*

An unsold seat on a cruise ship or airplane is worthless. Unfortunately, last-minute travel companies are hindered by the enormous cost of notifying clients of available trips. Using broadcast fax and fax on demand, an enterprising broker can easily and inexpensively notify her best clients of any available deals.

4. Distribute coupons for specials at the local market

Large supermarket chains can afford to run expensive free-standing inserts (FSIs) and full-page ads in the city papers. Local markets and specialty stores don't have this luxury. By offering broadcast fax to their best customers, these stores can fight back with precisely targeted promotion.

5. Transmit updated price lists

If a large business updates its prices monthly, the cost of notifying its 10,000 customers of each change can quickly become prohibitive. An alternative is to use broadcast fax to contact the most steady customers, while permitting intermittent customers to get the latest list using fax on demand. For example, a sports card broker could load his latest price list into the machine daily, eliminating confusion and frustration over old prices.

6. Broadcast news releases to the media

If your company has just won a national award or secured a major government contract, that's news. Unfortunately, by the time the postal service delivers a news release, it's old news. You may get more media exposure if you broadcast a release to editors by fax. Freshness is vital to the news media. The faster you can get your release to them, the greater the chance they will use it.

7. Broadcast product information to sales reps

Manufacturers often make slight changes to their products that will interest only a few customers. It isn't cost-effective to rewrite the product brochure. However, the company can fax details about the new features to its sales reps, who then tell interested customers.

8. Broadcast a newsletter to subscribers

Most newsletter publishers find that printing and mailing costs are two of their largest expenses. But if a publisher prints only one copy of her newsletter, and faxes it to subscribers in off-peak hours, she can save thousands of dollars. The subscriber benefits too, because he gets his valuable news more quickly.

9. Provide currency information

Currency prices change by the hour as the markets fluctuate. A company working on a major international deal can make or lose thousands of dollars, depending on the exchange rate when the contract is signed. A bank could fax frequent updates to its biggest customers, earning lots of goodwill for very little money.

10. *Advertise seat availability on airplanes*

When an airline offers a major fare reduction, its switchboard is over-whelmed with callers, many of whom are unable to find available seats at the advertised price. This frustration hurts the relationship that the airline is trying to build. The airline could offer a simple fax-on-demand system that would identify the flights with the most availability on a given route.

11. *Supply auction information*

A major auction house like Sotheby's could fax information on pieces up for auction to clients who have previously purchased similar or related items. Collectors who bought a Max Bill abstract sculpture last year, for instance, may be very interested in the upcoming auction of a Sonia Delany.

12. *Send record release information to radio stations*

DJs are always looking for bits of news and trivia to drop into their patter between records. A record company can fax a one-page sheet of interest-ing tidbits about a new CD ("Did you know that the new Cockroaches album was recorded in the Paris sewers?") to hundreds of DJs several days before the record arrives in the stores, creating listener interest at the most crucial time.

13. *Provide instructions for office equipment*

Technical consultants can spend hours answering straightforward ques-tions such as, "How do I change the toner cartridge on my photocopier?" A fax-on-demand system can solve this problem by allowing users to request instruction sheets for various common tasks. Everyone benefits: Users get clearly printed information and drawings, and consultants get more time to answer complicated questions.

14. *Provide how-to instructions for homeowners*

A publisher of do-it-yourself books can set up a fax-on-demand system offering tips on fixing common household problems. On each tip sheet, the publisher prints an ad for a related book. For instance, the sheet on fixing leaky faucets includes an ad for *The Complete Guide to Home Plumbing*. Even if the customer doesn't buy the related book right away, the publisher has positioned itself as an expert in home repair.

15. *Distribute medical advice to parents (sponsored)*

A hospital might set up a fax-on-demand service to provide medical infor-mation to couples who have recently had babies at the hospital. A related business, such as a baby food manufacturer or a children's clothing store, would cover the cost of the service by paying a fee to advertise on the information sheets.

16. *Produce special reports*

Supplying fact-filled reports on issues of importance to potential clients can create goodwill for your company before you even make a sales call. A nursing home could fax a report on changing trends in elderly care to people who subscribe to a seniors' publication. The recipients will be grateful for the hard-to-find information, and will remember the home's name if they are ever seeking extended care for a family member.

17. Broadcast lobbyists' position papers

Lobbyists often face a daunting challenge: getting new information out to hundreds of U.S. Representatives just days before a crucial vote. By faxing their position papers directly to each office, they get the information into the right hands quickly without the hassle of playing telephone tag with busy legislators.

18. Augment ads

A picture really can be worth a thousand words. A cycling equipment company can run a magazine ad featuring pictures of its most popular bikes, gloves, helmets, and cycling shorts, with a brief description and a code beside each product. Readers can dial the fax-on-demand number displayed in the ad, punch in the codes of products, and receive more information than could ever be printed in a magazine ad.

19. Distribute catalogs on demand

A mail-order company selling women's casual and business clothing may notice that some of its customers buy sweatshirts and leggings but never buy business suits. The firm can offer these customers the option of receiving a casual-only catalog by fax. These customers get only the information they need, and the company saves on printing and mailing costs.

20. Provide photos and layouts of houses that are for sale

A real estate company can set up a fax-on-demand service offering prospective home buyers information on houses for sale, broken down by price, neighborhood, size, or other characteristics. The fax answers the buyers' basic questions. An agent can call them a few days later to discuss more detailed concerns.

21. Advertise car dealership specials

Car dealers carry dozens of used cars, each unique. By offering a regular update of the stock on the lot, the dealer can save the shopper time, and increase the number of motivated prospects.

22. Send phone lists to politically active supporters

An oil spill has just clogged a major harbor, and an environmental group wants to urge its members to call local, state, and national authorities to demand a quick cleanup. The organization can immediately fax lists of legislators' telephone numbers to active members. It can also send the list via fax on demand to people who respond to a newspaper ad — generating a list of potential members as well as political action.

23. Distribute charts and tables from government data (sponsored)

The government creates reams of data — most of it unseen by the general public. An information publisher can capture this data and make it available to the public through fax on demand.

24. Supply job seekers' résumés on demand

An association of freelance writers can send a directory of its members to editors across the country. If an editor wants more information on a particular writer, he can call the association's fax-on-demand service to receive a detailed résumé and samples of the writer's magazine articles. Similar services would work well for employment agencies, unions, and student placement bureaus.

25. Transmit job descriptions on demand

A Fortune 500 company places a career ad in a national newspaper and is suddenly flooded with calls for more information on the three positions advertised. A fax-on-demand system can send job descriptions to callers automatically, helping interested people target their applications more precisely.

26. Broadcast sports information and lineups (sponsored)

The local hockey team can make the game's roster available to interested fans at virtually no cost by providing it through fax on demand.

27. Distribute travel brochures

A customer may want to find out about yak tours of Tibet or luxury villas in Spain, but most travel agencies only have enough room to stock brochures on all-inclusive Caribbean resorts, bus tours of France, and other popular packages. A fax-on-demand system, however, can offer interested clients a choice from thousands of brochures, increasing the agency's potential to make a sale.

28. Supply inventories of comic books for sale

Collectors are searching for particular comic books, but answering every inquiry is a time-consuming task. By placing the shop's entire inventory on fax on demand, collectors can quickly find the object of their search.

29. Broadcast poison and snake bite information (sponsored)

Six months to a year after a baby has been born at a hospital, the hospital's poison control center could send information on child-proofing medicine cabinets — just as the baby is learning to walk and open doors. A pharmacy could advertise on each sheet, covering the cost of the service.

30. Broadcast dental appointment reminders to existing patients

Every Monday morning, the receptionist at a dentist's office can fax a standard reminder notice to patients who have appointments scheduled that week.

31. *Broadcast bills*

Utilities can broadcast one standard bill to all customers paying the same fee, saving money on printing, envelopes, and postage. Database-driven fax broadcasting can send out personalized bills, further decreasing the utility's cost. A discount could be offered to those willing to receive bills this way.

32. *Handle reservations for a popular restaurant*

When a hot restaurant opens, the owner must deal with overflowing phone lines and angry people who couldn't get a reservation. By allowing individuals to request seating information through fax on demand, everyone wins.

33. *Provide information on the status of truck shipments*

Truckers have become far more sophisticated in their ability to track shipment status. Database fax can take this sophistication one step further, offering up-to-the moment written information.

34. *Provide proof of delivery*

Federal Express has captured most of the market for overnight delivery. But a competitor could offer automatic fax confirmation, sending a fax to the shipper the moment the package arrives. The cost to the competitor — less than forty cents a shipment.

35. *Distribute a large corporation's capabilities brochures*

An international consulting firm offers many services, such as accounting, outplacement counseling, public opinion research, and policy analysis. Every month, the company gains new clients, which it would like to mention in its literature. Instead of frequently updating one general brochure — a costly procedure — the company can distribute finely targeted, up-to-date brochures on each of its services through fax on demand.

36. *Distribute book samples*

The promotional ads for a new romance novel say the book is "hot, hot, hot," but the owner of a small bookshop is not convinced. She's stocked books based on that claim before, only to have her regular customers complain after buying them that they were about as exciting as C-SPAN. A fax-on-demand system would allow her to read selected scenes and plot synopses from books before they're published, and decide whether they would appeal to her regular customers.

37. *Offer a sneak preview of the latest issue of a magazine*

The publisher of an entertainment magazine can fax excerpts of an interview with a notoriously reclusive director to those interested by a teaser campaign. Certain to boost newsstand sales.

38. *Provide transcripts of a politician's position papers and latest speeches*

If a politician suddenly rises to national attention, her office may be swamped with media requests for information on her earlier career. A simple fax-on-demand system would allow reporters to obtain copies of position papers and speeches that would lend depth to their profile pieces and analyses.

39. *Supply international stock information*

A stockbroker can fax updated information on international stocks to important clients on a regular basis. By supplying hard-to-find data, the stockbroker positions himself as a knowledgeable expert. And the investors, confident that they are well informed, may buy more stock than they would without the information.

40. *Provide portfolio information*

Stockbrokers and mutual fund administrators spend a lot of money printing and mailing portfolio statements to investors. Many investors may prefer to receive this information by fax.

41. *Distribute application forms*

Universities publish scores of application forms for different groups: undergraduate students, Ph.D. candidates, foreign students, aid applicants, and more. University admissions offices spend hours each day answering phone calls from students seeking specific forms. A fax-on-demand system would allow students to receive forms immediately, at any time, and would free up admissions officers to deal with complicated questions.

42. *Create a fan club newsletter*

Fans of a pop singer could get daily updates on their hero through a fax-on-demand service. Cost to the singer — less than $2,000 a year. Certain to increase his concert sales and album play.

43. *Provide up-to-date sports scores*

Many sports fans can't get out to afternoon games, and can't listen to the radio at work, but they still want to know how their favorite teams are doing — especially during the playoffs. A radio station could build loyalty by broadcasting up-to-date results to interested fans.

44. *Answer frequently asked financial questions*

To attract new clients, a financial planner can advertise a free fax-on-demand service that offers answers to common financial questions, such as "How can I save for my child's education?" or "What are the advantages of mutual funds over savings bonds?" The service lets potential customers try out the planner's services in a nonthreatening way. The planner can then contact these prospects directly to set up a follow-up appointment.

45. Supply information on the top-selling products of the week

A record store or bookshop can fax information on the week's top-selling albums and books to local media outlets. The press attention will translate into increased store traffic.

46. Distribute company profiles

An organization that fields constant requests for company information, such as a credit-checking firm, a municipal Chamber of Commerce, or the local Better Business bureau, can make standard company profiles available through a fax-on-demand system.

47. Promote ways to improve gas/oil/electricity usage (sponsored)

An environmental group can team up with a utility to share the cost of faxing seasonal tips on saving gas, oil, or electricity to utility customers who request the service. In the summer, the tip sheets could outline ways to cut down on air conditioner use, while in the fall they could urge customers to clean their furnace filters.

48. Supply demographic information

Market research firms that have compiled detailed demographic information can make that data available to clients for a fee through a fax-on-demand service. The client would punch in a ZIP code and receive information on the age, income, family status, and buying habits of the area's residents.

49. Share mailing lists

A tourism and convention bureau in a major city can earn some money and save time by making mailing lists of its members available to marketers through fax on demand. Marketers, who would pay a fee for the lists they request, could get a list of all the bureau's members, or lists broken down by neighborhood or type of business.

50. Broadcast product recall/safety notifications

A car company can ensure that its customers receive immediate notice of recalls by broadcasting the information by fax. The car company saves postage costs, and the customers will be happy to know about possible safety problems as quickly as possible.

51. Notify interested parties of deadline changes

When a government department extends the deadline for bids on a contract, potential bidders need to know that information as soon as possible. And all bidders need to know about the extension at the same time, to ensure fair competition. By broadcasting the information by fax, the department informs all bidders of the extension quickly.

52. Provide exhibit information for trade shows and conventions

By faxing information to potential exhibitors, trade show and convention organizers can contact many more companies than they could afford to contact by mail. This increases the chances that the organizers will be able to fill all the available booths.

Fax Resources

Service Bureaus

Delrina Communications Services
895 Don Mills Rd.
500-2 Park Centre
Toronto, Ontario
Canada M3C1W3
(800) 792-0329

Delrina is a provider of fax mailboxes, a service that stores your faxes until you're ready to retrieve them. Your PC will never be left on, senders will never get a busy signal, and your own phone line will always be free. You can retrieve your faxes from anywhere in the world simply by downloading them to WinFax PRO 4.0 or forwarding them to a fax machine. Delrina also provides fax broadcasting. Compose documents using WinFax PRO 4.0 and distribute them using Delrina's phone lines.

Instant Information, Inc.
5 Broad Street
Boston MA 02109
(617) 523-7636 fax (617) 723-6522 demo
(800) USA-XPORT (The Export Hotline)

Instant Information is a full-feature service bureau specializing in fax on demand and fax broadcasting services. *Forbes, Fortune, Voice Processing*, The Export Hotline, and others have set up systems through Instant Information. Instant Information is the recipient of the first Enhanced Fax Award for Service Bureau Excellence by *Voice Processing* magazine.

The Kauffman Group
324 Windsor Drive
Cherry Hill NJ 08002-2426
(609) 482-8288 fax (609) 482-8940

The Kauffman Group is an enhanced facsimile services consulting firm that focuses on the sales, marketing, and communications benefits of fax technology. It often launches enhanced fax applications to solve a particular problem or augment a marketing campaign. Clients of The Kauffman Group come from a broad range of industries. The company can manage applications, evaluate delivery methods, evaluate and recommend products or applications, and do application strategic planning.

MarketFax
One Bridge Street
Irvington NY 10533
(914) 591-6301 fax (914) 591-0017
fax line (800) 227-5638 ext. 105 or 106

MarketFax is a proprietary fax-on-demand service that sends information from any touch-tone phone to any fax machine anywhere, 24 hours a day, 7 days a week — instantly, automatically, and unattended. It can be accessed via an 800 number using any touch-tone phone including cellular.

MarketFax can track all pertinent caller information, including date, time of call, caller location, fax and phone numbers, caller frequency, and more. You can change or update information on the MarketFax system as often as you wish — on demand. You can also access response activity reports at any time. According to the company, closing ratios of converting callers to sales via MarketFax range from 20 percent to 70 percent.

SprintFAX
(800) 366-3297 fax line (800) 877-1272

SprintFax offers fax on demand, broadcast fax, and interactive voice response systems. It also offers SprintFAX OnLine software for Windows, DOS, or Macintosh. Broadcast distribution features include automatic retry, smart retry (if an error occurs in mid-transmission, transmission will resume beginning with the last page sent), management reports, and alternate delivery. Volume discounts are available.

Touch Tone Services
P.O. Box 2994
Renton WA 98056
(206) 271-7200 fax line
(800) 791-1082, request document 101 for general information

Touch Tone is a telecommunications service bureau specializing in interactive voice and fax applications. It offers fax broadcasting, fax on demand and custom voice-fax programming for large and small clients. This service bureau is an innovator in bingo card fax on demand and database to fax systems.

Hardware and Software Providers

Copia International, Ltd.
(708) 682-8898 fax (708) 665-9841 fax line (708) 351-2266

Copia International provides FaxFacts, a union of a PC, voice, and fax board featuring easy-to-use pull-down menus. It allows you to create the prompt menu yourself in your own voice. Copia holds the patent on the one-call system. This system and the call-back system can operate simultaneously.

Ibex Technologies
550 Main Street
Placerville CA 95667
(916) 621-4342 fax (916) 621-2004 fax line (800) 289-9998

Ibex Technologies provides software, called FaxLine for Windows, for businesses interested in setting up their own fax-on-demand system. Named one of the 50 Best Buys for 1993 by *Corporate Computing* magazine, FaxLine provides users with an easy-to-use, data-driven Windows interface for building fax-on-demand applications. It also has a broadcast feature.

SpectraFax Corporation
3050 Horseshoe Drive, Suite 100
Naples FL 33942-7908
(813) 643-5060 fax (813) 643-5070
info line (800) 833-1FAX

SpectraFax is a market leader in providing fax and voice information retrieval/delivery systems to corporations, associations, government markets, and service bureaus. The Special Request product provides all fax and voice information retrieval/delivery applications, including fax on demand, data on demand, fax broadcast, fax order processing, and fax messaging. Other hardware includes devices to connect Special Request with LANs, fax boards, and more.

Reference Sources

National FaxList
P.O. Box 9777
Trenton NJ 08690
(609) 584-0047 fax (609) 584-0048

The database of National FaxList is claimed to be the largest compilation of business fax records in the country. It helps users reach multiple points in specific industrial or regional markets via fax. Each record in the database contains an address, telephone and fax numbers, an executive contact, and a business classification that allows the creation of groups of records selected by type of business in any area of the country. The National FaxList database comprises more than 940,000 records. National FaxList also offers clients with an existing database of businesses without fax numbers a match-up service that updates their records.

Sarah Stambler's *Marketing with Technology News*
$99/year (12 issues) available from
TechProse, Inc.
370 Central Park West, #210
New York NY 10025
(212) 222-1765 Orders (212) 222-1713

This four-page monthly newsletter is distributed solely by fax. It covers businesses' use of alternative electronic media to market and deliver their products. Alternative media include fax broadcasting, fax on demand, videotext, CD-ROM, multimedia, FM subcarrier, cellular communications, audiotext, and more. *MWT* examines the companies using these techniques, compares competing techniques for different applications, analyzes new trends, and reviews new products.

Other publications available from TechProse include ($84 each) "Selecting a Fax Broadcast Service Bureau," 24 pages, "Selecting a Fax-on-Demand Service Bureau," 24 pages, "Selecting an In-House Fax-on-Demand System," 25 pages. The first two reports include a comparison table of major service bureaus.

Fax Glossary

Bingo card fulfillment: an automated advertiser-response system used by magazines. Each ad in the magazine is given a code number. Readers can request information on advertisers by calling a central number and keying in the relevant code.

Call-back fax on demand: a system in which customers call a number from their phone, enter their fax number, and request documents. The documents are then sent to their fax machine.

Database to fax: a fax-on-demand system in which the documents are not pre-scanned. Instead, the computer compiles information from a database and sends it to the caller.

Dots per inch (dpi): a method of measuring how clearly a fax machine will reproduce a document. The higher the dpi of the receiving machine, the clearer the document will be.

Enhanced fax: any system of using fax technology other than for basic transmissions. It includes fax on demand and fax broadcasting.

Fax broadcasting: a form of fax marketing in which personalized documents are sent out to current or prospective customers en masse.

Fax marketing: using a fax machine to provide information to customers, sell products, or provide support.

Fax on demand: a form of fax marketing in which documents are available to customers upon request. A customer dials a number and requests the appropriate document. The document is then sent to the customer's fax machine.

One-call fax on demand: a system in which customers call a number from their fax machine and request documents. The entire transmission is completed with one call, at no additional expense to the marketer.

Service bureau: a company that provides enhanced fax services. It offers an alternative to an in-house system.

AUDIOTEXT

Despite all the hype about the Information Superhighway, there's currently only one interactive device that's available to everyone. It's simple, easy to use, rarely breaks, and has a great reputation. The telephone is about as interactive as many of us get.

During the 1940s, every phone call was connected by hand. Phone use was growing so fast that one Bell System estimate predicted that if current growth continued, every single woman in America would have to become a phone operator in order to keep up with demand.

Fortunately, the automated telephone switch was developed, preventing the collapse of the phone system. Two decades later, touch-tone telephones, digital phone switches, and computers have changed, once again, the way telephones work.

Until audiotext was developed, every phone call had to be answered by someone — there was a one-to-one relationship between customers calling a business and employees at the business answering the phone. The cost of living up to the promise of "operators standing by" scared off quite a few businesses from widely publicizing their phone numbers.

Now the paradigm has shifted. A virtually infinite number of people can call your business — and they'll all get an answer on the first ring. You can offer a huge range of information and services to customers. You can conduct polls, and inform people of product or price changes.

What Is Audiotext?

Audiotext is based on a technology called interactive voice response (IVR). Customers use the keypad on their touch-tone telephones to respond to prerecorded or digitally created instructions. Without ever having to speak to a live operator, callers can obtain information about a product or service, respond to a survey, enroll in a sweepstakes promotion, or track a lost Federal Express package.

Audiotext is available for both large and small usage installations. One system can handle more than 10,000 phone calls simultaneously, making it a viable tool for live radio and television promotions.

But you don't have to do business on such a large scale to benefit from audiotext. Many computer companies sell audiotext circuit boards that plug into a personal computer. These boards allow you to build a simple audiotext system that will work on a single phone line.

Think about audiotext from the computer's point of view. All we're asking the machine to do is accept a simple input and then generate a simple output. Most people use keyboards to get access to a computer, but there's no reason not to think of the keypad on a telephone as a primitive keyboard.

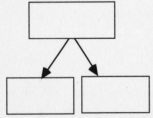

A flowchart tells the system exactly how to respond to any input from a user. It's simple. If the caller presses 1, the system jumps to one portion of the flowchart and delivers a message. If, however, the caller presses 2, a different part of the chart comes into play.

When integrated with a database, audiotext becomes an even more powerful tool. Federal Express uses audiotext to speed delivery information to customers. Dial (800) 238-5355 and the system will ask you to input the airbill number of your missing package. Within seconds, the computer searches the FedEx database, finds the status of your package and reads it to you. Federal Express saves time and money, and the caller avoids the hassle of being put on hold or explaining his problem to an operator.

Is this marketing? Sure it is. By investing in a system that makes life easier for its customers, FedEx has created goodwill. If the customer has a warm feeling about the company, he'll keep coming back. And because the inquiry is handled by computer, Federal Express can easily keep track of which customers are eager to track their packages, and even better, which customers are most often disappointed. By personalizing their service on a mass scale, Federal Express has avoided a classic danger of growing big.

When choosing an audiotext strategy, consider pricing first. For many consumers, price is a real issue. While a toll call will put a cap on your exposure, a toll-free call is guaranteed to increase response, even among business callers. And for many potential callers, a high-priced 900 number is out of the question.

More than 300,000 American businesses have one or more toll-free lines, and these lines are estimated to generate revenues of more than $7 billion each year. New digital technology means that service can be installed on existing telephone lines. Toll-free numbers are now portable, so you can keep one if you relocate or change carriers. Compared to mail-in response marketing, where the marketer pays for printing and postage, toll-free lines are relatively cheap.

Using Audiotext

I n its simplest form, IVR can answer incoming calls automatically, allowing you to provide 24-hour service without hiring round-the-clock operators. Do you get frequent calls requesting catalogs, coupons, or dealer location information? Use an audiotext system to provide prerecorded answers to common questions and to record names and addresses of callers who want catalogs or other publications. Your staff will then have more time to deal with complex customer inquiries. Be sure to keep track of hang-ups. A system that saves you time but costs you leads is no bargain.

You can also use IVR to expand your customer base and generate promising leads, as in the following examples.

Sample and Coupon Distribution

The makers of Mott's Applesauce created a marketing program to inform the public that the product could be used instead of sugar or vegetable oil in some baking recipes. The company used an 800 number to distribute a free recipe booklet, product coupons, and substitution hints. Put a sample or coupon into consumers' hands, tell them how versatile the product is, and you'll generate sales as customers put the product to new uses.

The Minwax company also wanted to showcase its products' versatility. It published a magazine of decorating ideas, woodworking projects, and expert advice called "Wood Beautiful," which it promoted through TV ads and point-of-purchase displays. Consumers could call an 800 number to receive a free copy.

"A refund or cents-off offer will not bring new users," says Seth Bostraom, promotional services manager at Minwax. "The book was developed to give consumers new ideas and ways to use the products, thereby encouraging more product purchase." Of course, everyone who received the free magazine is now in Minwax's computerized database of hot leads for future launches and promotions.

Makers of nutrition products or cosmetics can link their products to specific physical benefits by positioning a brand name in the midst of valuable health information. Smith Kline Beecham used a toll-free audiotext line to promote its Os-Cal line of calcium supplements. Callers registered to receive calcium-related health information and product discounts throughout the year.

Warner Lambert, makers of Lubriderm skin care products, also ran an audiotext-based promotion. The company placed print advertisements inviting consumers to measure their "Skindex," which gauged their susceptibility to skin problems. Callers dialed an 800 number and answered audiotext questions about their lifestyle, exposure to pollution and tobacco, and exercise habits. The company mailed callers the test results and a coupon good for 75 cents off any Lubriderm product. Audiotext allowed the company to collect a gold mine of intimate consumer information.

Just as important as the database, Warner Lambert gained customer loyalty and respect. By offering valuable medical advice at no charge, it established a relationship with the consumer — one that could lead to one purchase or a lifetime's worth.

Evaluate Media Placements

Systems such as Media Tracker, developed by Scherers Communications, Inc., of Worthington, Ohio, let companies monitor the effectiveness of their ads easily. Companies using the system add the phrase "ask for operator xx" to ads featuring their phone numbers. Each television or radio spot, point-of-purchase display, free-standing insert, newspaper or magazine ad, or classified listing has its own "operator number." When customers call, the audiotext system asks them to key in the operator number. Scherers can then supply a report showing how many callers responded to each ad, and when they called.

Before audiotext, operators would ask callers that perennial question: "How did you hear about us?" Many callers couldn't remember, so it was impossible to relate their call to a particular ad. Audiotext conquers this problem. Callers need the operator number to get access to the system (of course, those who forget are helped along by a human operator).

Contests and Promotions

You can develop eager, engaged consumers by inviting them to play a skill-related game. When the marketers of 15-Year-Old Pinch Scotch wanted to attract young sophisticated buyers, they launched a phone-based stock market game with ads in *The Wall Street Journal* and *The New York Times*. Contestants began with a set amount of "play" money and made it grow by investing it in the stock market. The person who made the most money won a trip to Scotland to see how Pinch Scotch was made. This contest was particularly suited to audiotext since telephones are integral to buying and trading stocks in real life.

But such a link isn't vital to a contest's success. Contests for limericks, slogans, mottoes, jingles, and new product names have traditionally been run by mail, but you can run them more efficiently using audiotext. If contestants record their entries, you can quickly select a few dozen finalists which can then be transcribed. You don't have to sort through paper entries, hire additional staff, or decipher illegible handwriting.

Customer Polling and Surveys

The less inconvenient and costly it is to answer a marketer's questions, the more likely it is that consumers will do so. The publishers of *McCall's* magazine knew this when they opted for an audiotext format to gauge consumer satisfaction of their magazine. Instead of inviting readers to fill out and mail back a lengthy questionnaire, or hiring a focus group, they mailed a list of questions to subscribers and invited them to respond via an 800 number. The response rate was high. Readers obviously appreciated the convenience.

Telephone polling has another advantage: it can generate almost immediate response. Right after President Clinton's 1994 State of the Union Address, pre-selected viewers called an 800 line at CBS News to comment on the speech. There is no reason why companies couldn't use the same kind of polling to record consumers' opinions on new products or advertisements.

If you sell through retailers, you can use instant consumer feedback to track which items are selling the fastest, which retailers are providing the best service, and how your pricing compares with the competition. The technology is simple and relatively inexpensive. It's also extremely flexible — you can change your questions within minutes.

Polling can also be used as a fundraiser. In 1993, Ralph Nader's advocacy group, Public Citizen, proposed a bill that would forbid lobbyists and special interest groups from influencing congressional legislation. The group encouraged concerned citizens to dial a toll-free number. Callers could pay Public Citizen $5.75 to send letters to President Clinton and their U.S. Representative on their behalf.

Register Applicants for Prizes and Drawings

In sweepstakes, unlike contests, winners are chosen at random. Popular mail sweepstakes run by Reader's Digest, American Family Publishers, and Publishers Clearing House have given these companies a nationwide profile. Other companies are finding similar success with toll-free telephone sweepstakes. Consumers like these sweepstakes because they're completely free — not even a postage stamp is needed — and easy to enter. Companies like them because they're easy to monitor and they generate thousands of leads.

During the 1993 football season, Coca-Cola ran television advertising promoting its "Monsters of the Gridiron" sweepstakes. Coke drinkers could win prizes by calling a toll-free number and punching in a special code printed on the bottle. The promotion generated an astounding 32 million calls, and marketers could prove the TV ads were effective because the number of calls often jumped dramatically right after an ad aired. While most marketers would have trouble paying for 32 million phone calls, Coca-Cola was delighted. It gained insight into its customer base, built a database, and most importantly, enhanced its relationship with its consumers. The NutraSweet company ran an innovative sweepstakes that used every NutraSweet product as a game piece. It invited consumers who had purchased NutraSweet products to call an 800 number. By using a touch-tone phone to key in the UPC code on the side of the package, the caller qualified to win a $10,000+ shopping spree. During the heaviest response times, calls were coming in at a rate of 52,000 an hour.

Thanks to the flexibility of interactive voice response, you can run a sweepstakes in conjunction with other marketing programs. Xerox Corporation set up a hotline offering businesses new ideas on how to use existing color copiers. Callers on the toll-free line could use a menu of recorded information to enter a sweepstakes, or transfer directly to a live operator or a color copier dealer.

NOTE: Before running a sweepstakes (in which skill isn't involved), check the legality of using the telephone to run the game. If there is a charge associated with the call (not a problem with 800 numbers), then there may be regulatory difficulties. Ask your lawyers first to be safe.

Operators Standing By

Y ou can give customers more reasons to choose your company over a competitor by providing automated services over the telephone. Charles Schwab, the discount brokerage firm, has established an interactive voice response system called Telebroker that allows customers to obtain stock quotes, trade options, and short-sell stocks using a touch-tone phone. Callers can make up to eight different transactions in one call. They even get a 10-percent discount on commissions for using the service.

Harper Leather Goods, a Chicago-based pet product manufacturer, encourages customers to register descriptive information about their pets in a computerized database. The company sends the customer a special pet collar with a phone number on it. If the pet is ever lost, the finder can call the number and Harper will contact the pet owner. For its efforts,

Harper Leather Goods collects a database of concerned pet owners and important information about the pets themselves.

Registration day at most universities is an unqualified nightmare. Many courses are filled on a "first come, first served" basis, so students camp out overnight to get the classes they want. Lines are long and tempers are short. But several universities have set up IVR systems that allow students to register by phone. At the University of San Diego, a dial-up computer verifies students' eligibility, then the caller picks courses using simple commands. The system can handle up to 18 calls at once. Students save time and frustration, and schools are reporting annual savings of $100,000 or more.

At the University of Nebraska at Kearney, students can use a system called EASI (Electronic Access of Student Information) to find out their individual grades or their grade point average, get information on class schedules, or even register for two consecutive terms at once. The school's financial aid department offers several IVR services, including an answer line for routine inquiries, and a missing documents information line to inform students if they need additional paperwork to complete their aid application.

Barrington Capital Management's audiotext information service, Fluent, provides up-to-date investment advice. Investors call five to ten times every day, and the system handles approximately 24,000 calls daily.

Vanity 800 Numbers

Vanity numbers are dialing codes that spell a word or short phrase such as 800-ICANSKI or 800-ILOVENY. If audiotext is a cornerstone of a marketing campaign, it may be a good idea to find a catchy phone number to help make the campaign memorable.

Hooked On Phonics, Inc., sells an audiocassette reading program. What phone number could be easier to remember than 1-800-ABCDEFG? In fact, the entire business was built around this phone number. Before spending a dollar on marketing or product development, the company paid $10,000 to another company to entice it to change its number and allow Hooked on Phonics to take the number over.

Teleway Florists knows the power of a good vanity number. The company that runs 800-FLOWERS has been so successful, it is reaching out to Spanish-speaking customers. More than 50 percent of the Hispanic population buys flowers each year, so the company has launched a second number: 800-LASFLORES.

900 Numbers

Horoscopes? Sex entertainment? Psychic talk networks? These are the businesses that come to mind when premium pay-per-call 900 numbers are mentioned. Some companies refuse to operate 900 lines because they're afraid the exchange alone will make them look like a fly-by-night operation.

The stigma hasn't always been there. In fact, the first national application of 900 pay-per-call technology was undertaken by NBC in 1980, to gauge the country's response to a debate between candidate Ronald Reagan and then-president Jimmy Carter.

Like a long-distance call, a 900 call costs the caller money. But the sponsoring company, along with the phone utility, receives the money spent on a 900 call. That's the appeal of these numbers to companies. The fees raised from charges to callers can help cover the cost of whatever service is offered on the line.

Sales via 900 numbers rose steadily throughout the 1980s, cresting at nearly one billion dollars a year. The market tumbled in the early 1990s as public annoyance at the seamy side of the industry grew. Parents discovered that their children were racking up hundreds of dollars in fees to listen to a prerecorded message from Santa Claus, or, worse, dialing the adult numbers.

The major carriers responded by offering call blocking and by refusing to pursue collection for unpaid 900 charges. Uncollected charges didn't hurt them because their revenue came from service providers who paid a per-call rate to lease the 900 exchange. Service providers were forced to absorb the uncollected "chargebacks." When unscrupulous callers realized the charges would not be aggressively collected nor their credit harmed, they called the 900 services with impunity, forcing many entrepreneurs out of business.

The industry is undergoing a slow but steady rebound. Sex-oriented pay-per-call lines are here to stay, but many carriers have set aside a separate exchange for them, leaving room for less controversial pay-per-call services. In New England, lottery information lines are the most frequently dialed 900 service, followed by personals services, sports lines, and events listings.

Entrepreneurs who offer quality services, desirable premiums, or valuable information will always be able to find a profitable niche in the 900 pay-per-call industry.

DON PEPPERS AND MARTHA ROGERS ON REVERSE-900 NUMBERS: ELECTRONIC COUPONING AND TRACKING

Marketers distribute three hundred billion coupons in this country every year, mostly as freestanding inserts in newspapers. About 8 billion are redeemed, a little less than 3%, but some industry experts estimate that 20% or more of these are redeemed for the wrong product, the wrong size, or for a fraudulent sale.

However, coupon issuers have overlooked a new, addressable technology — a new, 1:1 medium — right under their noses.

Local phone companies provide 900-number services to marketers. If you want information, you dial a 900 number, and a charge appears on your phone bill. Identifying every incoming calling number, 900-number technology ensures that the caller's phone bill is properly charged for the call. Such "900" numbers, provided by long-distance phone companies, collect money from individual consumers for information or entertainment services that other companies provide over the phone.

Why not use the same exact method of transferring money — via the phone bill — to pay consumers for their interactions? If a 900 number charges a customer's phone bill in exchange for information a customer wants, why doesn't a marketer credit the customer's phone bill in exchange for information the marketer wants — about the customer?

Suppose, as a packaged goods marketer (or any other kind of coupon issuer), you were to place a different, individual ID number inside each product package, to serve as a "proof of purchase." Then, instead of printing millions of coupons and placing them inside newspapers, you run an ad in the food shopping section of the paper that lists your products and the types of coupon rebates you're offering for each. Your ad could publicize the fact that you are rewarding first-time buyers with a special bonus for sampling your product. The ad might read:

"After purchasing a family-size box of Eggo Frozen Waffles, call 1-900-KELLOGG, punch in the 'proof of purchase' number found inside the box, and we'll credit your phone bill with a 50-cent rebate. First-time Eggo users will get an extra $2.00 — so if you haven't tried Eggo Frozen Waffles, try them now. It's our treat."

How would this work? Very easily, and totally automated. Using currently available telephone and computer technology on your own end, your computer will be able to identify the incoming calling number as each call is received. (Think about it: The phone company has to know whom to bill for current 900-number services, right?) If you've heard from that phone number before, your computer will know it. When the unique proof-of-purchase number is punched in by the caller, you'll know whether a 900-number coupon for that type of product has ever been redeemed by that particular calling household. Each proof-of-purchase number can only be redeemed once.

Naturally, since Kellogg is a multiple-product agency, a caller might call in to redeem more than one coupon at a time, for more than one type of Kellogg's product. The smart marketing company will have one reverse-900 number to call for all coupon redemptions, to encourage multiple coupon redemptions on the same call, and minimize telecommunications expense. Fraud would be far more controllable than for paper coupons, too.

When each phone call is connected and the computer identifies the calling number, you should offer different, additional values to different types of users. You might offer multiple coupon users additional, "hidden" coupons (not printed and distributed with the Sunday papers, but communicated over the phone during incoming calls from such coupon-sensitive households). First-time coupon users could be offered extra values for their second purchase, in addition to the high values they received on their initial purchase. And while you have a caller on the line to receive some coupon rebates, why not ask one or two multiple-choice questions for extra money?

The biggest advantage to you as a marketer, however, is that this kind of system is a perfect means for electronically differentiating one individual household from another, addressing tailored offers to each, without using the mail. You could use reverse-900-number couponing to begin identifying and tracking your own customers inexpensively today, in much the same way that airlines do, without ever having to deal with the postal system.

Once you get a customer on the line, engaged in an interchange of some type — even a "touch-tone conversation" with your computer — then you can begin to identify how much more business that customer does, and which of your competitors is getting it now. The more you can get a customer to communicate to you, the more likely it is that you'll be able to secure a greater share of his business. Paying for his time and trouble, with added services "on the house," or additional coupon rebates, or money, is often a wise investment.

What ought to be clear is that the benefits of this kind of program would be immense, but only if you are prepared to re-orient the way you visualize your marketing task. When you can differentiate your customers individually, then a whole new dimension of competition is possible — a share-of-customer dimension, building your business one customer at a time. If you aren't the first in your industry to adopt a 1:1 perspective, you may still be one of the first to feel its effects, as your competitors begin to pick off your own best customers, and keep them, leaving you with the dregs.

Earlier, we mentioned the possibility of reverse-900 numbers, using technology currently available to credit customers' phone bills in exchange for interacting with you. Reverse-900 numbers offer variable-value coupons for optimal incentives, and also provide a way to track customer transactions and participation.

Even if you don't print coupons on a regular basis, you could use reverse-900 numbers for a wide variety of other customer-differentiation purposes. Gathering survey information, for instance, would be much easier if you paid a customer to interact with your computer telephonically.

You could tie a reverse-900 number to a commercial, or an infomercial, so that if a viewer watched your video long enough to hear the "control" number, then he or she could call it in for a monetary credit — and you get the name, phone number, and address of a genuine prospect. You could combine 800- and reverse-900-number technology, so when a customer calls your customer service line you offer a small payment as a refund, or as compensation for a minor complaint, or in return for information about other brands being shopped.

Imagine how this might work: Locate owners of VCR Plus, the handheld device that controls program recording on your VCR when you enter the string of numbers from the TV listings. Using Polk or other syndicated data, you match up owners of VCR Plus with cable TV subscription and, say, certain car ownership. A postcard encourages recipients to record your infomercial, which you run on inexpensive cable time slots. In exchange for calling in the code words which will be revealed on audio during the program, you will credit the viewer's phone bill $5.00 — a small price to pay for 25 or 30 minutes of a prime prospect's — or current customer's — time and attention.

In a world such as ours where enough money is spent on advertising and promotion for every American to be exposed to 2,000 to 3,000 messages every day, this kind of explicit bargain will characterize advertising in the one-to-one future.

Professional Services

M ichael Cane, president of TeleLawyer, warns entrepreneurs away from attempting to launch a pay-per-call advisory service in professional fields such as law, medicine, or accounting. Citing different state licensing restrictions, and the difficulty of providing responsible service over the phone, Cane says only professionals who happen to be entrepreneurs should wade into the 900 waters. Of course, Michael Cane runs such a service himself, so take his warning with a grain of salt.

It's true that you're unlikely to profit from a stand-alone service that does nothing but offer advice by phone. But if you use an audiotext advice service to enhance your existing business, it may be a dynamite combination.

An accountant, for example, could offer quick advice on a 900 number for $3.00 a minute, then offer callers an in-person consultation at a fraction of that rate.

Every day, about 2,000 people call the Small Business Administration's 900 number, which provides general information to small businesses. The perceived quality of the information, along with the urgency of the callers, explains the public's willingness to pay for this information.

Cadwalader Associates, an architectural firm, lets potential customers try before they buy. Callers on the company's 900 line can discuss residential home and design problems with a licensed architect for $4.99 a minute. They can also fax drawings and sketches during the consultation. Cadwalader probably won't make much money on the 900 service, but they will gain the goodwill and trust of hesitant customers.

Consumer Savings Information

A customer will spend a few dollars on a 900-number call if she thinks the information will save her money in the long run. Many companies have had success with these information lines. La Onda, Ltd., runs a 900 line that links people looking for discount travel with airline companies that have empty seats.

A.M. Best Company, which publishes Best's Insurance Reports, lets consumers check their insurance company's solvency on its 900 line.

If you're thinking of setting up such a line, make sure that the information you plan to distribute isn't easily available for free elsewhere. You must also keep the number before the public by advertising constantly

— an expensive, time-consuming job that has doomed many would-be infopreneurs.

Polling/Surveys

Polling can increase a TV audience's involvement with a program. Fox Television invited fans of the show *Living Single* to call a certain number to choose which character would go out on a date with a new beau. The proceeds from the call went to Literacy Volunteers of America, Inc.

TV newsmagazines such as *Hard Copy* and *A Current Affair* use the pay-per-call format to solicit opinions about splashy stories such as the O.J. Simpson case. And *USA Today* invites readers to "vote" on controversial editorial issues through its 900 line.

Many callers enjoy giving opinions on their favorite shows or current issues. That enjoyment is the reason they spend money on a 900 call. But promoters in the manufacturing sector must combine a 900-line survey with a premium, a valuable coupon, or some other enticement in order to make the call worthwhile for the customer.

Pay-per-call Corporate Customer Service

Microsoft, like some other companies, has recently switched part of its free helpline to a 900 number to offset the cost of staffing a support services department. While they continue to offer service over a standard phone number, the callers to the pay-per-call service get priority.

Game software publishers use 900 numbers to provide support to their customers. For 75 cents, players can call the LucasFilms Video Games line to get tips on navigating the higher levels of popular games such as *Indiana Jones and The Last Crusade*. Chargebacks to these numbers are low, even though many callers are young.

But be careful. In many cases, customers will become angry if they have to pay for service. On the other hand, companies can save money without offending anyone by offering different levels of service. A software company could charge $3 a minute for immediate access to a top-notch technician, while offering toll-free service to the average consumer who is willing to sit on hold for a few minutes to save the fee.

Even banks are using this approach. Customers of the Society Bank of Ohio, First Interstate Bank (California), and Wells Fargo Bank can call a 900 number to verify checks. The banks recoup some of the costs of providing a service that customers value.

Replacing Traditional Media

Newspapers and newsletters survive because they provide information too timely or too complicated to be delivered in other ways. But with the immediacy of audiotext, a marketer can grab part of this pie.

Brite Voice Systems, Inc., has set up an audiotext version of that perennial newspaper moneymaker, the singles ads. Callers can place an ad describing themselves at no charge. Other callers pay to listen to the ads. In 1993, the number of calls to the system rose 250 percent, and the number of customers jumped by an astonishing 376 percent.

Audiotext may soon give radio traffic reporters a run for their money. Project Northstar, a service of NYNEX, provides travel information and traffic updates in metropolitan New York, New Jersey, and southern Connecticut. Callers can request directions, traffic reports, names of restaurants and service stations, and so forth. Avis has equipped 60 of its rental cars with cellular telephones and asked customers for feedback on the service. Avis has conducted similar tests in Florida and San Francisco. If this test is successful, nationwide service may not be far away.

Combining 800/900 Services

Some businesses take advantage of both toll-free and premium pay-per-call options. Marianne Szymanski uses a toll-free number to attract new subscribers for her toy safety newsletter. In addition, she operates a 900 line which offers callers information on current toy research, for $2.00 a call.

Corporations can combine both types of calls with a service called Vari-A-Bill. When callers contact the company through an 800 number, they are offered a menu of services that includes some 900-style pay-per-call options. This hybrid is currently under review by some legislatures, but offers some legitimate advantages if used properly.

Getting Started in Audiotext

To provide audiotext services, you need a phone system linked to a computer that can receive calls, answer automatically, provide specific caller-prompted information, and, in some cases, record customer voices. While a single-line service is cost-effective and relatively easy to install, the cost of setting up a major in-house system with dozens of lines is prohibitive for many companies. In most cases, it makes more sense to lease time on an existing system through a service bureau.

Like the building contractor who coordinates the efforts of plumbers, electricians, carpenters, and masons on a job, the service bureau links you, the major telephone carriers, and the customer. A service bureau can:

- *Provide automatic response services or live operators*

  Some promotions use both touch-tone response systems and live operators to ensure all customers can get access — including customers who may be confused by the prompts, or those who have pulse or rotary telephones (amazingly enough, as many as one-third of all American phones don't use touch tone).

- *Verify credit cards*

  Uncollectable credit card debts are a huge potential liability. If cash is exchanged in your promotion, you must be able to verify credit cards during transactions.

- *Provide statistical data on incoming calls*

  A service bureau can record the frequency of calls, broken down by geographic area. Some can even fax hourly call reports to your office — an important service if you're tracking the effectiveness of television or radio spots.

When selecting a service bureau, keep your needs firmly in mind. For instance, do you really need a service that can handle 10,000 calls every 90 seconds?

Check references carefully. Call some of a bureau's existing programs. Place orders and see how long fulfillment takes. Contact the local Better Business Bureau, and ask about any association memberships. According to the Secret Service, there are many scam operations in this industry. Keep your eyes open.

Budgeting for Audiotext

How much does it cost to operate an 800 or 900 number? It depends. A number that generates thousands of calls a day will cost more than one that gets only a hundred. A complicated application will cost more up front than a simple service. Be prepared to pay a one-time fee to get a service up and running.

If you can't afford to pay for an unlimited number of toll-free calls per day, make sure your service bureau can limit the number and length of calls.

Most service bureaus are wary of new 900-number accounts. They will ask you for references and a substantial deposit to cover the cost of potential chargebacks. (If someone calls your $2-a-minute number, stays on for five minutes, and doesn't pay her bill, you're liable to the service bureau for at least $6.) Until you've tested this area thoroughly, limiting the number of calls received each day on your 900 number is a prudent policy.

52 Ways to Use Audiotext Technology

1. *Provide movie schedules*

The local multiplex may have 12 different movies playing on any given evening. Audiotext can give callers basic information such as show times. It can also be used as a more aggressive selling tool to entice callers to see movies they might not have considered. At the touch of a button, callers could listen to plot descriptions, reviews, and bits of "behind-the-scenes" gossip about current features.

2. *Provide automated banking services*

Many consumers rarely enter a bank. They pay their bills, transfer funds, check on their account status or make investments by calling a toll-free number and keying in information on their telephone keypads.

3. *Offer railway schedules and prices*

A sophisticated audiotext system can provide callers with detailed schedules for any route they want to follow. Callers select a departure point and a destination from a menu, and receive a list of schedules, seating options such as coach or sleeper, luggage restrictions, ticket prices, and ticket availability.

4. *Supply a variety of catalogs*

An automobile parts supplier may have dozens of different catalogs, for different makes and models of cars, or for different products such as touch-up paint, mufflers, or radios. By listing them all on an audiotext system, the company not only relieves its operators from the job of answering multiple catalog requests, it creates a powerful sales tool: callers who didn't know the company supplied certain products will discover the fact as they use the audiotext menus.

5. *Offer basic tax information*

An accountant could set up an audiotext information line to answer callers' questions about deductions, credits, and other basic tax information. Then she can phone the caller back and offer a free, no-obligation consultation on tax preparation.

6. *Supply comparison-shopping information*

An enterprising infopreneur could set up a 900 line to offer pay-per-call information on the prices of big-ticket items at major stores in a particular city or region. Callers to a computer shopper line, for instance, could choose options from menus to get the current prices for a popular model of laptop computer or desktop publishing package at eight different stores — all without leaving home or contacting a salesperson.

7. *Let students register in continuing education courses*

School boards, colleges, and independent organizations often offer hundreds of courses in a given semester, on everything from Spanish for beginners to car repair to Indonesian cookery to massage for couples. An audiotext system allows students to peruse courses and register at their leisure.

8. *Take requests for cookbooks*

To encourage consumers to buy and use more milk, milk marketers can print a toll-free number on thousands of cartons of milk. Callers can use menus to choose from a variety of enticing recipe books — *Decadent Desserts, Great Shakes, Rib-Sticking Casseroles* — and have them delivered right to their home.

9. *Provide information on colleges*

High school students face thousands of choices when it comes time to pick a college or university. Popular printed guides to schools exist, but an audiotext line can offer something a printed book can't: information that is as up to date as today's newspaper. Students could call to find out whether a particular school has secured an important grant, approved a sexual harassment policy, or finished building a new athletic center.

10. *Distribute public health information*

Understaffed government public health offices have to handle hundreds of information requests every day — thousands if a crisis such as a measles epidemic or a food-poisoning scare is in progress. An audiotext line could give callers basic information such as AIDS prevention tips, and the hours and locations of public health clinics.

11. Offer schedules of events

A city magazine can increase its profile in the community by offering a free local hotline that readers can call for information on upcoming concerts, plays, and exhibitions. By positioning itself as an authority, the magazine gains credibility. By offering timely information in a convenient format, it fosters goodwill.

12. Provide information on new CDs

A chain of record stores could set up a phone line to promote new albums. Callers could narrow their search by choosing a type of music — country, classical, hard rock, folk, or pop — from a menu. Then the system would provide them with a list (and sample cuts) of all the new releases that are arriving in the stores that week in that category.

13. Offer programming information

Unlike TV listings, information on radio programming can be difficult to find. A station that broadcasts talk shows, documentaries, or ethnic programs can make its schedule available through an audiotext line. It can promote the service through ads in publications that reach its target market.

14. Get feedback on drivers

If you run a trucking company, you want to know if your drivers are driving safely and responsibly. You can paint the number of your 800 line on the back of every truck. Callers will be prompted to enter the license plate number and location of a truck they want to complain about, then asked to leave a detailed message.

15. Promote a comedian's career

A struggling comic offers excerpts from his routine by phone. He publicizes the number by mailing it to booking agents and media across the country.

16. Provide information on physicians

Newcomers to a city need to find a new family doctor. An automated information line, paid for by local physicians, can give callers information on doctors accepting patients, broken down by neighborhood and specialty.

17. Ask for feedback on a programming change

A radio station that has just switched formats can solicit feedback from listeners about the change. Listeners can call an audiotext line to answer detailed questions about the new format. Would they like fewer commercials? More music by The Carpenters? A new morning DJ? Audiotext can collect detailed information more efficiently than a telephone surveyor.

18. Run a free draw for your products

If you've just introduced a new brand of videocassette recorder, promote it with a toll-free contest. Callers, who can make a maximum of two calls to the line, test their wits on a movie trivia quiz. Callers who get all the answers right are entered in a draw to win one of your VCRs. All callers, of course, supply their names and addresses, which you can add to your mailing list.

19. Supply information on popular toys

Remember the Cabbage Patch doll craze? In the weeks before Christmas, distracted parents ran from store to store in search of the sold-out toy. Today, a manufacturer can set up a toll-free hotline to let shoppers know the location of the nearest shop that still has some of this year's hottest toy in stock.

20. Provide employers with information on contractors

A volunteer association of freelance editors can set up a hotline that matches people looking for an editor with members seeking new assignments. Callers key in information on the type of job, such as magazine editing or technical editing, and the system supplies the names and phone numbers of association members with experience in that area.

21. Provide up-to-date information on city buses

When it's cold, there are few things worse than waiting at a windy bus stop for a bus that's 20 minutes late because the driver got caught behind a traffic accident. The city bus company can run an audiotext service that lets riders key in the number of their bus stop to find out whether the bus is running on time — before they even set foot outside their house.

22. Offer news and gossip for soap opera fans

A TV station can keep interest in its afternoon soaps high by offering a phone-in service for dedicated fans. Callers can find out what happened on their favorite soap that day, hear bits of new trivia and gossip about the main hunk, or listen to teasers about upcoming episodes. That way, when they forget to watch or tape the show one day, they don't lose the thread of the story and stop watching the program altogether.

23. Provide information on hotel rates and room availability

A local tourism bureau or group of hotels can share the cost of operating a toll-free hotline that gives callers current information on available hotel rooms. The information can be broken down by price range and neighborhood, and can include additional details on each hotel's services.

24. *Offer free samples of magazines*

A company that publishes ten different magazines can offer free samples of one or more of them to interested callers — and send a subscription form and a discount offer along with the free issue.

25. *Distribute information on benefits*

The personnel office at a large corporation may spend hours each day answering routine questions about the company's benefits plans: Does the dental plan cover root canal work? How do I apply for self-funded leave? What are the maternity benefits? All of these questions can be handled easily by an audiotext line. Callers can request specific forms or brochures, which the system can have mailed or faxed to them.

26. *Offer stress management tips*

People working on tight deadlines are caught in a double bind: the deadlines cause stress and don't allow them any time to relieve the stress. A psychologist who sets up a phone line offering free, quick stress management tips will find a grateful audience. Several weeks after a call, when the caller's life may be somewhat more sane, the psychologist can contact the caller to offer a personalized stress management session.

27. *Handle account inquiries*

Credit card customers often need to verify their balances or increase their credit limit in a hurry. With the proper security precautions, an audiotext system could handle these routine inquiries quickly.

28. *Offer information and trivia about a rock band*

A record company or savvy manager could set up a 900 line that gives eager rock fans information on a band's upcoming concert dates or lets them answer a quiz about the group's history. Callers would receive advance notice of the release of the band's next album, and discount coupons for t-shirts and posters.

29. *Promote a law firm*

By providing basic information on a number of topics, a law firm can inexpensively make itself an on-call expert. The system can record the fax number of callers and send them even more information on the topic.

30. *Give members information on programming and services*

A professional association can set up a toll-free line to give its members basic information about upcoming seminars, member benefits, or an upcoming national conference. Nonmembers can also call to find out more about the group and request a brochure or application form.

31. *Provide fashion advice*

Are hemlines long or short this year? What are the hot colors? A busy executive probably doesn't have a lot of time to spend reading *Vogue*, but she needs to keep on top of the latest trends. An upscale clothing store can offer this sort of information on audiotext — and then contact the caller to offer a shop-at-home service or discounts on silk blouses.

32. Run a fantasy sports league

A national sporting goods chain can run a contest to attract the attention of diehard hockey fans. Fans create their own "fantasy teams" by picking a set number of players from all the players in the league. Contest entrants can check their rank in the standings as often as they like by dialing a toll-free number. At the end of the season, the fan whose "team" has scored the most points wins a package of sports equipment from the store (and all the other callers get a copy of the store's catalog).

33. Survey constituents

A congressman wants to know how his constituents feel about an upcoming bill, but knows his staff will be paralyzed if he asks everyone to call his office. He can set up an audiotext number that constituents can call to record their opinions. He can also use the line to poll constituents for their views on less urgent issues, or even on his success as a representative.

34. Provide updated weather information

Sailing clubs and private airports can set up audiotext lines that provide short-term and long-term weather forecasts related to their particular activity (wind speed for sailing clubs, visibility for airports).

35. Offer pet care advice

A veterinarian can offer answers to simple pet care questions on a free local line, such as how to prevent cats from getting hairballs, or how to get skunk scent out of a dog's fur. Later, he can send the caller a discount coupon for a service related to his or her type of pet.

36. Give companies municipal information

Economic development offices, which try to encourage companies to set up shop in their city or region, can make information on zoning, tax incentives, the local work force, and vacant commercial properties available on an audiotext system. A sales representative can then contact the caller and arrange to present a detailed slide show about the city and its advantages.

37. Sell antique cars

The market for antique cars is small. But because these cars are such high-ticket items, a dealer can benefit from an audiotext line. Callers can select from a menu to choose the make they're interested in, and get details on the price, color, and condition of any available models. They can also request photographs or other printed information.

38. *Offer photography tips*

A camera manufacturer could promote its products with an 800 number offering tips on taking pictures at night, underwater, or on foggy days. When appropriate, the tips would mention lenses, flashes, or filters made by the manufacturer that would help the caller take better pictures under various conditions.

39. *Give diet and fitness tips*

A publisher that produces health and exercise books can run a phone line offering callers basic advice on diet and fitness. Callers could also order books on related topics through the system, or add their names and addresses to the publisher's mailing list.

40. *Distribute travel discount coupons*

A group of hotels, restaurants, and attractions in a particular region can share the cost of an ad in the travel section of a newspaper in the next state. The ad would promote packages of discount coupons that callers could get by calling a toll-free number. The system could offer several packages of coupons, aimed at segmented groups such as families, seniors, or honeymooners.

41. *Provide real estate information*

A real estate agent can provide house-hunting tips and current mortgage rates on an audiotext system. It can also promote upcoming open houses. Callers can key in information about the sort of house they're seeking — neighborhood, size, price range — and request that an agent call them back with a list of suitable properties.

42. *Supply answers to common library reference questions*

The overworked reference staff at a public library can set up an audiotext line to answer common questions, such as the populations of various countries, names of state capitals, names and terms of office of various presidents, and dates of famous battles. The system could also give callers information on library hours, overdue fines, reserved books, and library locations.

43. *Create an alumni directory*

Alumni of a university can pay a small fee to have their addresses and phone numbers listed in an audiotext system. Other alumni can call to use the service to track down information on fellow students they've lost touch with over the years.

44. *Provide information on projects in process*

A repair center can permit customers to call in to discover the status of the work on their broken computer. Or a furniture manufacturer can give the patient customer a chance to track the progress on their six-month-back-ordered etagere.

45. Run a contest for TV fans

A local TV affiliate can whip up interest in television programming in general by running a contest in which callers try to guess the winners of the upcoming Emmy Awards. Each menu would let callers choose one show or actor from a list of nominees. Callers with the highest percentage of right answers are eligible for a draw for a big-screen TV.

46. Supply transcripts

A university can set up an audiotext line to allow students and alumni to order copies of their transcripts, a replacement diploma, or other official documents.

47. Provide game schedules

A basketball team can provide its schedule for the entire year on an audiotext system, including dates and locations of out-of-town games, and information on special promotions like two-for-one nights or specials for families.

48. Offer information on action campaigns

A wildlife association can set up an audiotext system to give callers information on endangered species, boycotts, and letter-writing campaigns. It can also promote its fund-raising products, such as books, posters, and t-shirts. Every nonmember caller would later receive a direct mail package asking her to join the association.

49. Provide information on lowest prices

A consumer watchdog group could regularly update a recording pointing out the best buys on certain items.

50. Provide hospital information

A hospital can set up an information line that allows callers to find out visiting hours and the room numbers of various patients, get information on outpatient clinics, or make a donation to the hospital's fund-raising campaign.

51. Offer lottery information

Lottery ticket buyers want to know if they've won. A 900 number listing the winning numbers in a variety of lotteries, going back several months, can save anxious ticket buyers hours of scanning back issues of newspapers in the local library.

52. Advertise available spaces at a campground

Travelers looking for a place to camp could call a central number from a pay phone on the road to find out which parks are full and which still have room for more campers. The line could also provide general information on each park and campground, such as which locations have shower facilities, supervised beaches, or snack bars.

Audiotext Resources

Call Interactive
2301 N. 117th Ave.
Omaha NE 68164
(800) 428-2400

Call Interactive, a business unit of First Data Corporation, is one of the nation's largest interactive 800 and 900 service centers. Call Interactive can provide fulfillment, real-time updating, database management, and crisis management. Call Interactive also has a patented telephone broadcasting service, Corporate Communiqué, which lets companies link thousands of callers at one time with a guest speaker. The company's clients include AT&T, CBS, and Avon Products.

Intervoice, Inc.
17811 Waterview Parkway
Dallas TX 75252
(214) 669-3988

Intervoice, Inc., is a public company that builds voice automation solutions for customer service applications. Intervoice has designed a turnkey software package that can answer your phones for you. The Robot Operator System handles routine calls by promptly providing callers with routine information. It answers on the first ring, 24 hours a day, 7 days a week and never puts a caller on hold. The smallest package runs from $27,000 for a 4-line system. It includes the application, and interface with the database and the user.

Matrixx Marketing, Inc.
2121 N. 117 Ave.
Omaha NE 68164
(800) 351-1000

Matrixx Marketing helps to design and execute telemarketing programs for leading advertisers who use 800 numbers to sell products, offer services, or provide information. The company specializes in closed-loop marketing using inbound and outbound marketing, and dealer locator information. Its services are best suited to programs that generate at least 5,000 calls per month. Some of the companies they have worked with include Motorola, Clairol, Microsoft, and Quaker Oats.

Network Telephone Services, Inc.
6233 Variel Ave.
Woodland Hills CA 91367
(800) 727-6874

With more than five years of experience, Network Telephone Services handles thousands of numbers and answers hundreds of thousands of calls per day. The company offers 800, 900, and 976 numbers with recorded or live service. It answers calls, processes billing, and provides 24-hour customer service, daily call reports, and advertising support. Customers can choose from every access and caller billing option available in the U.S., as well as the company's own proprietary plans. Network Telephone Services has worked with such companies as Capitol Records, Warner Brothers Records, NBC Gemstar, Revo Sunglasses, and Pizza Hut.

Phone Programs, Inc.
40 Elmont Rd.
Elmont NY 11003
(516) 775-5410

Founded in 1972, Phone Programs creates phone-based programs designed to develop an ongoing dialogue with a target audience. PPI blends technology, full-service creative capabilities, and computer database technology with in-house marketing support services, including media buying and fulfillment. It also offers fax-on-demand services and automated transaction processing via phone. The list of companies for which Phone Programs has developed campaigns includes American Express, Cadbury Schweppes, and PepsiCo.

The Product Line
2370 South Trenton Way
Denver CO 80231
(800) 343-4717

The Product Line is an 11-year-old, fully automated 200-position telemarketing service agency that provides inbound telemarketing, outbound telemarketing, and fulfillment services to national clients. It can take orders, refer dealers, make sales, and qualify leads. Among the technologies in use at the company are automated scripting, predictive dialing, and voice response (see glossary). The Colorado Board of Tourism is one of The Product Line's clients.

Scherers Communications, Inc.
575 Scherers Court
Worthington OH 43085
(800) 356-6161
Scherers provides a variety of 800/900 services, including passive and interactive audiotext, polling for marketing purposes, and live operators.

Telecompute Corporation
1275 K St. N.W.
Washington DC 20005
(800) USA-VOICE
Telecompute was founded in 1986 and has been providing AT&T 800 service ever since. It provides direct or online connections to a variety of vendors, operators, database matching services, and credit and/or phone card debiting facilities through the use of dedicated circuits, its own switched network, and the public network. Over the years, the company has worked with many types of clients, including local radio and TV stations, software support offices, and nonprofit associations.

Teleshare 900
227 North University Ave., Suite #103
Provo UT 84601
(801) 377-0600
Teleshare 900 is a service bureau that specializes in programs for entrepreneurs, small businesses, and professionals. The company hosts training workshops all over the country, aimed at new information providers, on topics such as evaluating a 900 idea and using broadcast media effectively.

Zycom Network Services, Inc.
200 South Los Robles, Suite 305
Pasadena CA 91101
(800) 880-3061
With more than six locations in the United States, Zycom Network Services, Inc., processes more than 10 million calls annually. Zycom has the capability to capture 1,500 leads per minute. It helps clients manage everything from initial program design to the implementation and day-to-day operation of their programs. The company's services include voice and data capture, passive and interactive programs, and fraud control.

It has worked with many Fortune 500 companies to set up 800 audio-text programs and self-liquidating 900 numbers (see glossary).

Audiotext Glossary

Audiotext: the technology that allows a computer to stand in for a human telephone operator.

Automated services: in audiotext, the use of a telephone and a computer to do work formerly done by an operator.

Automated transaction processing: using computers to verify charge cards and generate databases.

Chargeback: a chargeback occurs whenever a cardholder or cardholder's bank disputes a sale or credit transaction posted to the cardholder's account. If the dispute can not be proved as legitimate, the operator of a 900 line will have to cover the cost.

Circuit board: an insulated board on which interconnected circuits and components such as microchips are mounted or etched.

Contest: a promotion in which entrants have to submit entries to be judged or answer skill-testing questions in order to win a prize.

Freestanding insert: a stand-alone advertising circular stuffed into newspapers that usually contains a business reply card or coupon.

Inbound telemarketing: fielding calls that come from consumers in response to advertising.

Interactive voice response (IVR): the technology that allows callers to interact with a marketer through the telephone by using the keypad on their touch-tone phone to respond to prerecorded or digitally created instructions.

Outbound telemarketing: calling consumers, either at home or at work, to sell a product.

Point-of-purchase promotion (POP): a display or demonstration that takes place at the physical place where the purchase or sale occurs.

Predictive dialing: a computer-aided system that allows an outbound telemarketer to dial more numbers per hour.

Premium: goods offered either free or at low cost as an incentive to buy a product or service.

Response rate: the number of people who respond to a particular marketing vehicle, such as a television ad. Companies use this number to evaluate and compare the success of marketing techniques.

Self-liquidating 900 number: a service in which the income from 900 numbers matches the cost to the marketer of providing and advertising the service.

Service bureau: in audiotext, a company that specializes in telephone marketing. A service bureau usually provides services such as setting up a telephone number, answering a large volume of calls at one time, and sending products and literature to interested callers.

Sweepstakes: a promotion in which winners are chosen at random and not as a result of a special skill or judged entry.

Toll call: a telephone call for which a higher rate is charged than the standard rate for a local call.

Voice and data capture: a type of database system that will remember the inputs and voice messages left by callers.

Voice response: a type of system that can recognize voice commands in addition to touch-tone signals.

MULTIMEDIA

*Ten years ago, computers revolutionized
publishing. Desktop publishing programs
made it easy and inexpensive for anyone
to create handsome documents.*

*Three years ago, the same technology
came to video. Using computers and video
technology, it is relatively quick, cheap, and simple to
create multimedia presentations that combine
the impact of television with the interactivity of computers and the flexibility of print.*

*Multimedia uses text, graphics, video, animation,
and audio recordings to convey information.
It has great potential as a marketing tool.
If you sell, promote, explain, or educate,
you can use multimedia to meet your
objectives in all kinds of new ways.*

If you need to capture the attention of consumers already addicted to computer games and video movies, a printed brochure just isn't going to cut it anymore. Multimedia can bring your products to life right before a consumer's eyes, in living, moving color. Why settle for two-dimensional, static black and white?

What Is Multimedia?

That's a hard question to answer. Some multimedia products use a TV or computer monitor to display video and sound. Others use inexpensive devices at the point of purchase to attract the prospect's attention. Many encourage interaction: viewers can stop the action, focus on a particular image or fact, and get more information.

To set up a multimedia presentation, you need a computer or chip, a storage medium, and a way for viewers to interact with the presentation.

The computer that runs the presentation can be as complex as a custom-designed kiosk or as simple as a $300 CD-I player or a $4 chip in a point-of-purchase display.

Because they take up huge amounts of memory, many multimedia products are stored on a CD-ROM — a compact disk that holds data instead of music. A standard CD-ROM can store the equivalent of 500 floppy disks. But there are other storage options, including inexpensive custom chips for point-of-purchase displays, and online systems (see the Internet chapter).

Multimedia is appealing to both marketers and the public because it invites consumers to touch, to play, to get involved. Some presentations use touch screens, while others bring people in with a mouse, a keyboard, or a joystick.

Using Multimedia

The uses of multimedia are only limited by your imagination. The technology is particularly effective for point-of-sale kiosks and displays, electronic catalogs, sales presentations, and training tools.

Warning! Just using multimedia technology to do business the old way is a direct route to failure. Many large companies are transferring traditional flat media (brochures, catalogs, etc.) to multimedia without reaping the benefits of the new technology.

Using multimedia at the store level is one of the best uses of the medium. It's the critical moment: the consumer is in the store, wallet in hand, wondering which product to buy. Grab his attention with an arresting kiosk or point-of-purchase (POP) display.

Which system you choose depends on your product, your budget, and your potential customer. Kiosks are multifaceted, expensive devices that can be very useful if consumers are motivated to use them. POP is far cheaper and easier to use, and doesn't require much effort on the consumer's part.

Kiosks

T he most familiar type of interactive kiosk is the automatic teller machine (ATM). More than half of all Americans use ATMs regularly. While ATMs are merely computer terminals capable of spitting out money, multimedia kiosks offer more flexibility.

Kiosks are incredibly powerful. Virtually any consumer can use them. They attract curious passersby and hold their attention with sophisticated graphics that demonstrate and promote your product in vivid color.

Because they're interactive, kiosks can both distribute and collect information — piles of it. Users can print out answers to very specific questions, and you can collect massive quantities of data for use in future marketing efforts.

These freestanding units can set your product or service apart from your competitors by providing "branches" of your company in many locations — all without the expense of hiring a human attendant.

American Greeting Cards played on consumers' fascination with interactive technology by developing Create-A-Card kiosks. Users choose options from a menu, add a name, and the kiosk prints out a personalized card. The company installed the kiosks in drugstores and gift shops — places where customers were already comfortable buying cards. The system is essentially a gimmick, but a popular one.

But kiosks can be far more practical. IBM Kiosk Integration Services group has designed a kiosk that allows Minnesota Twins baseball fans to buy tickets at any number of locations, at any time of day. Using a handsome, easy-to-understand screen, fans can check the schedule, search for available seats, and even see photographs of the view from different areas in the stadium. The Twins have found a low-cost way to keep their fans happy. Buying tickets is now a quick and easy transaction, not a drawn-out ordeal.

Consumers' Catalog Showroom has installed in-store kiosks that let customers display pictures or full-motion video ads of selected items, search for competitive products, and make purchases. The kiosks also serve as active sales tools, much like a knowledgeable salesperson: when a customer makes a purchase, the kiosk suggests related products. If someone buys a camera, for instance, the kiosk may ask the customer if she is interested in film, filters, or a tripod.

The kiosks have led to a 50-percent increase in sales of in-stock accessories, and a 100-percent sales increase for special-order accessories that are mailed to customers or picked up at a later date.

The i•Station, discussed in the database marketing chapter, is another example of a multimedia kiosk. The kiosks allow listeners to sample five short selections from an album, view album art, watch music video clips, read record reviews, and obtain information on upcoming concerts. The i•Station, developed by Intouch, Inc., currently provides information on 32,000 compact disks. At a store in St. Louis, i•Stations were responsible for a 6-percent increase in sales, prompting Randy Davis, an executive with Streetside Records, to roll out the kiosk to all 24 of his stores.

Think about the i•Station from the retailer's point of view. Instead of hiring a platoon of expensive, intelligent salespeople, the store can rely on the wide-ranging expertise of the i•Station. It has complete information on more than 30,000 records, never calls in sick, and is rarely rude.

But the kiosk doesn't simply replace salespeople. It increases sales by actively helping the user find new music. For instance, it can recommend an early Steely Dan disk to anyone buying a Michael MacDonald record. The consumer might not have realized that MacDonald sang on these albums, and will be delighted to take a minute or two to listen to a cut. And the more the kiosk learns about an individual customer's buying habits, the more useful it becomes to him. Soon, the customer can't imagine buying CDs anywhere else.

Blockbuster, Inc., is testing video kiosks that let customers preview tapes at 20 of its outlets. Many video store customers head straight for the new release racks, and are invariably disappointed if all the copies of the latest hit movie have already been rented. According to the Video Software Dealers Association, as many as 65% of all video renters leave the store without renting anything. By using the kiosks to promote lower-profile movies that customers might not notice otherwise, Blockbuster can decrease the chance that customers will leave the store empty-handed.

Singers have a hard time finding sheet music, especially music transcribed to the key they need. Often, they have to buy music in another key and transpose it by hand. Musicwriter, Inc., has developed the

Notestation, an interactive kiosk that will print out music in any key for $3.95 per song — about 50 cents higher than the price of traditional sheet music. For an additional charge, the customer can get accompaniment on a diskette. The kiosk can hold thousands of songs, dramatically decreasing the cost of carrying inventory, a particular problem for small stores.

Clairson International, manufacturers of Closetmaid organizers, uses small interactive video units to dispense information about its do-it-yourself organizer kits, including easy-to-follow video installation instructions. By avoiding the untrained retail sales clerk and going straight to the consumer, Clairson is able to control the transaction and boost sales.

K-Mart Canada uses interactive kiosks to provide store directories, dispense coupons, and inform customers about special promotions and events. Since the kiosks were installed in 1993, sales of highlighted products have jumped by an average of 70 percent. Some products showed an astounding 500-percent increase in sales.

Bissell, Inc., makers of the Big Green Clean Machine, has installed multimedia displays in some warehouse-type retail stores. Shoppers can see demonstrations of various features of the product on a small, interactive video screen. The unit keeps track of which features users ask to see, and records users' responses to a set of questions about the product. Because the company originally introduced the cleaner in an infomercial, it already had a lot of footage to use in the display, reducing production costs.

Kiosks work extremely well at trade shows. They give visitors a risk-free way to obtain information. Users are more likely to ask for information if they're not afraid of being trapped by an aggressive salesperson, and they can walk away from a kiosk at any time without appearing rude.

AT&T's Network Systems had a problem with trade shows. The company's Integrated Services Digital Network (ISDN) technology is hard to explain quickly, especially in the festival atmosphere of a trade show. However, people had to understand the technology before they would consider buying it.

Multimedia bridged the gap. Customers turned off by complex concepts and confusing jargon didn't mind using a kiosk at their own pace to find out more about ISDN. As a result, they developed a greater understanding of the product.

Not only did AT&T make more sales, it also saved money. The company spent $30,000 to develop the multimedia program, and another $2,500 in computer hardware and monitors for the kiosk itself. But it saved about $100,000 per year by dispensing with expensive presentation tools such as live ISDN lines. In addition, it could decrease the number of staff needed to run the booths.

Stew Leonard's, an innovative supermarket in Connecticut, has an in-store kiosk called the Cuisine Screen. Customers use the kiosk to find and print out recipes, then go through Stew's and buy the ingredients. Not only does the kiosk generate increased food sales, it makes shopping at Stew's more fun, giving the store a competitive advantage.

Multimedia and Database Marketing

The opportunities to integrate these two cutting-edge technologies are tremendous. For database marketing to work, you need to know who's buying what. Customers will line up at a multimedia kiosk to give you this kind of information, because the kiosk gives them valuable coupons, information, and other feedback in return.

Imagine a fast food outlet where a talking kiosk takes the customer's order. The customer slides a membership card through the reader, and immediately the kiosk "knows" her name, her favorite sandwiches, and whether she likes extra ketchup with her fries. Using this data, the kiosk suggests daily specials that might appeal to her. Of course, it also keeps track of her frequent buyer points, automatically giving her a free sandwich after ten visits.

Even better, a kiosk at a pharmacy could keep records of every customer's medical and shopping history. In addition to filling his prescription, it could make sure he isn't allergic to the medication, automatically file his insurance forms, give him coupons on other items in the store and suggest items that he bought a while ago but hasn't stocked up on lately.

POP Displays

Point-of-purchase devices sit on a store shelf or in an aisle display. Using audio or an LCD display, they give consumers a chance to get accurate information on the spot, before choosing a product.

Interactive Audio: It's easy and inexpensive to create a tiny POP audio device. Think of the power of a celebrity's voice promoting your product whenever a customer presses a button on a display. Or imagine a display in a drugstore that plays a message every time a customer removes a bottle of shampoo. The message could offer the shopper an instant discount on the shampoo, or encourage her to pick up a bottle of the same brand's conditioner.

An audio device can also play a message every time someone walks by, drawing customers' attention to a product on display. But be careful of noise clutter! Push-button displays might be better suited to high-traffic areas.

These devices are usually battery-activated. Simple devices start at $50 each in quantity.

Interactive LCD: While sound is an impressive gimmick, you can't use it to present much information. For slightly longer messages, try LCD displays. With these low-cost devices, which use the same technology found in digital watches, you can present one or two lines of text, prompt consumers with questions, or answer simple queries.

Warner-Lambert Canada, a pharmaceutical company that sells cough, cold, and allergy medicines, created an interactive LCD it calls the "Cough, Cold, and Allergy Relief Directory." Consumers use a keypad to respond to questions about symptoms, then the device recommends a product to relieve them. The computer in the product is programmed to recommend one of about a dozen different remedies. Eight are made by Warner-Lambert. Pharmacists like the device because it takes a burden off them and helps their customers.

You can use LCD POP displays to collect basic information. For example, if you own a winery, you could place an interactive LCD device in wine retail shops that asks people what foods they typically eat when they drink wine. You may learn that most respondents eat foods that go best with white wine. Using this information, you can create a white wine promotion. Or, if you know a particular retailer carries 75 percent red wine and 25 percent white, you can use these statistics to convince him to carry more white wine.

Electronic Catalogs and Brochures

W hy should you consider an electronic catalog? CD-ROMs can hold much more information than a printed catalog — a boon for manufacturers with large product lines. Photographs can be as large as a computer screen, not simply the size of a standard printed page. Most importantly, an electronic catalog is "smart." Once it learns the likes and dislikes of a consumer, it can skip some pages, highlight others, and present new items that are particularly likely to interest the user — just like a smart salesperson in a high-end specialty store.

Most electronic catalogs are used in point-of-purchase locations, because relatively few households have computers equipped with CD-ROM drives. Still, some home markets exist. MCS Group, Inc., developed a CD-ROM catalog for buyers of *Star Trek* paraphernalia. Selling for $79, *Greenberg's Guide to Star Trek Collectibles* describes 3,000 items and includes 400 pictures along with pricing information. Because there's a huge overlap between Star Trek fans and CD-ROM users, the match is perfect.

Business-to-business applications are more common. Pacific Bell Information Services publishes an electronic catalog of PC networking software and hardware. For $99, subscribers receive four quarterly issues of *ReSource* on disk. The catalog covers thousands of products and features interactive advertising.

The cost savings can be substantial. A CD-ROM can be duplicated for less than 75 cents, and mailed for another 50 cents. A four-color catalog is expensive to design, expensive to print, and expensive to mail. And for buyers with the right hardware, a CD-ROM is likely to have more impact and absorb more of a prospect's attention.

Even Hollywood has discovered the benefits of multimedia. Casting agencies, which used to keep huge files on the actors they represent, now store the same information on CD-ROM. The catalog of present and future stars not only displays their photographs and résumés, but also short video clips of their acting styles. Users can enter desired attributes, such as "tall, blonde, attractive, unknown, 24 years old," and the software will list all the actors on the disk who meet the description. Actors pay about $100 each to appear in the catalog.

Apple's new CD-ROM catalog, *en Passant*, features well-known direct-mail merchants like the Pottery Barn, and allows the user to cross-index them. For example, if the user is searching for a $25 wedding present that can be used in the house, *en Passant* might present candlesticks from one company, a vase from another, and a tortilla press from a third. Press a button and the *en Passant* catalog will display all the ordering information. Future versions will allow a user to order by modem, guaranteeing fast delivery and avoiding any time-consuming phone interaction.

Techno Marketing helps companies create interactive floppy disks to promote their products. The disks cost about $1.50 each to produce and mail to prospects. After using the disk, prospects are encouraged to print out a form and fax it back to the company. The form is encoded so that Techno Marketing can see how prospects used the disk. How many times did they look at the disk? What information did they select, and what did they ignore?

One major car manufacturer created a floppy disk about one of its high-end cars that gave users information about available colors, the engine, the tires, the stereo, and other features. Researchers analyzed the forms users faxed back and discovered that lots of people had looked at information about the engine and colors, but nobody was really interested in finding out more about the tires. Armed with this data, the company can delete the tire information from future disks and replace it with something else. Even better, the company can instruct its salespeople to talk about features that really interest customers — anything but the tires.

A salesperson can use a CD-ROM catalog to bring a business-to-business sales call to life. Using a color laptop computer, she can show the prospect video clips and testimonials, and cross-index products according to the prospect's needs. She can even print out a spec sheet on the spot.

Let's say you make roofing shingles. While visiting a prospect, you can input the dimensions of his house into your laptop computer. The multimedia program will create a diagram showing the house with new shingles. You can also produce a spreadsheet that shows the customer exactly how many shingles he needs to buy and how much they will cost.

On-disk Presentations

T he overhead projector, light pen, pointer, slide projector, and VCR that used to be the tools of the presenter at trade shows, sales seminars, and client meetings have been replaced by a single freestanding monitor with a disk drive and a mouse.

At its Resource Center in Atlanta, the State of Georgia uses a multimedia presentation to sell businesses on the advantages of relocating to Georgia. The system provides information on infrastructure, taxes, and educational facilities in each of Georgia's 159 counties and cities. State officials can even design 3-D models of a theoretical "plant" and transfer the image to different sites across the state, so clients can see the layout that works best. The center produces 40 to 50 of these custom presentations each year. It will even transcribe the presentations in either text or video format so the client can take the information back to company headquarters. "It goes a long way in making a sale," says Roy Plott, Resource Center manager.

Multimedia presentations are not limited to the size of a computer screen. The following companies manufacture video scan converters, which allow you to put your multimedia presentation on a large-screen or projection TV.

Adda (510) 770-9899
Advanced Digital Systems (800) 888-5244
AlTech International (800) 882-8184
Boffin Limited (612) 894-0595
Communications Specialties (516) 273-0404
Computer Friends (503) 626-2291
Consumer Technology Northwest (800) 356-3983
Dextra Technology (800) 339-8725
Digital Vision (617) 329-5400
Dih Shin International (602) 978-8014
Extron Electronics (800) 633-9876
Genoa (800) 934-3662
IEV International (800) 438-6161
Jovian Logic (510) 651-4823
KDI Precision Products (800) 377-3334
Magni (503) 626-8400
MediaFX (714) 993-9988
Telebyte Technology (800) 835-3298
UMax (800) 562-0311
VideoLogic (800) 578-5644
Visionetics (310) 316-7940
Willow Peripherals (718) 402-9500

It's not necessary to have all your viewers in the same room at the same time to run a successful multimedia presentation. Harvard Graphics for Windows 2.0 has a conferencing feature which allows the user to distribute a presentation to up to 64 systems simultaneously over a network.

At the simplest level, a multimedia presentation is nothing more than a series of slides created on a computer. You can add sound and movies for a more sophisticated, professional presentation. It's easy to import videotape into a computer, especially if you use a Macintosh.

While most multimedia presentations aren't interactive, it's not difficult to make them appear to be. If you can anticipate your prospects' questions ahead of time, you can build pieces into your program that let you present answers to these questions if they arise.

DON PEPPERS AND MARTHA ROGERS ON USING CD-ROM TO MAKE A COMPLEX SALE

A friend of ours runs an advertising agency, and one of his clients is a major maker of corporate aircraft.

Now, selling airplanes to corporations has to be one of the most daunting and difficult of all sales tasks. Imagine the obstacles to the sale. First, there is the simple question of expense, which is enormous. But more than the simple dollar amount, a company must deal with the justification of it, when this enormous cost is being spread over the T&E budgets of a relatively few, high-level corporate executives.

Then there is image. While many, if not most, corporate executives may personally aspire to the status and power of being flown around in a small private jet, the truth is that for most firms the image of senior officials being pampered so luxuriously is not something to be cultivated.

In any case, convincing an executive that purchasing a corporate jet is worthwhile requires a good deal of persuading. Buying a corporate aircraft is truly a "considered purchase." The decision to buy can only be made after a great deal of thinking, analysis, and, in many cases, soul-searching.

There are many questions a potential aircraft purchaser will ask himself or herself before agreeing to such a sale. What about the cost of operating and maintaining the aircraft? How about its usefulness in reaching out-of-the-way destinations? Would it be better just to lease an aircraft on an occasional basis? What's the advantage of a jet over a turboprop, or is there one? What about weather? Pilot hiring and scheduling? Range before refueling? Dependability?

Then, after he's asked himself all these questions, the prospect is also likely to ask himself if he can really visualize himself with such an expensive "toy." What will his business associates think? His stockholders and investors? His employees?

The only reason to go into all this is that our friend was wrestling with the task of helping his client sell more jets, and he already knew that selling more jets was not something for which traditional advertising would be much help. Rather, he wanted to figure out how to equip his client's sales force with some kind of tool to help answer prospects' questions, and overcome the obstacles.

So our friend hit on the idea of an interactive CD, which could serve as an ideal reference tool, in addition to helping the salesman use personal references to resolve even the "soul-searching" issues!

It should be easy to understand how the reams of charts, specifications, and illustrations that are traditionally used to explain a product as complex as a jet or turboprop aircraft could be more easily carted around, and accessed more quickly, by using a CD-ROM device. But that was the easy part. Our friend had other ideas, too.

Imagine the aircraft manufacturer asking a number of aircraft owners and recent purchasers to speak about their own experiences with the firm's product. When is having a dedicated aircraft really indispensable? Does it save cost in terms of valuable senior-executive time? How hard is it to resolve scheduling conflicts? How about hiring pilots and maintaining the aircraft? And what strategies have been useful for explaining the need for the jet to stockholders, or to employees?

Now imagine that the firm conducts such an interview, asking all the most difficult questions, with each of several hundred current owners. Don't forget that each has already spent a good deal of time wrestling with these very questions, and justifying, to his own satisfaction, the benefits of owning a corporate aircraft, when compared to the costs.

Each executive interview is tape-recorded, and each interview is subdivided into the sections that answer various specific questions. The interviews are also keyed by industry, by size and nature of company, by geographic location, by flying patterns, and by the name, position, age, and gender of the interviewee. Each executive is also photographed once or twice.

Then these tape-recorded interviews and photographs are stamped onto a compact disc and indexed for CD-ROM retrieval. The firm's sales people are given laptop machines with CD-ROM drives. They are now armed and dangerous.

Consider the possibilities: Maybe a sales prospect is in the wholesale-distribution business. While he's a small company, he's rapidly growing, and he's often required to go somewhere off the beaten path of scheduled airline travel. Occasionally he's had to charter aircraft, and he's now trying to decide whether it makes sense to own one. So the salesperson asks him if he'd like to see other wholesale distributors who currently use the firm's planes.

"Oh, you know Bill Weston at Weston Warehousing? Here's what he says about his new turboprop…"

And with that the photo image of Bill Weston comes up on the computer screen, while his voice is heard explaining how he first decided that getting an aircraft was the right thing to do, particularly when he found himself chartering aircraft to get to those smaller destinations. He talks about missing an important sale once because he couldn't get there in time, and he couldn't get a charter. That, he says, is when he decided to take the plunge.

"Here are the specs on the first aircraft Bill Weston purchased, although he's now on his second upgrade."

"Here's a list of the other executives who travel a lot to the upper midwest, like you do…"

"Here's how one executive dealt with the issue of scheduling the aircraft…"

You get the picture, right? But the example we just gave is only from one industry. CD-ROM could be used in any number of industries and situations in the same way — to resolve complex product and service questions, as well as to provide references and recommendations from currently satisfied customers.

If your business is selling to other businesses, especially if you use a direct sales force, chances are pretty good that a CD-ROM tool would prove very helpful.

Interactive Training Manuals

I n 1993, businesses spent $47 billion on staff training. For many marketers, training the staff who deal with the public — salespeople, receptionists, operators, and technicians — is the most important, and most difficult, part of their job.

Using multimedia, you can standardize your training sessions, build in performance tests and make changes in a flash. It's often cheaper to hire a programmer and buy the necessary computer hardware than to hire a tutor or send employees to orientation programs. More and more large companies are opting for this approach.

A 1993 survey revealed that 45 percent of Fortune 1000 companies use multimedia applications for in-house training. By combining databases, text, audio, video, and interactive computing, multimedia creates a learning environment that can be more efficient than tutor or text-based learning. One study showed that trainees remembered only 10 percent of the material presented by a live trainer or textbook. But if they used a multimedia application for the same length of time, they remembered 50 percent of the information presented. Trainees using multimedia are not passive. They are reading, listening, watching, and keying in commands on a computer in the same lesson, all at their own pace. Some analysts believe that's why they remember more.

Federal Express installed 1,200 interactive training sites in 800 of its 1,400 service centers. As a result, the company reported a 30 percent reduction in errors and cut training time by 60 percent. Holiday Inn had the same sort of success. It reduced training time for employees from 14 days to 6 by using multimedia training programs.

Since multimedia does not have to be text-based, a company could create a CD-ROM training application for foreign employees that uses animation, video, and graphics to communicate its message. A copier technician could see exactly how to replace a component by watching a video clip of the process. Pictures speak louder than poorly translated words.

When United Airlines added the Airbus A320 to its fleet of planes, Airbus offered to help train United's employees. The two companies produced a tutorial on CD-ROM and delivered it, along with the machinery to run it, to flight attendants worldwide. The interactive software cost $150,000 to produce, but it cut training time from 8 hours to three.

United estimates it saved $9 million in travel, hotel, and other expenses by using this tutorial.

Getting Started in Multimedia

ultimedia disks are created using computers, disk recorders, and special authoring software. If you want an interactive introduction to the world of multimedia, you can order "The Guided Tour of Multimedia" for $39.95 by calling (800) 942-4000.

Authoring software gives the programmer step-by-step instructions for compiling the different media into a seamless production. *Multimedia World* magazine has reviewed the following 12 packages designed for people who want to create multimedia presentations quickly and easily:

Company	Software	Phone Number
Gold Disk	Astound 1.5	(800) 982-9888
Micrografx	Charisma 4.0	(214) 234-1769
Macromedia	Action 2.5.1	(415) 442-0200
Asymetrix	Compel 1.0	(800) 448-6543
Q/Media	Q/Media 1.2	(604) 879-1190
Lotus	Freelance Graphics 2.0.1	(617) 577-8500
SPC	Harvard Graphics 2.0	(800) 234-2500
Microsoft	PowerPoint 4.0	(206) 882-8080
Ask Me Multimedia	Super Show & Tell 1.0	(612) 531-0603
Corel	CorelDraw 4.0	(613) 728-8200
Zuma Group	Curtain Call 2.0	(800) 332-3492
WordPerfect	WordPerfect Presentations 2.0	(800) 451-5151

You create and test the software on a computer with a large hard drive, then transfer it onto a blank CD-ROM using a recorder. The PlayWrite recorder from Microboards works with DOS, Unix, and Macintosh systems and lists for $3,899. (Prices are dropping fast.) For more information, call Microboards at (800) 225-4414.

Making copies is as easy as running blank disks through the recorder and downloading the information from the PC. With blank recordable CD-ROMs costing less than $20, short-run reproduction is relatively cheap. For longer runs, you can send a master CD-ROM to a duplicator, who will copy it for as little as 70 cents per disk.

Marketing Reference Information Available Through CD-ROM

T ools available to marketers fall into three basic categories: census and demographic data, information for generating telephone lists and mailing labels, and atlas and geographic marketing information.

Census Data

Marketers of everything from toasters to cars need to know the demographics of their potential audience. After all, if you know how many Hispanic households there are in Seattle, you'll have a better idea of how much to spend there.

Fortunately, the U.S. Census Bureau has compiled an astounding array of information on every American, available in virtually any format. You can find the wealthiest 9-digit ZIP code in the U.S., the home of the most disabled veterans, and the percentage of homes with pets in San Diego. Until recently, however, this data was expensive to decipher. No longer. There are many resources out there if you need demographic data. Try some of these products, available through *American Demographics* magazine, (607) 273-6343.

Key Indicators of County Growth 1970-2015 is available on floppy disk created by NPA Data Services, Inc. This product provides basic demographic and economic data for all 3,096 counties in the United States on one disk. State and national totals are also provided, along with twelve basic growth factors for eight different years.

1993 MSA Profile is available on floppy disk created by Woods & Poole Economics, Inc. This disk contains metropolitan area forecasts to the year 2015 and historical data back to 1970. Census data for all states, metropolitan statistical areas (MSAs), primary MSAs, consolidated MSAs, and regions are included. You can look up information such as ethnic makeup, population numbers, employment makeup, and income per capita.

CEDDS: The Complete Economic and Demographic Data Source is available on CD-ROM created by Woods & Poole Economics, Inc. More than 2.8 million statistics and the equivalent of more than 3,600 pages of demographic and economic data are stuffed onto one CD-ROM. The database lets you analyze the data, prepare special reports, and generate graphs.

Demographics USA Zip Edition 1993 is available on CD-ROM created by Market Statistics. This product sorts and summarizes 40,000 ZIP codes on one CD-ROM. The enclosed software lets you rank, search, analyze, and customize the data to your needs. The disk includes information about retail sales projections, buying power indices, consumer expenditures, employment, and more.

Telephone and Mailing Labels

The huge data capacity of CD-ROM has dramatically increased the availability of other data as well. Several vendors offer phone numbers for every household in the country, with various levels of search capability. With a few keystrokes, for example, you could find everyone named Wong in Tucson. The more sophisticated products allow you to print a mailing label for each person you find.

The software is even more useful for marketing to businesses. You can find companies by SIC code (which identifies the type of business) and hit, say, every butcher in the Southwest.

Some of the available packages are listed below.

- *PhoneDisk* from Geographic Data Technology, Inc., (800) 331-7881, Matchmaker/2000 (software). This geocoding system contains more than 12 million address ranges and can match street addresses with ranges of longitude and latitude coordinates.

- *Business America on CD-ROM* from Optical Products Division, P.O. Box 27347, Omaha NE 68127, (402) 593-4565.

- *Phonedisc USA Business* from Digital Directory Assistance, Inc., 6931 Arlington Rd. #405, Bethesda MD 20814, (617) 639-2900.

- *Phonedisc USA Residential* from Digital Directory Assistance, Inc., 6931 Arlington Rd. #405, Bethesda MD 20814, (617) 639-2900.

Atlas and Geographic Data

For $125, Street Atlas, USA offers detailed street-level maps of the entire United States on one disk. The atlas includes ZIP codes, place names, phone exchanges, and even address ranges for metropolitan areas. Anyone managing a territory or planning new store sites will find this software useful. Available through software retailers.

Global Explorer is a world atlas that includes street maps of 100 world cities, comprehensive country profiles, and a network of world air routes.

New software from Microsoft and other companies will allow marketers to overlay statistical data on geographic areas, then produce colored maps of the result. For example, such a map could show that certain neighborhoods in Buffalo are buying more than twice as many Twinkies as other neighborhoods. This visual data representation can turn mind-numbing statistics into mind-blowing facts.

52 Ways to Use Multimedia

1. *Create a ticket-generating kiosk for your travel agency*

Put the kiosk in an easily accessible public place, such as a supermarket or mall. After booking a trip by phone, clients can print out their tickets at the kiosk. Clients can even use the kiosk to complete simple transactions, such as booking train tickets, without involving the agency at all. The agency can reach out and gain new customers with this convenience.

2. *Provide information on available seats*

Ticketing companies and performance halls can create an interactive kiosk that provides reviews of current plays, schedules of upcoming events, and ticket information. Users can call up a diagram of the venue for a particular performance that shows which seats are still available. Users select the seats they want, the kiosk prints out tickets, the customer pays for them with a credit card. People are more likely to pay $100 or more for tickets if they know the seats will be good ones.

3. *Recommend albums to record store customers*

Some record stores are installing a multimedia system that gives customers background information on artists and types of music. Customers can conduct searches by artist, name of song, name of album, or a host of different options. If a customer tells the system which bands he likes, the system can recommend related albums he might also enjoy, and play sample cuts from them.

4. *Offer more specialty goods to customers*

A company that makes expensive niche items such as crossbows, for example, might have a difficult time convincing a major retail chain to stock them. But the company could set up an in-store interactive kiosk so that customers can get information on the products and buy them directly from the manufacturer. The manufacturer makes more sales, the retailer can "carry" new products without spending money on stock, and the customer can easily purchase unusual goods.

5. *Present and modify blueprints*

Architects and contractors can show a client blueprints and drawings on diskette using a multimedia program. If the client wants modifications, these can be done on screen instantly, with no need to make new drawings.

6. *Provide how-to information to increase sales*

Customers can use an interactive display in a hardware store to get instructions on simple household repair jobs. The display can list the materials required for the job, provide prices for various brands, and even direct the customer to the aisle where the items are stocked.

7. *Help customers choose pet food*

A pet food manufacturer can place an LCD display on the shelf in the grocery store to help customers determine which kind of food is best for their dog. Customers can punch in what type of dog they have, how much the dog weighs and how old he is. The display will tell the customer which food to buy and when and how much to feed the animal.

8. *Show customers how they'll look using various cosmetics*

Place a video camera and computer screen in your store. Offer to scan in photographs of your customers. On the screen, you can use a multimedia program to show customers how different brands and colors of eye shadow, blush, foundation, and mascara can change their appearance.

9. *Distribute personalized catalogs*

Did a customer place a big order with your mail-order clothing company last month? Send her a personalized catalog on floppy disk that features items to go with her earlier purchases. If she bought a red skirt, for example, her personalized catalog could include a matching red striped blouse, a navy jacket, red pumps, and red-and-blue earrings.

10. *Put all your catalogs on CD-ROM*

If you put all your catalogs on one CD-ROM, you can save your customers time and increase your sales. For instance, a customer looking for a birthday present for his mother could specify the type of gift he wants and how much he wants to spend. The CD-ROM will take that information, search the different catalogs, and propose an appropriate gift package.

11. Sell carpeting

A carpet manufacturer could use a floppy disk to calculate how much carpeting a customer needs to buy for a room of a specific size. A good graphics program can even show her what it will look like when it's installed.

12. Propose interior design ideas

Designers and interior decorators can use multimedia to show customers how specific carpets, upholstery, drapes, wall coverings, and furniture will look in combination. Customers can easily make changes and try out endless variations — with no need to thumb through endless books of upholstery swatches, wallpaper samples, and paint chips.

13. Produce customized dress patterns

A pattern company can set up an interactive system in fabric shops that asks customers for their measurements, then prints customized versions of standard patterns for each user. Customers are happy because the finished item will fit better, and the company gets useful data on the measurements of actual users of its patterns.

14. Mail promotional CD-ROMs to prospects

A company with an extensive product line, such as an automobile manufacturer, can send a CD-ROM to prospects' homes that gives detailed information on complex features like anti-lock brakes and computerized navigational systems. The disk might have separate files for dozens of models.

15. Produce sophisticated instruction manuals on disk

Complicated products such as computer workstations can require instruction manuals that are several volumes long. Now, manufacturers can provide detailed instructions, including video clips and audio information, on a CD-ROM. It is easier for the customer to use, and cheaper for the manufacturer to produce.

16. Put extensive price lists on disk

A hardware company that makes thousands of types of nuts, bolts, screws, and nails can produce a price list on diskette for its biggest customers, and update it frequently as prices change. That way, customers can easily calculate the cost of a large order without scribbling down prices from an outdated catalog or calling the supplier for an estimate.

17. Provide an easy-to-use store directory

A large department store can make its store directory available through a touch-screen video kiosk. Customers could select the department they wish to find, see a picture of it on the video screen and print out a diagram showing the route from the kiosk to the selected department. The kiosk could even print out discount coupons for items in that particular department.

18. Suggest books

In a bookstore, a customer could use a multimedia terminal to request a bibliography of books on a certain topic or a list of books by a particular author in stock. Based on information he keys in about his favorite authors and reading habits, the system could suggest books he might enjoy.

19. Create custom cassette tapes

Record store customers could use an in-store kiosk to make customized tapes. The customer would key in a list of 10 songs and the kiosk would copy them onto an audiocassette.

20. Answer questions at a trade show

At a trade show, an electronics manufacturer could provide a display panel that lets buyers ask questions about the company's products. If the user wants to place an order, he can press a button to summon a sales representative.

21. Handle information requests

Visitors at a trade show could input their name, address, and information requests into an interactive display, so that exhibitors could send them information or arrange a sales call after the show.

22. Run an attention-getting interactive game

By setting up a multimedia game at a trade show, exhibitors can attract attention. If players have to enter the name and address of their company, the exhibitor can collect a database of hot prospects.

23. Demonstrate new hairstyles

A hair salon could scan a client's picture into a multimedia system, and then show her how different hairstyles would suit her face — before cutting even one lock of her hair.

24. Encourage multiple purchases

A small audio device in a display of perfume bottles can play a brief audio message when customers pick up a bottle, informing them that they'll save a dollar if they also purchase talcum powder in the same scent.

25. Provide information on artworks

A small gallery may represent dozens of artists, but it only has enough room to display a few of each artist's pieces at any one time. A CD-ROM system allows the gallery to maintain detailed information, including high-quality photographs, on all the works each artist has for sale, and to provide that information to potential buyers in a user-friendly format.

26. *Produce interactive travel "brochures"*

A tour company could produce an interactive presentation on its package tours. A prospective customer interested in a bus tour of Italy, for example, could use a kiosk at a consumer show to see a video clip of a gondola plying a Venice canal, hear Luciano Pavarotti singing in Milan, and print out detailed information on the tour company's prices and schedules.

27. *Market a specialized encyclopedia on CD-ROM*

Encyclopedias are extremely useful reference books, but they can be somewhat dry and unappealing, especially to children. But put an encyclopedia on CD-ROM, and you can liven up an article about the South American rain forest with video clips of brightly colored toucans in flight.

28. *Distribute electronic catalogs of craft supplies*

A craft supply store often stocks thousands of tiny items such as embroidery threads and ceramic beads, in dozens of colors. By putting its catalog on CD-ROM, it can show shoppers vivid, larger-than-life pictures of every item. To increase sales, it could include video instructions for dozens of projects using the store's materials.

29. *Demonstrate video games in a toy store*

A multimedia display would not only let customers try a game before buying it, it would allow them to find out more about the game, such as the price of the game and whether any games are left in stock, whether there are any related games available. It could also recommend other games the customer might enjoy.

30. *Provide information to writers at a conference*

At large conferences, editors are often besieged by eager authors looking for information. Most of the questions are similar: What types of novels are you buying? Do you have writer's guidelines? Do you accept multiple submissions? A stand-alone terminal and printer at an information booth could handle these routine questions, leaving the editors free to discuss prospective authors' manuscripts in more detail.

31. *Provide information to visitors*

In some popular tourist areas, the visitor information office in high season looks like Grand Central Station. A multimedia kiosk or two could take a lot of the pressure off harried clerks. Not only could it offer general information on attractions and events, complete with sound and video clips, it could provide up-to-the-minute information on vacancies at particular hotels. Of course, the computer will remember what questions were asked, allowing the town to alter its signage next year.

32. *Store documents from a historical society*

Local historical societies have archives of hard-to-find information, such as old diaries and letters, that writers and historians would be willing to pay to use. A small, volunteer-run society can't maintain a full-scale library. It could, however, record the materials on CD-ROM and sell the CD to researchers. That way, the society could make some money, distribute its materials more widely, and preserve the original artifacts from possible loss or damage.

33. Provide airport information

Kiosks scattered throughout an airport would be a great help to tired, often disoriented travelers. As well as providing information on flight arrivals and departures, the kiosks could give the users information on services such as duty-free shops, currency exchanges, and lounges for first-class passengers, complete with maps. Restaurants could put their menus on the system. Car rental agencies could offer users a discount.

34. Sell expensive homes

A multimillionaire from Texas wants to buy "a little vacation house" in New England — somewhere he can entertain, say, 35 guests for the weekend. He wants information on available properties. A Connecticut real estate agency can send him a CD-ROM containing information on dozens of exclusive homes, including detailed diagrams of every room, photographs of the view from various properties, and audio clips of the sound of the surf pounding the shore.

35. Train chefs

Let's say you own a nationwide chain of hotels. The executive chef at each property makes an innovative dish that has customers clamoring for more. You want all the chefs to learn how to make all of these dishes, but some of the techniques are fairly complicated, and it's impossible for all the chefs to get together at the same time. Produce a multimedia cookbook, with recipes and videos of each chef making his special dish.

36. Demonstrate exercise equipment

An exercise equipment manufacturer with a booth at a consumer show has several problems: he doesn't have room to display all his machines, and he doesn't have enough sales reps to demonstrate the ones he can display. By setting up a multimedia presentation, he can let prospects see videos of all his machines in use. Customers can also view price lists, watch testimonials from satisfied users, and read newspaper articles about the benefits of exercise.

37. Persuade prospective franchise buyers

A fast-food chain is trying to convince an investor to buy a franchise. After explaining that single people aged 15 to 29 are the chain's best customers, the sales rep can use a multimedia program on his laptop to call up maps of various cities, highlighting areas where the number and income of young singles is high. Then he can find out the price of each available franchise, and retrieve information on each city's tax rates, bylaws, and business climate.

38. Promote books to bookstores

A book is distinctly low-tech: just paper and ink. But a publisher can bring its upcoming titles to life for a bookstore buyer using a multimedia program. On a sales visit to the buyer's office, the publisher's sales rep could call up video clips of a famous actor who is profiled in an upcoming biography, and full-color pictures from a children's book.

39. Sell training materials to doctors in remote locations

In rural areas, physicians don't get much opportunity to watch top-flight surgeons in action or attend symposia on new drug therapies. A medical publisher can sell these doctors a CD-ROM containing videos of tricky new operations or of panel discussions from a conference. The disk could also hold hundreds of related research papers.

40. Produce a multimedia annual report for your investors

Companies produce expensive, four-color annual reports because they want to appear prosperous and exciting in the eyes of their investors. A CD-ROM annual report can give a company an even more attractive image. It can include a videotaped message from the president, clips of positive television stories about the firm, and massive amounts of statistics that the user can manipulate himself.

41. Promote community arts organizations

A group of local theatres, dance companies, art galleries, and ballet companies could pool its resources to set up a multimedia kiosk in a busy shopping mall. The kiosk could display videos of current productions, provide biographies of featured artists, list upcoming events, and even sell and print out tickets.

42. Reinforce your product's association with a current movie

Remember how E.T. loved Reese's Pieces? Today, the candy manufacturer could install an audio point-of-purchase device in high-traffic areas where its product is sold. Curious customers would push a button to hear a message like "I always choose Reese's Pieces" in the movie character's voice.

43. Help customers choose hair coloring products

A hair-care company could put an interactive LCD device near its product display. Shoppers would key in information on the length, natural color, and condition of their hair, as well as the color they wished to dye it, and the display would recommend the appropriate product.

44. Sell seeds

A seed company can produce a CD-ROM catalog showing every available variety in blooming color. The user can search the catalog to find out which plants grow well together and which survive best in the shade. Video clips could show how to transplant a delicate rose bush or get rid of aphids.

45. *Promote a flying school*

At a trade show, a flying school could use a simple multimedia presentation to show prospective students videos from inside the cockpit. Prospects could also print out information on course schedules and prices.

46. *Produce a portable fashion show*

Instead of mounting a full-scale fashion show in 20 different cities, a major designer could store a video of one show on a CD-ROM. Exclusive retailers could set up the presentation on an in-store monitor. Interested customers could stop the action to take a closer look at a particular dress, or call up detailed information on fabrics, colors, sizes, and prices.

47. *Promote a convention center*

A convention center could set up an interactive multimedia display at a trade show that would give prospects information on its facilities, diagrams and photographs of each convention hall, and sample menus from the catering department. The prospect could key in the number of people attending her upcoming banquet, select a menu, and hit a button to receive a price estimate.

48. *Survey customers of a bank*

Offer customers an incentive, such as no-charge checking for a month, if they take a minute to use an interactive kiosk to complete a survey. With the kiosk, your bank can gather information on your customers' likes and dislikes. Do they want faster service, longer hours, more locations, or free financial planning seminars? The kiosk can gather this sort of information in seconds.

49. *Provide route maps*

An auto club could set up a multimedia kiosk to provide route maps for club members. A user would key in his destination and interests. The kiosk could then print out a customized route map that indicates the locations of factory outlets, historic sites, amusement parks, or any other sites that might interest the user.

50. *Produce a video-by-mail catalog*

Many companies rent or sell videos by mail. A company specializing in foreign films could put clips of various movies, along with reviews and pricing information, on a CD-ROM, and mail the disk to people who recently bought tickets to a prestigious film festival.

51. Promote a lottery

An LCD device near the cash register of a convenience store could display information on the estimated jackpots of a dozen different lotteries.

52. Promote a children's camp

A multimedia display can provide parents with detailed information on a children's camp, including schedules and prices, video clips of kids riding horses or canoeing on the lake, audio clips of campfire singsongs, estimated travel times to the camp from various cities, and testimonials from happy campers.

Multimedia Resources

RTC Industries, Inc.
2800 Golf Rd.
Rolling Meadows IL 60008
(708) 640-2400
Interactive point-of-purchase specialists.

RTC Industries is a leader manufacturer in the world of point-of-purchase displays, merchandising systems, specialty packaging products, and premiums. They specialize in interactive point of purchase and develop programs for clients that involve one of three different types of electronic technologies — interactive audio, interactive LCD, and interactive video. RTC has developed interactive displays for clients such as K-Mart, Warner-Lambert Canada, Olin Chemical, and Sega Games.

The cost of RTC's interactive products ranges from as low as $50 for an audio unit to $2,500 for an interactive video system. RTC can take a stock product and tailor it to your needs or develop a unique interactive package for your product and/or retail location.

MediaShare
2035 Corte Del Nogal, Suite 200
Carlsbad CA 92009
(619) 931-7171
MediaShare is a business software and consulting firm that specializes in finding uses for multimedia applications in marketing environments. Since opening its doors in 1990, MediaShare has become one of the leading developers of interactive sales presentations. Using its own trademarked software package called PBPlus, MediaShare can incorporate your company information and product literature into a powerful multimedia sales tool.

MediaShare has also recently ventured into the world of interactive, electronic catalogs. They can take your product database and turn it into a full, stand-alone, catalog with full-motion video, audio, and an interactive order form. They specialize in being a one-stop shop for catalogers who need multimedia database design services, video and audio editing, graphic arts and animation design, and interactive software and hardware expertise.

Techno Marketing, Inc.

5170 West 76th St.
Edina MN 55435
(612) 830-1984
Creators of multimedia presentations and campaigns for marketers.

Techno Marketing, Inc., formed in 1987, produces custom-designed interactive multimedia programs created to meet each specific client's needs for a particular application or project. They can produce programs designed to run on anything from a single floppy disk to a complex interactive multimedia kiosk integrating CD-ROM, stereo, and touch-sensitive screens.

Even on a low-end platform, TMI can deliver such features as 3D animation, full motion video, voice and music, database searches, and personalization. And that's just scratching the surface. TMI has produced interactive products for clients such as Apple Computer, Holiday Inn, Lexmark, Carlson Companies, and the NFL. They specialize in producing multimedia solutions to sales presentations and interactive training.

Murray Multi-Media

Eight Carhart St.
P.O. Box M
Blairstown NJ 07825
Murray Multi-Media produces interactive multimedia programming for sales, public relations, point-of-purchase, promotional, and training applications. Their primary focus is on the creation of portable, interactive sales presentations using CD-I or CD-ROM technology. They have created presentations for Fortune 500 companies and their biggest success stories have involved *Forbes* magazine and Schering Plows.

Originally a design firm, Murray has evolved into its role as one of the top presentation designers in the market. They are a full production house, capable of writing your script, producing the audio and video, determining its interactivity, and mastering the disks.

Telestar Interactive Corporation
11541 Goldcoast Dr.
Cincinnati OH 45249
(513) 469-9800

Telestar manufactures a microchip speech technology used in the production of their interactive audio product called "Microtalk." Microtalk has been used as an audio point-of-purchase device by packaged-goods companies, fast-food restaurants, and automobile dealerships, among others. It allows customization of a series of interchangeable audio messages that can be triggered by either motion or push-buttons. According to Telestar, Microtalk increased product sales of eight national brands an average of 24% during controlled testing (without couponing).

Ohana Communications
233 East 70th Street
New York NY 10021
(212) 737-6906

Ohana Communications is the U.S. licensee of a multimedia software package called Engage. Originally developed in France and used internationally by companies like Mars and Kellogg, Engage is an interactive media technology used primarily at point of purchase in kiosks and CD-ROM applications.

Specializing in meeting the needs of the cosmetic, apparel, and computer industries, Ohana uses Engage to create entertaining interactive media and sales presentations and stand-alone kiosks for marketers. They also produce marketing programs that can be used online and, eventually, they hope to use the technology in the arena of interactive television and home shopping. Ohana can help you develop your interactive marketing campaign starting from concept and ending with installation and maintenance of the system.

Interactive Marketing, Inc.
2200 Pacific Coast Highway, Suite 103
Hermosa Beach CA 90254
(310) 798-0433

Interactive Marketing, Inc. (IMI), was created in 1992 by Andrew Batkin, one of the founders of the interactive industry. Since then, IMI has branched out into five divisions and has served a variety of Fortune 500 companies' interactive needs.

The Creative Services Group is an interactive media agency specializing in the use of a variety of interactive technologies for advertising, promotion, and marketing purposes. They have developed multimedia marketing campaigns for such clients as Anheuser-Busch, Coca-Cola, FOX Broadcasting, and Walt Disney.

IMI also produces the *Interactive Marketing Newsletter*, acts as an interactive consultant in the areas including interactive education and analysis, and produces interactive TV shows and CD-ROM titles. They have also organized and maintained the *Interactive Marketing Conference* Group, a series of educational and networking conferences for high-level corporate marketing executives.

Multimedia Publications

Multimedia World
(800) 825-7595 x501 to subscribe

Multimedia Glossary

CD-ROM (compact disc read-only memory): a technology that stores information on a diskette. A scanner reads the diskette and projects the information onto a computer screen.

DOS (disk operating system): the operating system used by most IBM-compatible PCs.

Download: to send information from one source, such as your computer, to another source, such as a disk.

Kiosk: a freestanding unit which uses multimedia technology to dispense consumer information.

Laser disc: also known as a "video disc." It is similar to a music CD, but it holds visual images as well as music. In fact, laser discs can store entire concerts. The signal is fed into your television or video monitor as with a videotape, but the quality is better.

LCD (liquid crystal display): a low-cost digital display device. Your digital watch uses an LCD to display the time.

Multimedia: a form of providing information that combines text, graphics, video animation, and audio.

Online: a term used to describe two or more computers that are communicating through a modem or a network. You need to get online to send or receive e-mail or to use a bulletin board service.

Programmer: the person who writes the coded instructions that tell the computer what to do.

Read only: a term used to describe a file you can look at and print, but not change.

Software: the instructions that make computers work.

UNIX: a software system that lets multiple users work on a computer network simultaneously.

Upload: to use your modem to put one of your files onto a network or an online service so other people can use it.

INFOMERCIALS

A NEW GENERATION OF LONG-FORM TELEVISION COMMERCIALS

What are infomercials, notorious for spray-on baldness cures and Thighmasters, doing in a book on cutting-edge marketing?

eMarketing is about establishing relationships with consumers — finding people who want your product or service and then cementing your relationship with them. For many markets, infomercials are the perfect first step in this process.

e

A Quick History of the Infomercial

Fifty years ago, direct-response magazine and newspaper ads were the marketer's most effective tool. These long, text-filled ads informed as well as sold. They often encouraged readers to send away for a free sample. Marketers turned these initial inquiries into sales.

This direct-response technique gave marketers adequate time to teach readers about a complex topic, answer questions and objections, and close the sale.

The introduction of television saw these ads make the transition to broadcast. The long ads just moved to the small screen, in the form of commercials that lasted as long as 30 minutes. Many marketers capitalized on the power of the televised sales pitch. In 1958, however, the FCC banned all commercials longer than two minutes in length. Short, expensive ads for easy-to-understand products such as soft drinks, toilet paper, and cigarettes became the norm. Marketers could use TV to generate name recognition and store traffic, but no longer had time to educate the consumer.

Cable television changed one part of the equation. With hundreds of alternatives to the big three networks, the cost of putting a commercial on the air dropped, and it became much easier to target a niche market. Then, in 1984, the FCC once again allowed long-form commercials.

Suddenly, infomercials were back.

Unfortunately, the first advertisers back on the air were the shlock artists selling forgettable junk at high prices. They had realized a fundamental truth of direct-response advertising: if your commercial generates more profit than it costs to run, you can dramatically increase your advertising budget instantly.

Using Infomercials

The days of overnight infomercial millionaires are gone. The market is too crowded now. The second generation of infomercial producers is relearning the lesson learned by early TV advertisers: an educated customer is a motivated customer.

Niche cable stations let marketers target their message more precisely than ever before. They make it more likely that the infomercial can successfully sift through millions of consumers to find the thousands who want the product.

The second-generation infomercials aren't an end in themselves. They're the first step in a two-step process. Their only goal is to generate a phone call from an interested consumer. Then the advertiser has to take the second step: scheduling a dealer visit or a sales call, or sending the caller a free sample.

Both steps are critical. The infomercial breaks down consumers' resistance to an unknown product or company. Once they feel comfortable with the company and believe the product might solve a problem for them, the second step can close the sale.

Volvo has a reputation for making safe cars. But it's hard to explain safety features in a magazine ad. So when the company introduced a new line of cars a few years ago, it created a half-hour infomercial that told Volvo's safety story in detail. The company obviously wasn't trying to convince consumers to pick up the phone and buy a Volvo on the spot. It simply wanted to create interest, so that qualified prospects would call and set up a test drive.

After the infomercial ran in Southern California, more than 20,000 people called Volvo for more information. At this point, one-to-one marketing took over. By handling every inquiry swiftly and personally, the company could make prospects feel like a valued member of the Volvo family. This second step was crucial, but dealers never could have taken it if the infomercial hadn't generated qualified prospects in the first place.

General Motors broadcast a half-hour documentary that described the creation and production of its new Saturn cars. Because the company was more interested in building brand identity than selling cars immediately, it didn't invite viewers to call. But the infomercial still taught a huge number of prospects about the new car.

Burger King understands that selling a franchise is far more complex than selling a hamburger. Unfortunately, it's hard to reach people who have the money to buy a franchise who haven't already considered the possibility. By using an infomercial, Burger King can tell a compelling story to a huge number of consumers, then winnow this audience down to the few who are both interested and qualified. With the fee for a franchise at well over $100,000, Burger King can afford to run quite a few infomercials even if the sales rate is low.

Do you market an expensive product? Then you know that a business-to-business sales call can cost well over $200. An infomercial, on the other hand, can cost just $3 to deliver to a likely prospect on videotape. For the price of one personal sales call, you can reach more than 60 qualified prospects with an infomercial. And you can do even more in an infomercial than you can in a sales call: discuss product specs, show product in use, use testimonials, show product construction, discuss guarantees, and make competitive comparisons.

Accountability

U nlike most television ads, an infomercial lets you measure results immediately. Within an hour, you'll know whether the ad generated any phone calls. Within weeks, you'll know if the calls resulted in sales.

Understandably, infomercials make some advertising agencies nervous. They've spent the last 40 years telling clients about the benefits of "brand building" or "awareness," confident in the knowledge that there was no way to measure the effect of particular ads.

There will always be image advertising and short messages. But effective infomercials are proving their worth as a way to give potential customers more detailed information.

TIMOTHY HAWTHORNE ON INFOMERCIALS

TIMOTHY R. HAWTHORNE is president of Hawthorne Communications, a leader in infomercial marketing. As the first agency focusing exclusively on Fortune 500 infomercial advertising, Hawthorne has gained tremendous experience using this medium as a two-step selling tool.

It's 1849; Sutter's Mill, California. The hills and valleys are alive with men and women dreaming of newfound fortunes. They come from all walks of life, merchants, farmers, laborers, even doctors and lawyers. A few hit the mother lode; most watch their dreams washed rapidly downstream....

Fast forward to 1984. Southern Californian Bob Murphy strikes gold. Only this time it's infomercial marketing. And word of potential riches travels as fast as it had 135 years earlier. Soon there are dozens of adventurers laying claim to the infomercial gold vein.

They're bankers, educators, computer executives, attorneys, fast-buck artists — no longer called "Forty-Niners," but entrepreneurs.

In 1849, all you needed was a strong back, a pickax, and a pan to reach millionaire status. In 1984, it didn't take much more. A unique product, a hot pitch man and an 800 telephone number. And within months, these TV direct-response moguls individually created 10 to 50 million dollars in sales.

The first generation of infomercial marketers peddled get-rich-quick homestead courses, diets, kitchen gadgets, health and beauty aids. If a product had a 300% mark-up, was not available in stores, appealed to the masses, appeared new and unique, and met common needs of greed and vanity, it was a potential infomercial gold mine.

For eight years, from 1984 to 1992, the mavens of TV infomercials harvested their fortunes, ignored by mainstream advertisers and traditional advertising agencies. Annual, industry-wide gross sales leapt from 10 million dollars to 750 million. While 1984 saw perhaps five infomercials launched, in 1992 nearly 200 long-form shows debuted.

The currents of change, though, had been flowing quietly all along. As more infomercials competed for a limited number of media time slots, the cost of a half-hour had risen dramatically. By 1992, long-form media buyers paid an average of three times more for the same time period than in 1984.

The consequences were twofold: 9 out of 10 infomercials tested were failures; and "successful" infomercials made less profit on the front end and relied more on "aftermarket" sales. Consumer response to infomercials hadn't gone down; it simply cost more in media expenditure to generate one sale. The net result: the long-form market was ready for a change.

That transformation took the form of a Texan riding in on a political white horse. His name: Ross Perot.

In the fall of 1992, only one Fortune 500 advertiser used infomercials: Time-Life. But when Perot premiered his fourth quarter 1992 presidential campaign infomercials, suddenly Madison Avenue woke up to the power of the half-hour.

Showing him sitting in a denlike setting, referring to hand-held charts, Perot's simple, inexpensive infomercials were revolutionary. With 8 to 10% of all TV households tuned in to watch, ratings were nearly 30% higher than the networks' entertainment programs Perot's shows preempted.

Immediately, in boardrooms across the nation, corporate execs consulted with their ad agencies. "Why can't we tell our products' stories in a half-hour?" they asked. Infomercials had come of age overnight.

From 1992 to the present, the corporations listed below have all tested infomercials.

Apple Computer, Inc.

Avon Products, Inc.

BankAmerica Corp.

Bell Atlantic Corp.

Black & Decker Corp.

Braun

Century 21

Club Med

Coca-Cola Co.

Dayton Hudson Corp.

Eastman Kodak Co.

Estée Lauder

Fidelity Investments

Fischer Audio

Ford Motor Co.

General Motors Corp.

GTE

HarperCollins

Hyatt Resorts

Johnson & Johnson

Mattel, Inc.

MCA Records

McDonald's Corp.

Norelco

Panasonic

PepsiCo, Inc.

Philips Electronics

Playboy Enterprises, Inc.

Prodigy

Prudential

Redken

Revlon

Scott Paper

Sears, Roebuck & Co.

Slim•Fast

Smith Kline Beecham

Texaco, Inc.

Time-Life

Visa

Volkswagen

Volvo

Warner Music Enterprises

Weight Watchers

Every major advertiser now has long-form TV advertising routinely considered as part of its marketing mix. But along with big corporate infomercials came a change in marketing goals and strategy.

Even at media prices averaging now five times the cost of infomercial time in 1984, half-hour media is still a bargain. On a per-minute comparison basis, infomercial media is roughly one-fifth the cost of a 30-second commercial. Established brand companies realized they could use an infomercial to accomplish marketing goals beyond the traditional one-step offer ("Use your credit card. Call the 800 number and order now.").

For Fortune 500 companies, infomercials could generate leads (the two-step offer), establish brand awareness, and become a powerful public relations vehicle. The Fortune 500 even revolutionized TV direct response with their discovery that infomercials can even drive retail sales. An accidental discovery....

In 1989, the entrepreneurial infomercial company named Quantum hit a home run with its Daily Mixer show. The product was an Italian made, handheld, single-stem food mixer priced at $129.95. Within one year, Quantum sold $50 million worth of mixers.

Coincidentally, the American division of the German manufacturing giant Braun had a like-styled mixer on the shelves at retail. When the Daily infomercial went big, Braun's mixer flew off the shelves. And when the infomercial died after 18 months, Braun's retail sales dropped significantly.

Braun decided to take control of its own retail fortunes. It asked Hawthorne Communications, the first Fortune 500 infomercial advertising agency, to make a new infomercial with Braun's mixer as the star. Rolled out in the fourth quarter of 1992, Braun's infomercial not only sold well direct over TV, but, as predicted, drove retail sales dramatically.

Braun's MaryAnn Connelly said, "Braun is particularly interested and impressed by the tremendous impact infomercials have on retail sales. Braun's ultimate goal was to cover most, if not all, of the cost of media with direct sales and drive sales for our retail partners. Braun's infomercials have met this goal admirably. We have seen retail sales increase dramatically."

The "retail driving" infomercial was a true advertising innovation. For 50 years, television direct-response commercials have typically sold products "unavailable at retail." The TV exclusivity was thought to build immediate telephone response. But a look at the numbers shows why infomercials impact retail sales.

Research has indicated that only 20 to 30% of consumers are inclined to buy a product directly from a television offer. Most Americans still like to touch and feel a product before purchasing. But 99% of consumers watch television. And they can't help but come across an infomercial sooner or later.

In fact, only 1/10 to 1% of all infomercial viewers actually pick up the phone to order. That means 99% of infomercial viewers have spent anywhere from three to 30 minutes learning about a product's features and benefits but don't call the 800 number to order, leaving millions of highly educated sales prospects much more willing to buy the product if they discover it at their favorite retail outlet.

Because infomercials have the power to inform and entertain so many retail buyers, in-store sales of an infomercial product can amount to two to 20 times the direct-over-TV sales volume. "Driving retail" is now the preferred strategy of the infomercial industry's second generation: major brand advertisers.

Philips Electronics successfully used this strategy to revive its listless CD-I (Interactive) sales. In 1992, Philips had spent nearly $12 million in image advertising, and struggled to move any product. In 1993, it spent half as much on an infomercial campaign and cleared retail shelves within three months. The infomercial, in fact, was briefly taken off the air until inventory could be restocked.

But creating an infomercial success is not as easy as it looks. Traditional ad agencies have thus far struggled with the format. There are different rules of persuasion for 30 minutes versus 30 seconds. The first "sit-commercial" was a classic boondoggle.

Bell Atlantic commissioned its agency to create an infomercial for its add-on phone services: call waiting, call forwarding, and the like. Bell's agency spent $750,000 hiring a Hollywood sitcom writer to craft a situation-comedy infomercial.

The plot revolved around an Archie Bunker-style family called "The Ringers." Ralph Ringer, a plumber, tried for 30 minutes to keep peace in his family by introducing them to the add-on Bell Atlantic phone features. Unique, innovative, entertaining…but the infomercial was unable to create sufficient response. A basic selling rule had been violated.

The writer had placed Ralph, a fictional character, in the role of "asking for the order." Periodically, Ralph stepped out of character, turned to the camera, described the phone features available, and asked the viewing audience to "call the 800 number on your screen now."

Those experienced in infomercial marketing recognized the blunder immediately: few people will do the bidding of a fictional character. Especially when it requires making a purchase.

Such are the lessons the Madison Avenue copywriters must learn in the emerging era of "elective" advertising.

Infomercials are the forerunners of this new era. A revolution is happening in how advertising will be delivered and viewed. The world of interactive television will make the 30-second copywriter useless.

For 50 years, television advertising has been based on "intrusion": interrupting viewers glued to *Jeopardy!* and *Home Improvement* to present a commercial message. Until 10 years ago, the TV audience had little choice when intruded upon: watch it dumbly or head for the kitchen or the bathroom. The 1980s gave the viewer another choice — zap commercials with his remote control. Forty-six percent of viewers now zap all commercials.

Interactive television presents an even more serious threat to advertisers than the remote control. When the home viewers can watch anything they want at any moment, how will we get them to watch our product message? Will anyone, given the choice, choose to watch ever again a commercial for Dove, Crest, Tide, Coke, or McDonald's? No. Not unless you give them an incentive.

Television advertising is moving from the age of intrusion to the age of "attraction." Viewers will elect to watch commercial messages for two basic reasons: they will be compensated by advertisers for their attention through product discounts, coupons, contests, cable TV fee discounts; or they will decide of their own volition they want product information because they're in the market to buy. The former category of products will be low-involvement, low-ticket items such as food and packaged goods; the latter category will be high-involvement, high-ticket items such as electronics, appliances, and autos.

No matter what the product, the ad messages will be required to be highly "attracting." Otherwise, the consumer will move abruptly to one of the 499 other viewing options available.

This "attracting" quality is exactly what infomercials have to possess even today. Audiences watch infomercials not because they have to, but because they want to. Long-form ads never intrude; viewers choose to watch them because they appeal to their desire for product information: information presented over a 30-minute period in an entertaining way.

In the TV interactive age, commercials neither will be 30 seconds nor 30 minutes long. Most likely, a product will have 6 to 10 chapters of information available to screen, each 2 to 6 minutes long. And the goal of the 21st century advertiser will be the same as the 1990s infomercial producer: keep the viewer watching as long as possible. The venerable merchants' axiom yet holds true — the more you tell, the more you sell.

Advertisers would be advised to learn the art of infomercial creation today, because tomorrow's advertising will follow closely in its footsteps.

Success Stories

G TE ran an infomercial for a new service. An astounding 70 percent of the callers to the 800 phone number ordered the service. GTE advertising manager Victoria Lins says she liked the infomercial because it was "100 percent measurable to sales. We saw greater returns than we did on some traditional ads." GTE is developing a second program.

Gemstar Development Corp. developed the groundbreaking VCR Plus. It lets users tape TV shows more easily. Instead of fiddling with a VCR timer, VCR Plus owners simply key in a code that appears beside each program in the television listings. After convincing newspapers around the country to carry the numeric codes, the company faced the daunting task of persuading consumers to try a brand-new technology.

Market research showed that most people had heard of VCR Plus but had never tried it. So Gemstar created an infomercial that demonstrated the product and featured testimonials about how easy it is to use. The infomercial is part of an integrated marketing strategy including radio spots and TV product placements.

Some people still associate infomercials with junk, but you can't get much farther away from shlock than The Salvation Army. As one of the country's three largest charitable organizations, the Army is continually struggling to maintain its presence, its impact, and its funding. The Army had never used paid advertising. However, following the lead of other nonprofit organizations, it created a 30-minute infomercial.

"The purpose of the campaign was to present a contemporary and accurate image of The Salvation Army and generate leads for people in service ministries, and to increase attendance at The Salvation Army," says Jeffery Goddard, president and executive producer of The Video Agency, which produced the infomercial.

The program, hosted by actor and AT&T spokesman Cliff Robertson, invited viewers to call an 800 number to request a free 10-minute videotape, "Happiness From Having a Life Money Can't Buy." A Salvationist delivered the tape to the caller's home. The nationwide campaign was so successful that the Army translated the infomercial into Spanish.

While compilation albums have always been sold on TV ("Now you can get every record ever recorded!"), leading record labels have rarely used TV ads. However, record companies such as Arista, Mercury, and Warner Music Group are now working on infomercials. These ads will use clips of music videos, concert footage, and canned interviews to jump-start sales of languishing acts — the same techniques that made MTV such a powerful force in the record business. The ads will encourage viewers to call an 800 number or visit a particular record store.

Playboy Home Video uses infomercials to market two of its best-selling videos: "Secrets of Making Love to the Same Person Forever" and "Ultimate Sensual Massage." The ads also offer audiocassettes of "Playboy's Music for Lovers," vitamin E massage oil, and jasmine massage balm. The company has overcome video stores' reluctance to stock its products by marketing directly to the consumer, with marked success.

Hoover used an infomercial to solve two problems: its difficulty in reaching male consumers, and its inability to control the way its product was demonstrated in retail outlets. The show featured the company's 16-gallon Hoover Wet/Dry Vac Supreme cleaner and a 12-piece tool set. It ran primarily on weekends during the day, and was originally released to promote Father's Day sales.

At first, Hoover was afraid that retailers would see the infomercial as competition. On the contrary, retailers appreciated the ads because they increased sales by educating consumers. According to David Gault, Hoover's Vice President of Marketing, "With fewer and fewer salespeople in any given outlet, the more demonstration and selling that takes place before customers enter the store, the better the sales will be."

Planning Media Placement and Distribution

T en years ago, you could buy a half-hour of local cable time for about $50. Today, that same spot will cost you $500 — if it's even available. As more companies have entered the infomercial field, time slots have become more difficult to find.

The placement of an infomercial has always been the single most important factor in its success. With rising prices and increased competition, it's more important than ever to study the market carefully before buying air time.

Most infomercials should be aimed at a niche, not the entire population. The tighter your focus, the more efficient your advertising. Fortunately, the explosion in the number of cable TV channels makes it easier than ever to target your market. There are channels devoted to food, golf, and talk shows — and several that will feature only infomercials.

Buying air time directly is a difficult and expensive undertaking. It's far more efficient to hire a media-buying firm. In many cases, these firms have pre-bought blocks of time around the country — cornering the market in some areas.

Remember VCR Plus, the technology that helps consumers program their VCRs easily? It's also a boon to infomercial advertisers.

Now, you can save money on placements by running your infomercial in the very cheapest time slot (3 a.m.) on the least watched channel, and letting prospects know they can tape it by setting their VCR Plus to your show's code. Of course, you can also tell other VCR users just to set their VCR timer. Either way, you can generate interest for very little money — if your infomercial truly offers useful information to your target market. No one is going to bother taping a straight sales pitch. You have to make it worth their while.

You can promote your infomercial in a variety of ways. CBS sells a package called Spot Plus+ that combines your dead-time infomercial with a series of short 30-second daytime commercials promoting the infomercial.

Tri-Star used Spot Plus+ to advertise the movie *Guarding Tess*. In its daytime ads, the company told viewers that it would air a 10-minute preview of the movie at 2 a.m., and that the preview would include information for a phone-in contest. Despite the extremely low cost of the 2 a.m. time slot, Tri-Star received 2,000 calls from people who had seen the preview and wanted to enter the contest. More than 75% of the callers had taped the preview.

To attract the attention of a more specialized market, you can use magazine, newspaper, and direct-mail advertising. Let's say you're running a 30-minute infomercial to explain the features of a new computer. You can promote the infomercial to computer-savvy consumers with full-page ads in *PCWorld* and similar magazines.

Or, like many advertisers, you may decide not to broadcast your infomercial at all. Instead of paying to beam your message to hundreds of thousands of homes with no interest in your product, you can send a videotape to likely prospects. For about $3 per 30-minute videotape — $2 to duplicate the tape and $1 to package and mail it — you can deliver a high-impact message right to a prospect's door.

Very few people will throw out a videocassette. And if your list is carefully targeted and you follow up, most of the recipients will actually watch it.

In 1991, Hart Schaffner & Marx, the men's clothier, replaced its Christmas catalog with a videotaped infomercial. Customer reaction was quite positive, and the company got hundreds of unsolicited calls for more video catalogs.

INTERVIEW WITH BILL THOMPSON

William M. Thompson is the president of TV Inc., an infomercial marketing and research firm in Largo, Florida. He is also the author of Inside Infomercials, *and is a recognized expert in the infomercial field.*

Q: **Who are the new major marketers entering the infomercial arena and why do you think they are entering now?**

A: Let's start from the beginning. In 1984, the government very quickly relaxed the rules on the amount of commercial air time that could be placed during any one half-hour or hour period. Any time there is an opening to a frontier, you get the Sooners. You know what a Sooner is?

Q: **The Oklahoma Sooners?**

A: Yes. They called them Sooners because when the government opened a strip of land, some people would sneak in the night before to stake their claim. The first into the market are like the carpetbaggers who went to Atlanta in 1865 to set up businesses and make money as quickly as possible and then get out of town.

These are the types of people who were involved in infomercials when it first got started. The slicers, the dicers, the diet program, that type of thing. Traditional marketers always sit back and wait to see how things shake out and what effect it is going to have because they have corporate images and major dollars to consider. Whereas an entrepreneur operates by quickly throwing a few hundred thousand dollars in this thing, making some money and seeing what happens.

As major marketers enter the game, the market is in transition. As a result, air time is becoming much more expensive. The consumers have stated that they are willing to watch half-hour-long or hour-long informational commercial programs. The major marketers in different industries, the Fortune 500, so to speak, are looking at long-form advertising as another vehicle they should consider.

Q: **Can you give me some examples of who you see of these industries that are entering now?**

A: We don't know of anyone who isn't. We have met with some of the top companies that are recognized on the American and New York Stock Exchanges, even entire *countries* that are looking into this vehicle. Infomercials have been established as consumer-acceptable. Since they are accepted by consumers, major marketers are now looking at how they can proceed into the market.

Q: **How do you think the new infomercial marketers are using the technology to build connections with their existing and potential customers?**

A: The weakest link in any distribution program is always the firing line. That's the person who is actually behind the counter, in the salesroom, who is talking to the potential customer.

In the past, salespeople were relatively well trained and usually worked on commission. That's expensive. With today's high-energy, fast-lane type of merchandising and marketing, you can not afford to put that type of person on the firing line. Yet consumers still demand, even more so as they get older, more and more information about the product they are going to acquire before they are willing to spend the money.

The infomercial gives the manufacturer the opportunity to speak at length, in a controlled way, with his potential customers about his product so they get the information. It is like having your very very best salesmen at the top counters all the time.

Q: **How does the concept of one-to-one marketing play itself out in the production and use of infomercials?**

A: The infomercial is exactly that; it is an information-based piece. No one ever bought a television to watch commercials. They bought a television for entertainment and for information. The infomercial allows the manufacturer to give the consumer entertainment and information at the same time that he's selling something.

The fine line between what is commercial and what is entertainment is now being totally erased. The product is becoming very much a part of the production itself, the entertainment vehicle.

With a 30-second, 60-second spot ad, where you're focusing on brand awareness, brand identification, and image advertising, you are asking the person to remember the name of your product when he gets to the retail marketplace, and hopefully to opt for that product over the competitor. An infomercial goes much further, because you can now tell the person all there is to know about the product, and you can develop a relationship with the customer through the television. So not only does he want to buy the product, but he knows as much about it as, if not more than, the salesperson behind the counter.

Q: Why do you think major marketers are using a two-step process versus a one-step process?

A: Because they are already in the distribution business. A company came to us and said, "We'd love to get this product out there on infomercials. The problem is, we have distributors, we have retailers, and we can not possibly appear to be competing with them directly. We've got to come up with a program that supports our retailers and moves merchandise at the same time."

Q: Do you think the reason for the two-step process is to create a long haul, whereas a one-step is for get-money-quick schemes?

A: I don't think that all one-step commercials are quick-money schemes. There are many one-step commercials that we have designed for $39, $49, or $59 programs. The whole idea was to develop a customer base, so you could sell to them again and again. Victoria Jackson has done that very successfully with cosmetics. Now there are still one-step, strictly one-step; Ginsu knives for example, Tony Robbins is a one-step, although he is moving into multiple steps by flooding the customers with mailings of this program and this vehicle. Don't forget the purpose of an infomercial is to build a customer base.

Q: Do you think the entrance of major marketers who can spend greater amounts of money will affect the infomercial market?

A: Not at all. And it won't for this reason: two-step, three-step, image-type infomercials require more prime-time, more conventional time base. One-step commercials require that you catch the person one hour after they wake up or one hour before they go to sleep. So those times are not of interest to major corporations.

Q: Do you think infomercials will become alternatives to prime-time programming?

A: They already are. Look at "Oprah Winfrey Interviews Michael Jackson Live." That was a two-hour infomercial. It was produced by CBS, who also produced his newest and latest album. They spent 90 minutes talking to Michael Jackson, and 30 minutes talking about his album.

Q: What about using videotape for infomercials?

A: The power and versatility is terrific. It's just one more step toward total control. You're not limited to making a 30-minute commercial and saying it is going to be on at 11:30 at night on channel 69. You can do anything you want because people are crying for and demanding more and more information. The video concept answers that problem.

Q: What has been the biggest problem for major marketers entering the world of infomercials?

A: Having dealt with a number of the larger companies, I have found they have a tendency to look at something innovative and then apply traditional techniques in order to get it solved. This kind of thinking typically has proved unsuccessful. In fact, I can't think of an infomercial that has been produced by a major company by its major agency (and those are two important things that have to be tied together) that has ever been successful.

Philips has done a decent job with their CD program on the continuity basis. Get the unit and then buy the discs and so forth from them. Eastman Kodak tried it. They have a one-minute spot for their photo device that puts them on a disc. But they have found that their short form, their one-minute spots, do much better than the 30-minute spots.

Q: Why do you think that is so?

A: The people who would use the product are already predisposed to it. You are talking about people who enjoy picture taking and would be willing to spend significant money in order to improve their picture-taking experience. They haven't pitched it to the non-converted as introducing something new.

Q: But isn't another goal to attract people who are marginally interested?

A: They found that it does. However, they found there is enough of a base already there that is more actively interested in taking advantage of it rather than having to re-educate. Re-education is a very expensive process. Now, if you have a million people who are willing to buy your product right now and you can reach them for $100, that's your first step.

If you have ten thousand people who are interested in buying your product and it is going to cost you $200 to reach them, well $200 isn't that bad, but if I could only spend $100 to reach the first group, I'd get that many more sales. So they prioritize. What is working best is what they are doing right now. I am not saying the infomercial didn't work. I am saying the short form was more effective financially.

Now, those are the only two that I know of that have actually produced significant results. Volkswagen just came out with one. It was a very nice infomercial about the car you love and the history of the Volkswagen — it tried to develop customer loyalty. They had an 800 number at the end and they wanted to drive the people to dealerships.

They weren't able to drive the people to the dealerships because when you dialed the 800 number, the person who answered the call would say "What's your ZIP code?" and you would say, "My ZIP code is 81818."

"Oh, okay, your local dealer is Fred Morris. Do you need his phone number?" That's the response they're giving them. They dropped the ball. They did not use effective receiving techniques. The telemarketing service did not do a sufficient job of completing the process. All the steps from buying air time to fulfillment need to be consistent. Volkswagen did not do this. Why? Because they are using traditional techniques in a direct-response atmosphere.

Why is it that DDB Needham, which owns one of the largest direct-response companies in the world, is talking to people like me to do their infomercials? If you look at a script for an infomercial that is really well done, you see you'll suddenly become just enwrapped in the story and you can't wait to get the product.

An infomercial is about the management of the whole marketing program as compared to buying some print space or running a 30-second spot, putting your finger in your ear and hoping somebody calls you. Infomercials are advertising vehicles that are accountable, and most agencies don't even want to think about that. We know immediately how well a program did. How well it did in the time slot, how well it did in the demographic, in the psychography. We know that within 24 hours. No other advertising vehicle allows that.

In the end, infomercials will be successful if people plan and execute the marketing strategy from the beginning to the end. As I have said before, "Future profits are not the result of technology alone, but the proper management of that technology."

Creating Content

I t's easy to make a bad infomercial. Remember the first wave of infomercials, with their unctuous, untrustworthy hosts delivering never-ending sales pitches? These "one-step" infomercials tried to convince viewers to buy immediately.

Infomercials have evolved. They now use the dramatically different "two-step" approach — educating the viewer before trying to sell to him. Remember, the viewer can and will change the channel the moment the program stops interesting him.

Don't underestimate the willingness of a consumer to get into details. In an infomercial for a car, you can visit the factory, explain the computer-controlled antilock braking system, or discuss tire design. Any information that will help your prospect make a better decision benefits both of you.

Producing Mini-Infomercials

T o date, we've talked about infomercials that are widely distributed. But infomercials designed to be seen by 1,000, 100, or even one person can be just as effective.

If you can identify a targeted audience that needs to know more about your products or services, it may pay to deliver your message on videotape instead of using a traditional brochure.

Hard Manufacturing is the nation's largest producer of hospital cribs. There are just 2,000 hospitals in America big enough to buy more than a few of these $1,000 to $5,000 cribs.

Hard mailed the head pediatric nurse in each of these hospitals a 30-minute video on crib safety. Produced in conjunction with a cable TV network, the video consisted primarily of an interview with the president of the company.

Evidently, many nurses watched the video. The whole promotion cost less than $15,000, but it led to more than $50,000 in new crib orders.

Producing an Infomercial

I t may be tempting to produce your infomercial in-house, but that's rarely wise. Production expenses are a tiny fraction of the total cost of your infomercial campaign. Don't skimp.

Technology has substantially lowered the cost of creating broadcast-quality video in the last five years. Dozens of companies now specialize in infomercial production. When assessing a production company, start by asking for its reel, which will include excerpts of past infomercials. Try to ignore the product being sold and focus instead on the quality of the script, set, and lighting.

Remember that you can create 30 minutes of infomercial for just about any price. Your goal is not to pay the least, but to be sure that you get what you pay for. Instead of asking producers for a price estimate, ask them to describe what they can deliver for a given amount.

If you're doing a mini-infomercial, you may not be able to afford a production house. However, you may be able to cut a deal with the local cable station to shoot your commercial during the day, when many cable studios are empty.

DON PEPPERS AND MARTHA ROGERS ON HOST COMPUTERS: THE MARKET IN INFORMATION EXCHANGE

Imagine you're watching a Mitsubishi commercial sometime in the interactive future. You've been thinking about a new car, and this one looks pretty good. So you punch your remote to call up some information about leasing, warranty, and options currently available — even though you're not sure whether to buy just yet.

As you sit down to dinner that evening, however, the local Mitsubishi dealer calls you to discuss things personally. The next day, the local auto insurance companies drop by your office, and in a few days, your mailbox is crowded with glossy automotive promotions and brochures.

You feel hustled. Would you ever raise your hand — electronically — again?

Today's mail-order and credit card information gets freely passed from marketer to marketer. Buy clothes from a catalog and you'll soon get more clothing catalogs in the mail. Make a donation to muscular dystrophy, and pretty soon the heart and cancer people will also hold out their hands — either in the mail or on the phone.

But the interactivity available on the Internet will speed these practices intolerably, creating junk mail at light speed. Consumers will soon loathe the volume and pace of commercial solicitations, and the invasions of privacy that accompany them. Transaction-happy mass marketers will have much greater power to track individual customers, but the customers themselves will probably stop responding altogether — thus crippling the economics of interactivity.

The solution lies within the technology that created the problem. Using currently available technology, tomorrow's media company must insulate consumers and marketers from direct contact with each other.

Imagine the media company of the future not as an information pipeline connecting marketer and viewer, but as an information pool instead — a repository of information acting as a buffer between marketer and consumer. This is the role the Internet could play, or else it will attract hosts who will themselves serve as buffers.

Such an information intermediary gathers detailed information from each user and sells it to marketers — including all kinds of information about the consumer — except the individual's identity or any form of address. In turn, the marketers who are most interested in particular individuals will make highly targeted offers to them — offers so attractive, or so narrowly focussed no marketer could make them available to every consumer, or even every consumer in a certain "segment" or "niche."

The offer can be made only within the host's own interactive system. With no name, Mitsubishi or Club Med or Waldenbooks cannot contact any customer by e-mail, phone, or snail mail. Nor can he sell the information to competing marketers.

The savviest marketers will realize that even if they get the customer's ID (which they will if the offer is just right), they are better off keeping the information to themselves. In the 1:1 future, success will accrue to those marketers with real relationships with consumers, and those relationships will be based on superior learning about each individual customer. One-to-one marketers will use the information they have about a customer to get a greater share of that customer's business, and will find that endeavor more profitable than selling off the information to competitors.

Thus the consumer's privacy is protected by the value of the relationship. The marketer holds information that gives a bankable competitive advantage. The intermediary host makes a living by serving as an information buffer. It's the only way consumers will play, and it's fast becoming the only game in town.

52 Ways to Use Infomercials

1. *Create a "news" program about your new car*

   Make a documentary about the development of your new family sedan.
   Ask designers how they came up with ideas for the vehicle. Show the
   state-of-the-art plant where the car is made. Interview workers on the
   assembly line about quality control, and ask them to demonstrate some of
   the ways they double-check the car's safety and structural integrity.
   Viewers will come away feeling confident about the product.

2. *Link your product to a charity*

   Do you sell books? Run an infomercial promoting a literacy foundation,
   showing how the charity uses your books to teach adults to read. Do you
   run a bakery? Produce a program about a food bank, and include an
   interview with the executive director mentioning how you have donated
   thousands of loaves of bread to the charity. You'll create goodwill for
   your company by associating it with a worthy cause.

3. *Conduct market research by inviting customers to call you with feedback*

   If you're promoting a diet supplement, tell viewers they can try it and then
   call your 800 number to give you their opinions. After a few months,
   update the infomercial by including some of the positive comments from
   the feedback line.

4. *Run a quiz show about a tourist destination*

   Are you trying to promote a popular tourist destination such as Mexico,
   Hawaii, or London? Produce an infomercial that combines alluring video
   of your destination with a series of trivia questions such as "Where are the
   Crown Jewels on display?" Viewers can mail in their answers for a chance
   to win a free trip. They'll feel more involved in the program, and you'll
   get a list of hot prospects for future marketing campaigns.

5. *Offer free samples of a new brand of energy bar*

   Many athletes put great stock in energy bars — bars of healthy ingredients
   and vitamins that are designed to boost performance. Manufacturers do
   detailed studies to determine the best combination of ingredients. In an
   infomercial, you can interview researchers, as well as successful athletes
   who have used the product. But viewers won't be convinced enough to
   buy a box of 24 until they've tried one themselves. A free bar can overcome their reluctance to buy.

6. *Promote a chair to new dentists*

   Using a mailing list from a dentistry school, send a mini-infomercial about
   your dental chair to new graduates. Show the chair in an actual dentist's

office and describe its features in detail. Does it tilt to 12 different positions, or include a retractable step to let children climb into it easily? Follow up with a sales call offering a delayed payment plan.

7. *Promote a video camera with samples of actual home movies*

Run a contest for your current customers, offering cash prizes for the best movies made using your camera. Put the best of those entries in an infomercial. Include interviews with the winning entrants, in which you ask them how they got such great shots with your product.

8. *Interview satisfied buyers of your vacuum cleaner in their homes*

This promotion works especially well if the happy customer has white carpeting, a dog, kids, and a lot of houseplants. As you chat with the customer, the dog can come tearing through the formal living room, followed by several small children. They knock over a plant stand, sending potting soil and begonia bits everywhere. When the serene customer sucks up every last bit of dirt with your vacuum cleaner, you'll have struck a chord with every frazzled homeowner.

9. *Create an educational program based on your encyclopedias*

Many potential encyclopedia buyers are afraid the books will sit on a shelf gathering dust after they buy them. Show these skeptics how they can use the books to pursue subjects they didn't have the time or money to study in school: art history, philosophy, physics, geography, world literature.

10. *Promote stained-glass supplies with a how-to program*

Stained glass can be an expensive hobby. Glass and soldering irons aren't cheap, and it can be hard to find quality supplies. People interested in the hobby may be reluctant to invest in the supplies if they're not sure they could use them properly. Produce a program showing how to make a simple project using your materials.

11. *Show viewers how your maid service will make their lives easier*

A short "before-and-after" program, showing one of your maids cleaning a typical house, can be a very effective sales tool. Viewers who feel guilty about their messy houses will sympathize with the hapless homeowner at the beginning of the ad, and feel wildly jealous of her at the end. Perfect for a local audience.

12. *Produce a public safety message to promote a related product*

A life-jacket manufacturer could run an infomercial on the general topic of water safety. The product could be mentioned frequently. Of course, in every shot showing boaters, swimmers, and campers how to behave responsibly around water, everyone will be wearing one of the company's life jackets.

13. *Challenge real people to test your product*

So you claim your suntan lotion is the best? Prove it to viewers. Go to the beach and offer free samples to sunbathers. Convince them to try your product. Later in the day, interview them and let them tell viewers that the product smells nice, isn't greasy, and didn't let them get so much as a freckle.

14. *Produce a talk show about books for a bookstore chain*

Many people are curious about authors. Unlike movie actors and rock stars, authors aren't immediately recognizable, although they may have millions of devoted fans. Use this cachet to promote several authors' books at once. Run a roundtable discussion about the books in which authors can describe the plots and talk about where they get their ideas.

15. *Show how your golf clubs can improve a player's game*

In a store, golf clubs are just lifeless pieces of wood and metal. To inspire people to buy, show real golfers using them to win games. All the brochures and persuasive retailers in the world can't equal the impact of an actual golfer booming them off the tee.

16. *Produce a show on veterinary health to promote your pet food*

Many pet owners are fanatical about their pets' well-being. Provide useful information on keeping pets well groomed, slim, and free of fleas, and you'll catch viewers' attention. Mention your full line of dog and cat food, and viewers will associate your brand name with good health and good advice.

17. *Broadcast a program showing how donors' dollars are used*

Some people don't like to donate to charities because they're afraid much of the money raised goes to administration. Allay their fears with an infomercial documenting your charity's work with underprivileged children, refugees, or endangered species. If your offices are small and cramped, include footage of them to inspire further confidence that money is really going directly to the cause.

18. *Test your company's car against the competition*

Seeing is believing, and many consumers are suspicious of auto manufacturers' claims that their vehicle performs better than a competitor's model. Run a road race pitting your all-terrain vehicle (in flashy red) against the competition (in dowdy beige). Have it sanctioned by an independent organization. When your car easily plows through bogs and tackles rough, winding mountain roads, while the competition breaks an axle, viewers will have visual proof of your claims.

19. *"Make over" customers to promote your cosmetics*

Cosmetics companies like Avon and Mary Kay have realized the power of in-home consultations for years. If you can't visit all your customers individually, do the next best thing — broadcast a step-by-step makeover. By showing viewers exactly how certain products make a real person look, you'll increase sales.

20. *Produce a photography show to promote camera equipment*

Amateur photographers are always looking for new tips on capturing sunsets, children, or historic monuments on film. Show them how to take better pictures, in a documentary featuring your lenses, filters, tripods, and cameras.

21. *Promote a tourist destination with a show about a typical family vacation*

Parents want to make very sure that a destination offers lots of fun attractions for kids before they undertake the ordeal of a long car trip. Put their minds at ease with a documentary showing an actual family seeing the sights in your city. Once they've seen other kids laughing at the aquarium, staring in fascination at dinosaur skeletons, and picnicking in a riverfront park, they'll feel much more confident about taking their own family there.

22. *Produce a cooking show to sell kitchenware*

You know your electric steamer is the best on the market, but consumers have told you in market surveys that they can't imagine buying a special appliance just to cook rice. In a half-hour cooking show, you can show customers dozens of ways to use your steamer. Show viewers how to prepare sole almondine, steamed puddings, and crunchy vegetables. Once they realize the appliance cooks more than rice, you've overcome their major resistance to buying your product.

23. *Produce a home-improvement show to promote hardware*

Home-renovation fanatics are already your best customers, and you've already sold them just about every type of hammer, wood screw, and varnish in stock. But many other homeowners don't know the difference between a jigsaw and a jigsaw puzzle. If you give them solid information on basic tools and simple household jobs, you may pique their interest in home repair. Suddenly, you've created a new customer who doesn't own so much as a pair of pliers.

24. *Share the secrets of your restaurant chain's best recipes*

Is your restaurant famous for its four-alarm chili and honey-garlic chicken wings? Ensure surefire viewer interest by sharing the recipes in an infomercial. Include lots of testimonials from satisfied customers eating in your restaurant. By positioning your restaurant as an "expert" on certain dishes, you'll improve your profile.

25. *Target one customer with an infomercial*

If your company is pushing for a million dollar contract from a major supplier, create an infomercial just for that customer. Allow them to meet your staff, see your facilities, and understand your enthusiasm. Deliver a copy of the tape, along with a rented TV and VCR, directly to the office of the president.

26. *Produce a show about the history of your product*

Do you make a product that's a household name, such as Coke or Levi's jeans? Many established products have fascinating histories. Draw in viewers who already enjoy documentaries with an infomercial about your product's background. Did Queen Victoria once buy it? Did it play a part in a presidential election? Does it have its own museum? Create a mystique for your product.

27. *Produce a video dance party*

A record company can get more airplay for some of its lesser-known acts by producing its own version of MTV. Copying the music station format, the company can use a "VJ" to introduce videos and include interviews with the artists themselves. Viewers could call a toll-free number to get a free CD sampler of songs featured in the infomercial.

28. *Run an educational program about computers*

The technical language of computers intimidates many people who might otherwise find the technology useful. If you produce an infomercial explaining basic concepts like "CD-ROM" and RAM "memory," you'll earn their trust. Offer a free booklet of definitions, and you'll get calls from people who are obviously interested in computers but don't yet own one.

29. *Introduce viewers to your language course by broadcasting the first lesson*

A language course on videotape is the perfect product to sell through an infomercial. With a brief introduction and a closing message urging viewers to call for more information, the first lesson can be your whole infomercial. Your production cost will be almost nothing, since you already have the video. And viewers can test the actual product for themselves before ever making a call.

30. *Produce a program on recent sleep research to sell beds*

Science documentaries have a hard-core group of fans. An infomercial that explores the reasons why we sometimes wake up tired after an eight-hour rest will attract these viewers. The infomercial can also contain information about your company's beds, showing how they can help viewers wake up refreshed. Why not run it late at night to reach insomniacs?

31. *Show how tough your dinnerware is*

Do you claim that your dishes are unbreakable? Use a funny infomercial to impress this point on viewers. Let a hockey team use one of your dessert plates as a puck. Support a Jeep on four overturned teacups. Drop ball bearings from a high diving tower into one of your cereal bowls. David Letterman has made himself a household name with these kinds of tricks. You can too.

32. *Show how your company makes your city a better place to live*

Raise your profile in your city by running an infomercial that demonstrates your company's impact on the community. You can show clips of your president participating in a food-bank drive. Provide statistics on the amount of money you pump into the local economy. Boast a little about your company's exemplary environmental record.

33. *Profile the lucky winner of one of your contests*

If you're responsible for promoting a state lottery, track down the winner of a previous jackpot and do an infomercial showing how her newfound riches changed her life. Take viewers along on her boat as she sails across San Francisco Bay, or put them in the passenger seat as she drives her Aston Martin up the California coast.

34. *Let your company president promote your products*

A Canadian line of private-label grocery products, President's Choice, used company president Dave Nicol in all its television advertising. Dave told viewers how he found the recipe for "his" jerk sauce on a recent trip to Jamaica, and fed his dog President's Choice kibble. The approach worked because Dave was so affable. If your president is similarly charming, this approach could work for you.

35. *Promote your newspaper with a documentary*

In the early days of newspapers, reporters resorted to outrageous tricks to beat their counterparts on competing papers to a "scoop." Some tied up telegraph lines for hours until the competitor's deadline had passed. Others siphoned fuel out of the rival's gas tank. Produce an entertaining infomercial showing the lengths your publication's writers have gone to to get a story.

36. *Show reluctant customers how to use dental floss*

Every day, hundreds of dentists tell thousands of patients about the importance of flossing. Every last patient agrees, but few actually follow up because they're afraid of cutting their gums. If you make dental floss, produce a short infomercial showing viewers how to use it correctly.

37. *Show the success of your diet plan*

You can produce a pair of two short infomercials. The first one introduces a dieter who is using your calorie-reduced milkshakes to lose weight. The viewers learn how much weight she wants to lose and how your product will help her. The second spot, which airs two months later, shows the newly thin dieter, who gives your shakes a glowing testimonial.

38. *Demonstrate unconventional uses for your product*

Show viewers how they can use your vacuum cleaner to inflate air mattresses or clean hot air registers. Use your hot chocolate mix in recipes for cappuccino or brownies. Tell viewers they can use your video camera to keep a permanent record of their possessions in case of theft.

39. *Sell furniture with tours of well-decorated homes*

Most people would be thrilled if their home looked like a picture in a magazine. But most people are also pragmatic. They need furniture that can stand up to Super Bowl parties, destructive cats, and rowdy children. Use an infomercial to show your furniture actually being used by real families who happen to live in fabulous homes.

40. *Produce a parody of a soap opera or old movie where the plot turns on your product*

Taster's Choice has had great success with this tactic in its traditional-length commercials, which show a witty urban couple pursuing a somewhat rocky romance over cups of coffee. Maybe your hero and heroine could spend a romantic evening cleaning their kitchen with your mops and brushes.

41. *Produce a fashion show featuring your brand of clothing*

Most fashion shows take place on a plain, boring runway. Use the flexibility of an infomercial to showcase your products in exciting locations. Models can dance in your evening dresses at a fashionable New York restaurant, frolic at Vail in your skiwear, or go hiking in Vermont in your 100% wool sweaters.

42. *Show male viewers how to buy gifts for their wives*

Allay men's insecurities by showing them how to gauge their wives' tastes, and you'll have customers for life — for your products.

43. *Push outdoor equipment to its limits in real-life conditions*

A gleaming mountain bike looks great in the store, but how will it perform in the real world? Produce an infomercial about a cyclist who travels across the country on one of your bikes. Let viewers see how well the brakes work in a rainstorm, or how steady the bike is on a rocky path. Test the bike in conditions most viewers would never even consider riding in.

44. *Interview writers from your magazine*

Travel and entertainment magazines are particularly suited to this approach because many viewers think writers for these publications live exotic lives. After all, wouldn't we all like to earn our living by relaxing on the beach in Bali or chatting with Harrison Ford? Even though the reality may be somewhat more prosaic, an infomercial about the fun side of your writers' lives can give your publication cachet.

45. Create a gardening show featuring your products

If you sell garden tools, produce an infomercial showing viewers how to start a brand-new garden. Viewers who don't know a rake from a Roto-Rooter will soon see how easy it is to grow beautiful roses and hardy tomato plants — easy, that is, if they use your products.

46. Promote your auto parts with a do-it-yourself show

Many people resent the money they spend at garages on simple maintenance jobs such as oil changes and tire rotation, yet they don't have enough confidence to tackle these jobs on their own. Give them step-by-step instructions, featuring your products, and you'll create brand-new, enthusiastic customers.

47. Set a detective show in your store

If your chain's stores have a standard layout, write a mystery (preferably one that doesn't involve violence and corpses) set in your store. The detective can search for "clues" — various products you wish to promote — in different departments, giving shoppers a feel for both your store and your merchandise.

48. Run a "reverse testimonial" to intrigue jaded viewers

We've all seen movie and TV stars promoting exercise machines, hair care products, and diet plans to regular Joes. But have you ever seen regular Joes promoting a product to a celebrity? Play on a celebrity's well-known habits to make a humorous infomercial. For instance, if a singer is famous for her outrageous, revealing costumes, have ordinary businesswomen trying to convince her to buy one of your tailored suits. They'll succeed, of course.

49. Present the science behind your product

Why does Alka Seltzer fizz? Why does a pregnancy test strip turn color? And what makes Jell-O set? An infomercial explaining the science behind your product can give viewers more confidence in the item.

50. Promote your driving school

Show viewers the value of driving instruction by producing an infomercial describing the accident-avoidance techniques students at the school learn. Include interviews with graduates of the school in which they describe how these techniques helped them avoid gruesome accidents.

51. Produce a biography of a successful graduate of your school

Did a famous CEO, singer, astronaut, or author graduate from your college? Produce a biography of one or more of these celebrities, in which they frequently mention the role your institution played in their future success.

52. *Promote a book of financial advice by interviewing successful investors*

A group of grandmothers from the Midwest has become one of the country's most successful investment clubs. The women have written a book about their methods. They also appear in a video, discussing how their investment success has allowed them to travel, build the home of their dreams, or pursue expensive hobbies.

Infomercial Resources

Publications

The Infomercial Producer Report
Published by Television Time, Inc.
178 Barsana Avenue
Austin TX 78737
(512) 288-6400
This report includes an index of infomercials, product categories, producers, and products.

Response TV
201 East Sandpointe Avenue, Suite 600
Santa Ana CA 92707-5761
(714) 513-8400
This company also produces a videotape called "Dynamics of DRTV." Response TV sells the video for $29.95 and you can order it by calling (800) 598-6008.

Steve Dworman's Infomercial Marketing Report
11533 Thurston Circle
Los Angeles CA 90049
(310) 472-6360
The leading newsletter in the field.

Infomercial Consultants and Associations

Brandt-Thompson Group
10810 72nd Street North, Suite 210
Largo FL 34647
(813) 544-8118
Consultants in all areas of the infomercial business.

William Thompson TV, Inc.
10810 72nd Street North, Suite 210
Largo FL 34647
(813) 544-8118
Author of *Inside Infomercials: The Industry Overview of Infomercials and Direct Response Commercials.*

Cannella Response Television
488 North Pine Street
Burlington WI 53105
(414) 763-4810
Company founder Frank Cannella has more than 15 years of experience in the television direct-market-response industry. The company offers introductory and exploratory consultations; analysis of media buying and results; on-site evaluations of existing offers and marketing methodologies; back-end review and recommendations; freelance media buying; brokering of national cable availabilities; and project supervision.

Hawthorne Communications, Inc.
300 N. 16th Street, P.O. Box 1366
Fairfield IA 52556
(515) 472-3800
Hawthorne Communications plans, produces, places, and manages infomercial campaigns for a wide variety of goods and services. These infomercials are aired on cable networks and broadcast stations across the country. In their book *The Great Marketing Turn-Around*, authors Stan Rapp and Tom Collins dubbed company founder Tim Hawthorne "King of the Infomercial." The firm's Fortune 500 clients include AT&T, Time-Life, Black & Decker, Braun, Nordic Track, BankAmerica, Weight Watchers, MCA/Universal, The Disney Channel, and Paramount.

Score Productions, Inc.
254 East 49th Street
New York NY 10017
(212) 751-2510
Score operates Infoscore, a music service tailored for infomercial production. Score will absorb the cost of producing the music for your infomercial in exchange for the writing and publishing royalties associated with broadcasting the infomercial. Score also works on a traditional fee schedule. Call for more information.

Jordan Whitney, Inc.
17300 17th Street, Suite J-111
Tustin CA 92680
(714) 832-0737
This direct-response television consulting firm publishes the *Direct Response Television Monitoring Report* and the *Greensheet TV Merchandiser* newsletters. It is also a monitoring agency that keeps track of direct-response TV infomercials appearing on national networks.

National Infomercial Marketing Association (NIMA)
1201 New York Ave. NW, Suite 1000
Washington DC 20005
(202) 962-8342
This association promotes the infomercial industry in the best interests of its members and the public. NIMA works to maintain and develop a commercial environment in which the consumer can make an informed choice, based upon the information provided through the industry's unique programming. NIMA advocates industry interests before state and federal government entities and enforces program content and advertising policies and guidelines among its members. Consumers, the media, and other interested parties use NIMA as an informational and educational resource.

Infomercial Production Companies

Blue Marketing, Inc.
20 Valley Stream Parkway, Suite 220
Malvern PA 19355-1407
(610) 648-9345
Blue Marketing takes a personal stake in the creation of a company's

infomercial by putting up its own capital. The company believes that this vested financial interest in the infomercial's success drives it to keep costs down and quality high. Blue Marketing's clients include insurance companies, manufacturers of both industrial and consumer products, associations, financial firms, nonprofit organizations, and travel firms. The company can provide marketing proposals, market research, media and list recommendations, creative supervision, production and fulfillment management, and analysis of results. It also develops sales and fulfillment packages, and telemarketing scripts.

Direct Hit Productions
3 Piedmont Center, Suite 300
Atlanta GA 30305
(404) 233-0370
Since 1981, the company has combined direct-response and image advertising into infomercial packages. Direct Hit can work with clients in any phase of infomercial development, from conception to production. Dick Bennett, the company's award-winning director, has 20 years' worth of TV productions to his credit. He has directed and produced more than 50 half-hour infomercials for major marketers including Bally's Health and Tennis, Time-Life Books, Time-Life Music, Six Flags/Astroworld, St. Jude's Children's Research Hospital, and The Regina Company.

E&M Advertising, Inc.
60 Madison Avenue
New York NY 10010
(212) 481-3663
Founded in 1980, E&M Advertising provides a full range of direct marketing services. E&M has aired client infomercials on more than 800 broadcast stations and cable networks. The company uses the Direct Response Media Analysis System, a Windows-based application that allows their buyers to create schedules, track response, perform analysis, and generate activity reports. In addition, E&M can channel clients' products through a variety of aftermarket vehicles. Through its marketing affiliate, MICO Productions, E&M provides clients access to a wide range of other media and sales vehicles such as catalogs, print, direct mail, bank card syndication, outbound telemarketing, and home shopping networks. The company's client list includes Parker Brothers, Pepsi USA, Showtime, Time, Inc., and RCA Records.

Guthy-Renker Corporation
42-080 State Street, Suite A
Palm Desert CA 92211
(619) 773-9022

Guthy-Renker sells products through infomercials, home shopping channels, and other media. The company began in business by marketing audiocassette series such as Napoleon Hill's "Think and Grow Rich" and Tony Robbins's "Personal Power." The latter is one of the most successful products ever marketed by infomercial and remains the number-one seller in the motivational category today. In its long-form commercials, Guthy-Renker works with celebrities such as Victoria Principal and Vanna White to drive sales through endorsement or partnership. Greg Renker voluntarily testified before a congressional subcommittee to provide the views of direct-response marketers, and Guthy-Renker helped found the National Infomercial Marketing Association (NIMA). In 1993, two out of the three top-selling infomercials were Guthy-Renker productions — an industry first.

McNamara & Associates
5301 Calhoun Avenue
Van Nuys CA 91401
(818) 907-6212

This creative production company specializes in direct-response spots and infomercials. Company president Jim McNamara has been creating direct-response TV advertising for almost 20 years. Infomercial successes include sales in excess of $120 million for Thighmaster, $65 million in sales for Mindpower, and $35 million for "How to Get a 2nd Paycheck Without Getting a 2nd Job." McNamara & Associates has worked with Estée Lauder, MCA/Universal, Jenny Craig Weight Loss, Easter Seals, and others.

National Media
1700 Walnut Street
Philadelphia PA 19103
(215) 772-5000

This producer of program-length infomercials has invested heavily in order to control media time. It pioneered a multichannel marketing strategy that capitalizes on the infomercial's ability to drive profits across all mass distribution markets. The company has built its own fulfillment and service center, and has expanded worldwide to take full advantage of proprietary air time on satellite and international cable channels. The company operates under two divisions: Media Arts International in the U.S. and Quantum International abroad. It has produced infomercials for a variety of products: automotive ("Colorcote 2000"), beauty and personal care ("Frankie Avalon's Zero Pain"), kitchen and household goods ("Power Steamer," "American Harvest Dehydrator"), self-improvement ("Megamemory"), and health and fitness ("Bruce Jenner's Stairclimber Plus").

Prescott/Levinson, Inc.
2727 Philmont Avenue, Suite 110
Huntingdon Valley PA 19006
(215) 947-4100
Prescott/Levinson is a full-service advertising agency that has specialized in direct-response advertising for more than 10 years. Although it develops advertising for its clients in all media — broadcast, print, and direct mail — television is the dominant medium. The company works with all types of clients, from large corporations to individual investors, to place both infomercials and short-form commercials on local and national buys. Prescott/Levinson can also provide complete creative and production services for infomercials and commercials.

Media Buyers
American Television Time, Inc.
178 Barsana Avenue
Austin TX 78737-9075
(512) 288-1156
American Television Time, Inc., is a media-buying agency specializing in cable and broadcast TV time. It offers media management and infomercial planning services, including daily and weekly profitability and costper-order reports. The company's clients include Ronco, Inc., Avon, Ginsu, Transglobal Media, Inc., Great Expectations, and Bill Clinton.

Barry Jacobs and Associates
5408 Nagle Avenue
Sherman Oaks CA 91401
(818) 780-1761
BJA is a direct marketing agency that consults on all production, creative, and marketing needs. It can also provide media planning and buying services. The company's clients include Guthy-Renker, National

Marketing Media, Clark National Products, Tony Robbins Research, and Vista Advertising. Media buying has been the cornerstone of BJA's growth.

Cable Shows Unlimited
422 Route 206, Suite 192
Sommerville NJ 08876
(908) 725-7026

This is the company that re-introduced the program-length commercial in 1983 with its "Showmercials," built around the concept that "The show is the commercial." The company pursues high-ticket, lead-generating products and services, such as kitchen remodeling, aluminum siding, and dating services.

Mediaworks, Inc.
1845 Walnut Street
Philadelphia PA 19103
(215) 567-3888

Mediaworks, Inc., specializes in TV direct response, tracking, and managing. Buyers and program managers use computer systems to analyze and negotiate results daily. The company has experience with both long-form and short-form commercials.

MercuryMedia
1750 Ocean Park Boulevard, Suite 204
Santa Monica CA 90405
(310) 452-3999

This media-buying agency specializes in the placement and servicing of direct-response paid programming accounts. Its buyers negotiate air time on broadcast and cable facilities throughout the U.S. and Canadian markets. The company has successfully rolled out such infomercials as Tony Robbins's "Personal Power," "Snakmaster," Victoria Principal's "Principal Secret," Popeil's "Pasta Maker," and Kathy Smith's "Fat Burning System/Walk Fit." Mercury can coordinate tape trafficking and videotape distribution, and package new-product test schedules to gauge commercial effectiveness and profit potential. In addition, Mercury can plan media schedules, analyze and track orders via an 800-number service, provide computer-generated profitability reports and airdate lists, audit station invoices, and prepare computerized client invoicing.

Meridian Marketing Management, Inc.
221 East Glenoaks Boulevard, Suite 200
Glendale CA 91207
(818) 552-4000

Meridian provides media buying and analysis services to the infomercial industry. It can work with clients and vendors to develop a targeted market test, analyze the test results and present computerized results along with recommendations. Meridian will negotiate targeted air time in designated markets. The company also provides additional services such as order tracking, tape traffic management, and consulting.

Williams Television Time, Inc.
3130 Wilshire Boulevard, Fourth Floor
Santa Monica CA 90403
(310) 828-8600

This full-service direct-response advertising agency, founded in 1987, specializes in media buying. The company believes strongly in the accountability of the infomercial. It can assess the success of an infomercial on a day-to-day basis and adjust strategy accordingly. CEO Kathleen Williams has years of experience in the industry and in buying media time. The firm's clients include Time-Life, Inc., Warner Music Enterprises, Philips Consumer Electronics, Braun, Inc., M&M/Mars, Inc., and The Hoover Company.

Infomercial Glossary

Back-end marketing: selling additional products to your existing customer base.

Call-to-action: a request during an infomercial for viewers to take action, usually by calling an 800 phone number.

Continuity: sales that continue on an ongoing basis, such as subscription programs that send a customer one product every month.

Dealer locator: a commercial that gives viewers a phone number to call to find out the location of the nearest dealer that carries the advertised product.

Direct-response TV: programming that provides a means for a viewer to interact by mail or phone.

Fulfillment: the process by which products are delivered to customers.

Image enhancement: the use of infomercials to increase brand loyalty and improve the image of a company or product.

Inbound telemarketing: the process of handling of incoming calls for product orders or information.

Infomercial: a commercial advertisement of at least 10 minutes in length.

Lead generation: the use of infomercials to produce names of potential customers for future marketing efforts, rather than to make immediate sales.

Long-form commercial: an infomercial.

Media buyer: a person who buys air time in which to run infomercials or other commercial programming.

One-step process: the use of infomercials to create immediate sales.

Outbound telemarketing: the process of handling outgoing calls for product orders or information.

Pledge solicitation: a television commercial designed to generate pledges or donations.

Psychography: the buying patterns of a specific viewing audience.

Reservation solicitation: a commercial that encourages callers to make a reservation.

Short-form commercial: a traditional television ad, usually 30 or 60 seconds long.

Tracking: the process of recording responses to an infomercial in order to make adjustments and assess the success of the program.

Two-step or multiple-step process: the use of infomercials to create interest in the product and obtain names of prospects.

BULLETIN BOARDS

Wouldn't your sales force of 50, located
around the world, be thrilled to have an inexpensive
way to check in with the head office daily?
Wouldn't your biggest customer love to
get direct access to your warehouse and find out
what's in stock? Wouldn't your customers
be pleased to get quick answers
to their most frequently asked questions?

You can make all these people happy with
one low-cost technology: an electronic
bulletin board system, or BBS.
All they need to use your system is a
computer, a telephone, and a modem,
a device that takes incoming phone calls
from other computers and converts
the phone signal into something
the computer can understand.

e

By now, you've probably heard about the tremendous success of CompuServe, America Online, and other commercial online networks. These huge bulletin boards allow millions of people to use a computer, a modem, and a telephone line to get access to vast storehouses of information stored in huge computers hundreds of miles away. Users can receive (download) files, send messages, and exchange information. Thousands of people all over the world can use these systems simultaneously.

Once online, users can choose from more than 20,000 different computer files on a huge range of topics, from typefaces and computer games to job leads and recipes. With about a million members each, these commercial services are as big as small cities, and provide their members with a form of electronic community.

While these services offer sophisticated technology and access to huge audiences, most marketers will get more bang for their buck using a home-grown bulletin board running on a personal computer (PC). In this chapter, we'll refer to services such as Prodigy and America Online as commercial bulletin boards, to differentiate them from the more common small-scale bulletin boards.

The Small-Scale BBS

For less than $5,000, you can create a BBS that will help you create and maintain a strong one-to-one relationship with your customers. A BBS combines the wide reach of traditional mass marketing with the immediacy and intimacy of the electronic world. You will reach lots of people, but you can still answer their questions individually. A BBS also gives your customers convenient 24-hour service. They don't have to call during business hours, deal with time differences, wait on hold, or wander the maze of voice mail.

Need to get a new technical manual to your 100 largest accounts? You can post the manual in seconds, and your customers can retrieve it at their leisure. Need to answer questions from customers? With a BBS, your technical specialist doesn't have to spend all day on the phone.

Charles Schwab, an investment firm, runs a bulletin board that gives customers access to real-time price quotes, stock trades, even market research and tips. Bulletin boards are particularly useful to investment companies because financial information changes rapidly, and customers want to know about fast-breaking news immediately.

How It Works

A BBS is nothing more than a simple PC with one or more modems attached. BBS software lets you create an electronic "bulletin board," where anyone can post a notice that anyone else can read. Your staff can check these notices regularly and post responses. You'll be amazed how many of your customers share the same concerns, and you'll wonder how you ever kept them happy before you set up your BBS.

A simple BBS might have as many as a dozen forums. Each forum focuses on one subject, such as "Pricing" or "New Features." Callers choose one of the forums, then type a note that all future callers will be able to read. For example, a user might write:

"I wish that the XL2000 provided a user-interrupt switch. My office spends at least an hour resetting it after a power failure."

The next day, another caller could read this notice and respond:

"Good point. We jury-rigged a user-interrupt with a Tandy 34-JT DIN switch. Call me with your fax number and I'll send some instructions right over."

With no effort on your part, the bulletin board has helped your business in several ways. Your engineering department now knows that customers want a user-interrupt switch, and one user was able to vent his frustration with the XL2000 and find a solution.

Except for conferences (see below), BBSs are not "real-time" systems. That means that only one notice can be posted at a time. On the plus side, however, the BBS gives you a clear record of customer inquiries that is easier to decipher and archive than a transcript of phone calls to your technical support center.

In addition to postings, BBSs now offer users several other services:

Electronic Mail

E-mail lets your customers or salespeople send private messages to one another or to you. This low-cost correspondence can dramatically change the way your company interacts with the outside world. It can save you time and money, and shorten many of your development cycles.

After a consumer electronics company in California installed e-mail, the development time for a new stereo speaker dropped from seven months to three months. Why? E-mail allowed engineers and marketers to communicate quickly, easily and, above all, clearly.

A sales manager can use e-mail to tell her entire sales force about price adjustments or sales contests, in seconds. More importantly, she'll receive constant feedback from the field — even if she's out of the office when a sales rep calls in.

Posting Files

Users can post large files on a BBS, including manuals, images (pictures of products, for example), and computer programs. Software companies, for instance, can just post updates of popular programs on a BBS instead of mailing an expensive floppy disk to users. They can also use the system to transmit short multimedia presentations to customers.

Conferences

Some BBS systems can now handle conferences, which are structured differently from any other element of a BBS. Conferences let several parties trade information simultaneously.

Using the conference feature, the company president might invite six customers and six sales reps to call in at a given time. The system displays each person's comments for all the others to see. For example:

- *President: What's the best feature of the new XL2000 you've been testing?*

- *Tom: We've found that the new voice mail management feature is terrific.*

- *Bob: Really? We haven't used it at all. It's too complicated.*

- *Susan: Complicated! Bob, you should have called me.*

- *John: I'm with Tom. We've got twice as many people using it in half the time.*

This real-time conferencing is far more effective than a voice conference, because only one person talks at a time. Better still, it leaves a written record for all participants to review.

Using a Bulletin Board

B ulletin boards are an invaluable way to monitor your existing customer base or "eavesdrop" on potential customers. Electronic discussions tend to be extremely frank. People seem more willing to say what they really think on a BBS than in a focus group or a survey, perhaps because they can't see or hear the person on the other end.

Here's an example of the way a BBS can help you read your customers' minds. A factory in Muskoka is having trouble with the tolerance level on your plastic-forming machine, and posts a notice on your BBS. Other customers see it, and suddenly you're hearing from a dozen other people with the same problem.

What happens next? Most commonly, one of your customers will post a solution, as seen in the earlier example about the user-interrupt switch. Alternatively, you may be able to help the customer yourself. If no one has a quick solution, ask your engineering staff to come up with a fix and to notify the customer as soon as possible.

Public postings make a lot of people nervous. "That gives my customers too much power," skeptics say. "If they realize that other people are having problems too, they may go to the competition." Actually, the opposite is true. If your customers are frustrated and you *don't* know about it, you're in trouble. But if you can "eavesdrop" on their complaints, you can satisfy their concerns quickly and create customers for life.

A BBS helps you anticipate and answer customer questions before they even post them. You can store answers to frequently asked questions, technical notes, or price lists in an electronic "library" where customers can download them at their leisure.

Other BBS Advantages

F ord Motor Company currently distributes a floppy disk containing detailed information on its various cars. If the company posted these files on a BBS system, it could reach thousands of other customers at virtually no additional cost.

Sometimes, you can use the enhanced speed and information of a BBS to create an entirely new business. SportsNet links 3,500 trading-card stores and dealers in the U.S. The service reports daily price changes and allows dealers and buyers to rate the collectability and quality of baseball and trading cards. First created as an information network by a dealer, SportsNet has become the dominant way to determine the final price and value of cards.

Up to $5 million worth of cards changes hands every week on SportsNet. Dealers can find a card anywhere in the country more quickly than they could by calling dealers directly. They can buy a spot on the bulletin board to post their buy-and-sell messages for as little as $49 a month.

A BBS can handle large amounts of information more efficiently than other automatic systems, such as those driven by touch-tone phone menus (see the chapter on Audiotext). For example, customers of a food broker could use a BBS to find out quickly and easily which of the company's 10,000 different items are in stock. Trying to find the same information on an audiotext system, pushing buttons for menu after menu, would be a nightmare.

Just a few years ago, only technowizards owned and used modems. But in 1993–94, 62% of all computers sold came equipped with modems — up from 39% in 1991. More and more consumers are finding out how fun and useful modem computing can be. So don't be afraid to set up a BBS because you think your customers will be reluctant to use it.

A BBS can even help your international marketing efforts because it helps overcome barriers of language and distance. Customers who might be hesitant to phone because they feel uncomfortable speaking your language will be much more willing to write you a message. In addition, you can send your reply any time, without having to negotiate international calling codes and time zones.

Setting Up a BBS

Once you've purchased the computer and software, the only cost of maintaining a BBS is the standard monthly fee for the phone line. Because users are calling you, not the other way around, you don't have to pay long-distance charges. The simplest bulletin boards allow only one incoming line. As the BBS becomes more popular, you'll probably want to add additional lines. Most popular BBS systems allow you to add up to eight lines without upgrading your computer, other than adding modems. Some systems let you add up to 64 lines.

Boardwatch magazine, which covers the BBS industry, asked its readers to rate various BBS software packages. Their top five choices were

TBBS (The Bread Board System), PCBoard, Wildcat!, Major BBS, and DLX.

If you want to set up a sophisticated BBS, you'll probably need to customize these packages. The software companies can recommend programming firms that specialize in customizing their software.

Before investing in one company's product, call up a BBS that uses the software you've chosen and try it out. The features and interfaces of each vary greatly.

Deciding Whether You Need a BBS

Ask yourself these questions before setting up a BBS:

1. *Do my customers and prospects care very much about our product?*

   Obviously, people who chew Wrigley's Gum are less committed to their product than factory managers dependent on a $1.5-million Heil web press that operates around the clock.

2. *Do my customers have computer access?*

   While some companies may find it worthwhile to buy computers for customers so that they can use the BBS, you'll probably want to make sure that your customers have their own machines.

3 *Is time critical?*

   A BBS isn't practical for a manufacturer of heart valves. Surgeons can't wait around in the middle of an operation for an answer to a critical question. They need 24-hour live technical support.

4. *Is there a manageable number of customers?*

   If you expect more than a few thousand people to use your board regularly, you should consider using a commercial service such as CompuServe (see "Commercial Bulletin Boards," below) or the Internet (see the next chapter).

5. *Will my sales force benefit from this sort of access to both customers and headquarters?*

   Even if your customer base isn't committed enough to use a BBS, your salespeople may be.

DON PEPPERS AND MARTHA ROGERS ON TAPPING IN: PUTTING YOUR BEST CUSTOMERS IN TOUCH WITH EACH OTHER

One of the most important roles for newspapers in rural America during the Agricultural Era was keeping local residents informed about happenings around the world as well as in their own community. The local paper provided a forum for citizens to voice their opinions and share ideas and viewpoints. The basis of the community was geographic, not only for the newspaper, but also for churches, schools, charities, and political groups.

The paradigm shift of the Information Age renders obsolete the need for geographic proximity. Residents of Telluride, Colorado, occasionally commute through the Denver airport, but more often over their phone lines and cable, using fax modems, teleconferencing equipment, e-mail, and other interactive media that allow them to communicate with offices and clients without leaving home. One futurist predicts that 80 million Americans will earn all or part of their living from their homes by the year 2000. Families are able to keep in touch from across the country more often and at much lower cost than our grandparents, separated from their loved ones, could have imagined.

Communication creates communities. Geography is, less and less, a factor in communication. And thus we see that electronic communication creates electronic communities.

Not long ago, a group of quilters met in person for the first time in Bowling Green, Ohio. But they had already exchanged quilting patterns as the Prodigy Quilting Club. (It should not be surprising that bidding was hot for the quilting software package that calculated yardage in the blink of a cursor.)

In April of 1994, Toyota went online. Finding 140,000 Toyota owners among Prodigy users, the company set up a bulletin board exclusively for these Toyota owners. Access to the bulletin board requires a Vehicle Identification Number (VIN), which qualifies the would-be participant as a Toyota owner. Those who wish to participate in Toyota Interactive can say anything they like; one topic area that emerged early was "I Love My Honda."

Early returns indicated that the positives far outweighed the negative comments, and many of the negative comments were about dealers by Toyota owners who loved the automobile but felt unfairly or badly treated by the local shop. (In some cases, nearby dealers have been recommended to the mistreated owners by other owners, which, as Toyota hoped, carries more weight than a recommendation from the manufacturer.)

Of course, Toyota can send messages to bulletin board participants, who themselves often choose to interact with Toyota, to request information about the cars or to make suggestions directly. Otherwise, owners solve each other's problems. commiserate over common obstacles, and share their sense of joy in Toyota ownership with willing listeners.

The goal for Toyota is to try to grow their share of each customer's business — to get trade-ins sooner, to get a greater "share of garage," to sell a bigger and better car next time to a customer who already has a relationship with the company through their own experience and now through the experience of others as well.

The next step for Toyota is to find a way for prospects to be able to ask questions of owners, without being contaminated by competitors' comments and queries. Present satisfied owners provide a credible and often enthusiastic sales pitch that carries far greater weight than the salesperson in a dealer showroom or the model brochure.

Commercial Bulletin Boards (Online Services)

The four largest online services (CompuServe, America Online, Prodigy, and Delphi) have approximately 4,000,000 members between them. They have consumer-oriented interfaces, and support sound and graphics. They handle tens of thousands of callers simultaneously and provide unlimited free technical support.

This combination of user-friendliness and technological prowess makes a commercial online service an attractive alternative to a private BBS for many companies.

How Commercial Services Work

Online services began as musclebound BBS systems. They use larger computers and support far more modems, but the philosophy behind them is the same. Every major online service provides support for:

- *Forums for posting messages*

- *Conferences (often called "chat")*

- *E-mail*

- *File storage and transfer (often called "libraries")*

These services also allow you to send e-mail to other services or to the Internet. Instead of reaching the 50 or 100 people who might be on a private BBS, a member of America Online can reach more than 20,000,000 people via e-mail.

Each online service has a distinct editorial bent and philosophy. On Prodigy, you'll have lots of online opportunities to entice users to your forum. On America Online and CompuServe, you'll have to do more offline promotion to attract users, but these services offer better tools and a more sophisticated interface.

You have less control over who uses your forum on a commercial service than you do on a BBS. Being online is like having a store in a shopping mall. Running a BBS is more like building your own store on a rural highway.

Deciding Whether to Use a Commercial Bulletin Board

Ask yourself the following questions:

1. Do we deal with a large customer base?

NBC, Microsoft, and DC Comics all benefit from using America Online (AOL). While a small widget company would be happy to have 100 or so users logging onto its BBS, NBC needs tens of thousands of responses to justify the expense.

2. Do we need sophisticated sound and graphics?

Some companies want to demonstrate their products in real time. The commercial services are quickly developing more sophisticated ways to deliver this data.

3. Do we have a technical support problem?

Novice users aren't comfortable with BBS systems. The leading commercial services have invested millions of dollars in teaching their users how to use their services. If you foresee a technical nightmare, it may be better to let them deal with the hassles.

4. Do we need to reach people we don't already have a relationship with?

A BBS is ideal for a company that wants to interact with current customers. If you want to attract new customers, a commercial service can bring hundreds of thousands of prospects to your electronic door. It may also offer ways to promote yourself online. Car companies, in particular, have had great success promoting themselves online.

The biggest downsides of using a commercial service? You lose control of the interface and the services offered. You lose confidentiality and ownership of your user base. Finally, customers must pay to use an online service ($5 to $8 an hour). This fee can be a significant barrier for individual consumers.

Commercial Online Success Stories

Toyota's service on Prodigy is available to owners of Toyotas only, who must provide a valid factory number from the dashboard of their car. Toyota collects information about users' likes and dislikes, and runs an online fan club. Customers can even make an electronic reservation to tour the company's plant in Kentucky.

Toyota hopes that, once a user discovers that other people like their Toyotas as much as she likes hers, it will increase her loyalty and generate positive word of mouth.

NBC broke records when it unveiled its service on America Online, which offers publicity stills of popular shows, news releases, scheduling information, and more. Within a week, more than 4,000 people had taken the time to download the Seinfeld cast photo onto their computers.

NBC quickly turned television — traditionally a one-way medium — into an interactive one. Writers and executives can eavesdrop on and participate in discussions about NBC shows, and viewers can get information they couldn't find before the service was introduced.

PC Flowers is one of the largest FTD florists in the world, yet it never deals with a customer by phone. Through its forum on Prodigy, the company takes orders for flowers, enters them into the FTD computer, and bills the user's credit card. This simple business has captured the imagination of Prodigy users. PC Flowers has blossomed into a company with sales of more than $10 million a year.

Quark produces a popular desktop publishing software package, Quark Xpress. Unfortunately, the company has long had a reputation for providing cranky, difficult-to-reach technical support. But its forum on CompuServe is changing that situation.The forum gives users a place to vent their frustrations and share information. It also allows the company's president to interact directly with users. When Quark tried to implement a controversial new pricing strategy, the outcry from CompuServe forum visitors was so great that the president came online to explain his reasoning. After further complaints, the company changed its pricing strategy. Without the opportunity to get direct input from users through a commercial service, Quark could have crippled its relationship with many customers.

The Illinois Bureau of Tourism runs a forum on Prodigy that gives users access to information about the state and allows them to post questions to a travel counselor. This personal attention has resulted in a measurable increase in the number of Prodigy members considering a trip to Illinois. While this small universe of people isn't going to make a dent in Illinois's economy, the questions Prodigy members ask help the bureau refine its marketing strategy.

Setting Up a Bulletin Board with a Commercial Service

A s the online services become more popular, their available "real estate" is dwindling. Most services will be delighted to help you set up a forum online, but only if you can prove that you have a wide universe of potential users.

The online services collect the fees users pay to participate in your forum, and pay you a very small royalty. While this royalty is certainly larger than the nonexistent income you'll generate by running your own BBS, don't be fooled into believing that your online forum will eventually become a profit center. Very few companies have made money through the online fees they've generated.

The online services provide the technical tools to establish your forum online. You'll be required to provide one or more individuals who will act as system operators, or sysops. These people will run the board, post the information, and answer questions.

When you're considering a service, it's vital to find out how much promotion you'll receive. The impact of a mention on the opening screen of a service (where every member will see it) cannot be understated. One mention on the Prodigy highlights screen can result in 10,000 people trying a new service.

To set up an online forum, contact one of the commercial services listed in the Resources section near the end of this chapter.

52 Ways to Use BBSs and Commercial Online Services

1. Distribute price lists

This is an ideal way to use a BBS if you have many products with many price options. Consumers can educate themselves quickly and make price-based purchasing decisions in the privacy of their own homes. You can also offer customers discounts, such as two-for-one deals.

2. Contact the sales force en masse

A company with a traveling sales force, or salespeople scattered through many branch offices, can communicate changes in product, price, or policy with a single mailing.

3. Encourage customers to ask questions about technical details

A VCR manufacturer can finally tell its customers how to get rid of the blinking "12:00" on their machines.

4. Open a suggestion box to improve your products

This not only provides you with a steady source of good ideas, it also shows your customers that you are open to input — even critical input. Prompt customers by asking specific questions. "We have just added a new line of French wines to our list. What did you think of them?"

5. Send samples of a new record album to loyal fans

Some commercial bulletin boards now let subscribers download snippets of songs. The hard rock band Aerosmith recently distributed some of its material this way.

6. Facilitate communication between your marketers, engineers, and salespeople

Set up weekly conferences to connect disparate branches of your company. Make sure to send the transcript to everyone involved so that they can take action on suggestions. Use the meetings to brainstorm.

7. Develop an automated pricing model that salespeople can use on sales calls

Using a laptop, a salesman can log onto your BBS and enter the specs for his client. The BBS will instantly respond with the latest pricing.

8. Distribute a short multimedia presentation to interested customers

A multimedia presentation, complete with pictures of appetizing dishes, a video of an aerobics class, and a clip of soothing music, can do more to sell your health spa than the most costly color brochure. Best of all, you can distribute it for next to nothing.

9. Post and update real estate prices and descriptions

Given the fast pace of change in any area's real estate market, a company can stand out from the crowd by giving its agents access to the very latest information on new properties. Alternatively, this can be a way to sell your own house. You could even start a bulletin board for people trying to sell their own homes, and charge them a fee to post their ads.

10. Post job openings in your fast-growing company

Sometimes your customers make the best employees. Nintendo hires expert players to staff its support line. Posting jobs also indicates that your company is going places, and communicates stability and strength.

11. *Establish an electronic industry association in which competitors can exchange information and ideas*

Some commercial online services have forums devoted to specific products. See if your industry gravitates to one service in particular. Professionals and artists, many of whom work independently or at home, find these services particularly useful. Members of the Romance Writers of America recently launched an online RWA chapter on CompuServe.

12. *Offer a contest or sweepstakes to customers online*

This is also a way to prospect for new e-mail addresses. Perhaps the prize can be free access to your service, if you charge a fee. Use the contest to promote new products.

13. *Start a fan club for your product or service*

If you are in a field where brand-name recognition is crucial, a fan club can be a source of testimonials. "The XYZ camera company has 30,000 customers who like us so much, they joined the club." Such a club can also become a springboard for a loyalty marketing program.

14. *Provide access for the media*

If your company has a wide range of position papers, product information, and news, you can allow the media to browse through your BBS to search for the information they need.

15. *Allow international customers to access technical notes after your regular office hours*

Make sure you keep your BBS running after hours, and that you have a menu option for languages other than English.

16. *Answer technical questions via private e-mail*

E-mail from the president of the company will impress a frustrated customer and build goodwill. E-mail is also the ideal way to send complicated information quickly. Someone working on a new computer program can refer to your message repeatedly without having to call your 800 number over and over.

17. *Provide a dating service to customers of your bar*

BBSs offer anonymity, but you can also allow daters to upload scanned images of themselves. In the 1980s, bars that put phones on their tables were trendy for a while. Perhaps the new trend will be computer terminals.

18. *Provide updated commodity pricing to farmers who shop at your feed store*

Farmers' fortunes rise and fall on the price offered for their crops and live-stock. Make it easy for them to keep up to date on the latest prices, and you've provided a service they'll really appreciate. Once you've secured their goodwill, build on it by offering discounts on your products.

19. *Provide instant portfolio valuations to your stock brokerage customers*

An industry that is going through a merger or other event might witness dramatic stock price changes every hour. Clients with hefty investments will need to know how they're doing so they can pick the optimum moment to sell or buy.

20. *Post rumors and news in an open forum for stock traders*

Trading on inside information is forbidden, but once the information is posted on your BBS, it becomes a full-fledged rumor. This is an effective way for a broker to stay close with frequent traders.

21. *Access your best customers' inventory situation so you can suggest reorders and restocking*

As well as giving customers access to your BBS, encourage them to give you access to theirs. An auto parts manufacturer can gain new insights from the BBS of a car company.

22. *Answer consumers' medical questions as a way of promoting your hospital*

By posting the answers to the most frequently asked questions, the doctors in your hospital can establish themselves as experts to a wide audience.

23. *Sponsor public conferences on controversial issues of interest to your customers*

A magazine or bookstore could host an electronic discussion on censor-ship or freedom of information. A gun shop could invite comments on new gun-control proposals.

24. *Sponsor an electronic symposium for doctors and scientists*

Many family physicians would love to attend more symposia, but they can't get away from their practices. If you sell pharmaceuticals or other products of interest to doctors, make it easy for these family physicians to keep up on the latest issues by running an online discussion. You can even upload detailed research papers.

25. *Publish full-color pictures of your products to help customers make purchasing decisions*

A clothing company can show exactly what its products look like and how the colors work together. Reproduction of the image depends to a great deal on the resolution of the customer's computer screen, but at the very least patterns should be obvious.

26. *Provide software upgrades to customers who have already purchased an earlier version*

A large number of software companies already do this, especially to fix bugs. The library of the CompuServe forum run by Microprose Software even includes software that allows people who play its games to cheat.

27. *Publish recall or product problem information to customers*

When there is a product problem, your BBS can be part of your communication strategy to reach your customers. By including the recall in the opening screen, you can save some customers connect-time fees and long-distance charges.

28. *Provide a job-search service that allows customers to post résumés*

If you run an employment agency, you can make life easier for both the employees you represent and companies seeking new staff. Post your clients' résumés on your BBS, where recruiters can scan them at their leisure.

29. *Allow loyal book customers to retrieve excerpts, reviews, and book covers*

Advance publicity is an important part of the book business. Post teasers of the latest works in the libraries. Set up special forums on your BBS devoted to particular books or authors. Perhaps invite the author herself online for a "chat" session with fans.

30. *Provide information on where to purchase your products in a customer's area*

A large company with a wide but weak distribution system will have to direct customers to particular stores. A specialty magazine may only be available in two locations in a medium-sized city. Help your customers find you.

31. *Allow customers to send e-mail and hold conferences with the executives of your company*

Include "office times" notices on your BBS explaining which executives will be online when, and which products they manage. Customers who absolutely love — or despise — those products will be the first to call.

32. *Provide prices on supplies, seasonal services, and animal health information to pet owners*

Pet owners can interact with each other, and with your company, through your BBS.

33. *Communicate with your clients on product specifications and production runs*

When speed is important and you want information to be in writing, using a BBS can be an ideal solution. Unlike with faxes, you can keep a digital record of everything that transpires.

34. *Post rates for various lengths of stays at your hotel, and provide information about what to do in the area*

By providing travel information, you can give incoming tourists exposure to your hotel at the earliest planning stages of their trip. When it's time to make a reservation, they'll think of you first. A Boston-only BBS, for example, is the natural place to start planning a trip.

35. *Allow mail-order customers to sign on and check on the status of their order*

Deal with customers' curiosity without taxing your support staff. Allow callers to monitor the status of back orders or get shipping information.

36. *Post information about a photography studio*

Allow potential customers to call into a photography studio's bulletin board to check rates, find out about package deals, and view an online portfolio of uploaded photos. By putting your portfolio online, you can provide a wide selection of photos of all types, including portraiture, commercial, and boudoir.

37. *Post pictures, supply lists, and instructions for craft projects*

A hobby store could provide such a service for its customers. By uploading a "Model Airplane of the Week," you encourage customers to call in more often, exposing them to more of your promotional materials.

38. *Allow car mechanics to look up specifications of parts in stock at your auto supply store*

If you include photos, mechanics can make sure they are ordering the right parts. If it increases sales, consider giving the mechanic a computer just to run the service.

39. *Allow customers to call in and confirm or change appointment times*

A doctor providing this service allows patients to call in and cancel appointments without the embarrassment of dealing with a human assistant. In the end, such a service saves everybody time.

40. *Help customers to troubleshoot and fix common office equipment problems*

A company selling fax machines can include files in its library that address unusual or rare problems. You probably don't have room in your manual to explain how to get chocolate cake out of a home fax machine. But one of your customers may have had to solve this very problem. Post his solution, and the next customer who faces this dilemma will be amazed at the extent of your customer service.

41. *Have patrons send in reference questions to the local public library*

This service allows librarians the chance to better set their priorities when answering questions. And if questions are posted in an open forum, other library patrons might provide their own answers, suggest obscure reference books, and argue about nuances of various replies.

42. *Notify preferred customers of special offers and sales in your store*

Set up a forum called "Frequent Flyers" for passengers who are part of your program. Other passengers who visit this section can see the advantages that accrue to more loyal customers.

43. *Notify customers of new magazine or comic book edition arrivals*

Collectors and magazine junkies want to be the first on their block to have the latest arrivals. By posting the daily inventory of what's in stock, you can alert your best customers as to when to come in.

44. *Allow customers to call their favorite restaurant in advance to find out what the nightly specials are and how long they'll have to wait for a table*

Use this opportunity to promote wines, desserts, and appetizers. In a restaurant that depends on high traffic, such as a deli, an online menu can also reduce ordering time.

45. *Allow bank customers to call in and check on account information, interest rates, and investment services offered*

Remind customers of the full range of your services with a comprehensive menu. Use evocative titles such as "Lower Interest Mortgages," "Special Plans for Students," "Effective Retirement Planning," and so forth.

46. *Alert sporting-goods store customers to upcoming events in the area*

Don't forget to post local sports scores. If you sponsor a team, run an online fan club. Encourage customers to make "reservations" online for lessons or personal fittings. You can also use your BBS to communicate skiing and surfing conditions, as well as basic weather information.

47. *Maintain a list of frequently asked tax-related questions*

An accountant can provide a free resource for posting tax questions and finding answers. He can also use the BBS to allow clients to upload their accounting files.

48. *Allow customers to access their billing statements 24 hours a day*

Allow them to flag errors, change their address, or request more information. Prompt waiting customers to explore the libraries for information on your other services.

49. Provide information about upcoming movies

A movie theater can offer coming attractions, seat reservations, and viewer reviews on its BBS.

50. "Eavesdrop" on customer discussions about your product

Do most forum members hate your pizza chain's tomato sauce? Does every second message about your jeans remark on the fabulous fit? Dell Computer has two full-time employees who do nothing but eavesdrop on conversations about the company.

51. Raise your newsletter's profile by offering advice

Judith Broadhurst publishes a newsletter for freelance journalists called *Freelance Success*. She's also an active member of the Journalism Forum on CompuServe, where she frequently participates in discussions about rates and markets. In the process, she sometimes refers to articles from her newsletter.

52. Increase customer loyalty by providing useful services

Create a BBS with e-mail capability and allow all your current customers unlimited free access. Changing providers means that they'll lose their e-mail account as well.

BBS Resources

Aquila
4438 E. New York St., Suite 281
Aurora IL 60504
(708) 820-0480

Illinois's largest bulletin board system offers a wide range of news, information, files, chat areas, and entertainment features. You can use the Aquila BBS to learn how bulletin board services work. In addition to offering free trial subscriptions, this bulletin board service provides technical support to subscribers.

BBS Software Manufacturers and Consultants

Galacticomm
4101 SW 47th Avenue, Suite 101
Ft. Lauderdale FL 33314
(800) 328-1128

Galacticomm develops and markets data/fax communications software and hardware. Its primary product is a software package called *Major BBS,* which helps users set up their own bulletin boards. The company offers free, unlimited technical support. Galacticomm software is available in seven foreign-language versions.

GW Associates
P.O. Box 6606
Holliston MA 01746
(508) 429-6227

This company promotes and supports information management systems for telecommunications. GW maintains commercial BBS systems, installs networks and software, and provides local, on-site support for your bulletin board. The company also provides software to enhance bulletin board systems, such as file searching, games, and file management software.

Mustang Software, Inc.
P.O. Box 2264
Bakersfield CA 93303
(805) 873-2500

This software company markets the *Wildcat!* BBS software used to start up and maintain a bulletin board service. *Wildcat!* offers graphics, mouse support, and tools for creating menus. You can also use it to offer fax, newsgroup, and e-mail features through your bulletin board. Mustang also offers a full line of other networking software for various applications and bulletin board systems.

Online Management Services
791 Del Ganado Road
San Rafael CA 94903
(415) 257-4146

This national provider of online services specializes in start-up consultations, setup, management, and support of online systems. OMS works with both commercial and private online services and provides corporate training for using online services for marketing and management purposes.

Commercial Online Services

America Online
8619 Westwood Center Drive
Vienna VA 22182-2285
(800) 827-6364
info@aol.com
America Online provides access to some features of the Internet and an extensive online service of bulletin boards and other features.

CompuServe
5000 Arlington Center Boulevard
P.O. Box 20212
Columbus OH 43220
(614) 457-8600
postmaster@csi.compuserve.com
CompuServe offers extensive features and bulletin boards as well as access to e-mail. Its marketing brochure outlines the company's rates and services for businesses, and provides complete demographics about the system's users.

Prodigy
445 Hamilton Ave.
White Plains NY 10601
(914) 448-8000
Prodigy provides commercial online service access and bulletin board features. Several businesses already use its bulletin board system for advertising, marketing, and promotional activities. Prodigy offers variable rate structures and can track users who access your information.

Publications

Boardwatch magazine
8500 W. Bowles Ave., Suite 210
Littleton CO 80123
(303) 973-6038

This monthly magazine covers issues related to using and maintaining a bulletin board of your own. It regularly features articles about businesses that are using bulletin boards, and devotes space every month to each of the commercial online services. The magazine also contains extensive listings of available bulletin boards and the services they offer. The noncomputer commentary is often juvenile and tiresome, but the scope of the magazine is unmatched.

BBS Glossary

Baud rate: the measure of how quickly computers can send and receive messages. Baud is usually discussed in terms of bits per second (bps), with the common measurements being 300, 1200, 2400, 4800, and 9600 bps.

Bulletin Board Service (BBS): a service that lets people use a phone and a modem (see below) to get access to information and services stored on a remote computer. Users can also leave messages, questions, and files on the BBS for other users. Often used to describe small services, while large ones are described as online services.

Chat (or conference): an area of a bulletin board service that allows two or more people online at the same time to have a real-time discussion. Participants can immediately reply to comments by typing in their responses, which other users will also see immediately.

Communications software: a program that, when used along with a computer and a modem, gives you access to bulletin boards, commercial services, and the Internet.

Electronic mail (e-mail): a system of sending messages between any two computers that are linked through a network or bulletin board. E-mail is similar to regular mail, only instant and free.

Files: Text, numbers, pictures, sounds, or programs. Files can be stored on a bulletin board for other users to retrieve, which makes them an ideal way for businesses to distribute items such as software upgrades to customers.

Modem: a device inside or connected to your computer that converts data transmitted over telephone lines into files your computer can read. It allows computers and other electronic devices to talk to each other.

Online: the general term for communications between computers or between people who are using computers. You are online when your modem is sending and receiving information for you.

Real time: instant interaction between computer and user, or between user and user. Most BBS transactions don't occur in real time, but chat and conferences do.

Sysop: the system operator of a bulletin board. The sysop is the person who runs the bulletin board, handles the technical details, and is responsible for the content or direction of the board. In some cases the sysop is also able to control who gets access to the bulletin board.

User interface: the environment users see when they use a bulletin board. Interfaces can be anything from a command line asking the user to type in commands to screens with sophisticated graphics that let users with a mouse click on items of interest.

THE INTERNET

*At last count, 22 million people were hooked
up to the Internet. Given the huge number
of newspaper and magazine articles
written about the Information
Superhighway, you'd have to believe that
at least a million of these users are
journalists. The rest are pretty evenly
divided among students, professors, businesspeople,
and ordinary consumers.*

*Imagine reaching a hundred thousand
interested prospects in less than an hour —
at almost no cost. Or placing your entire
catalog and inventory online so that any
interested consumer could browse through
it — for free. The Internet is a vast,
unregulated territory, an ideal site
for businesses willing and able to
experiment on uncharted ground.*

e

What Is the Internet?

While many articles make the Internet (often called the Net) sound like a complicated place, the theory behind it is quite simple. Imagine the network in your home office. You probably have a single computer hooked up to a printer. The network in a small office might consist of three or four computers, each hooked together to a printer. A larger network could consist of 100 or 200 PCs connected to each other and a big mainframe computer.

The Net links all of these networks to each other. This network of networks has no location. No one owns it and no one is in charge. You'd think this power vacuum would lead to anarchy, but most Net users have a self-policing attitude that keeps the Net functioning remarkably well. On the technical side, a series of rules (called protocols) determines how computers on the Net exchange information.

The Internet can connect you to virtually every university in the world, as well as many government computers (including supercomputers like the one at Lawrence Livermore Labs). You have access to CIA files, discussion groups on AIDS research, even the Coke machine at Carnegie Mellon University.

Features of the Internet

You can do two types of things on the Net. First, you can send electronic mail. This is a fast, easy, inexpensive way to communicate with millions of people. It's also one of the easiest Internet features for the new user to master. Almost all of the commercial online services (see the Bulletin Boards chapter) allow you to send e-mail to all other Internet or online addresses. E-mail is the perfect way to send information and brief messages to people you know.

The second feature of the Net revolves around real-time interaction with other computers. While e-mail works in a way similar to regular mail (address it, send it, and it will be delivered to its destination), real-time communications are interactive and immediate. As soon as you type in a message, someone else can see it and reply while you watch. This capacity makes your interactions more powerful — you can answer questions instantly or engage in a spirited debate with several people at a time — but it also puts a huge load on the system. You need a fast modem, and the computer you're accessing has to be idle enough to deal with your requests. Four of the Internet features that use this technology are Gopher, World Wide Web, Mosaic, and FTP/Telnet. This chapter discusses all four.

E-Mail

E-mail provides quick, nearly free communication with large numbers of people. Everyone on the Net has a unique e-mail address. For example, Oscar winner Holly Hunter is at HUNTRESS@AOL.COM. The first word is the person's user name. After the @ sign is the address of the computer system she's using (see "domain," below). Finally, the three letters after the period indicate whether the account is primarily for commercial (COM), educational (EDU), or military (MIL) use. General accounts end in NET. (My e-mail address is SETH@SGP.COM. Feel free to drop me a note once you get online.)

A note on domains: in the previous example, you saw that my domain name is SGP (it stands for Seth Godin Productions). These custom domain names are a little like vanity license plates — they're easy to remember and imply some sort of authority on the part of the owner. Catchy and relevant domain names make it easy for your customers and users to remember your e-mail address.

Available domain names are controlled by a group called the NIC. To find out if the domain name you'd like is available, you can Telnet to INTERNIC.NET (if you have access to Telnet services) and type WHOIS DOMAIN.COM where DOMAIN is the word you'd like to use as your domain name. If it is available, have your service provider reserve it for you. You get it forever and the cost is virtually nothing. If you don't have access to Telnet, you can send e-mail to refdesk@internic.net and ask for help in finding out if the domain name of your dreams is available.

E-mail offers many benefits:

- *Low cost.*

  Actually, there is virtually no cost once the system is in place. You may pay monthly charges to get access, but the money you save on fax and file transfers by using the Internet instead will more than make up for these fees. According to a recent analysis in The Internet Business Report, a full-blown corporate Internet set-up with a very fast line, dedicated computers, and full security, along with similar setups in 500 branch offices worldwide, is still cheaper than using Federal Express and fax.

- *Extremely fast delivery*

  Most e-mail arrives at its destination (around the corner or around the world) in seconds. The worst delay you can expect is 10 hours.

- *Permanent records*

  You can save and print messages, providing a permanent record of a discussion for future reference. You can save paper and time by e-mailing contracts back and forth during negotiations.

- *Flexibility*

  It's not unusual to send a two- or three-word e-mail message. e-mail provides the considered thoughtfulness of mailed correspondence with the quickness and informality of a phone call.

- *Elimination of barriers*

  An executive can open his door to e-mail without fear of being overwhelmed. Because e-mail is so easy to forward, an executive can easily read messages to see what's happening in the company, then forward the messages to the appropriate people for follow-up. Executives with public e-mail addresses include Bill Gates, Barry Diller, Ted Waitt (at Gateway 2000), and Bill Clinton.

- *Ease of communication*

  Replying to an electronic letter is simple and fast. Conversations last far longer than they might using traditional means.

- *Ease of replication*

  Because e-mail is digital, you can replicate a message as many times as you'd like. A company with 1,000 customers could alert all of them to a price change in less than one minute at a total cost of perhaps a dollar.

Auto Reply and Mailing Lists

An auto-reply mailbox is a very simple program that lets you send a pre-written document to anyone who sends mail to a given address. For example, anyone wanting a list of stores carrying your latest product can send mail to your address and receive two pages of listings within an hour. You can offer as many auto-reply mailboxes as you like, offering literally hundreds of different documents to interested people.

It's also easy and straightforward to create a mailing list of names.

Once you've compiled the list, you can send a document to the list server, which will automatically send it to every name on the list. There are mailing lists of every shape and kind on the Net, from those for fans of the Grateful Dead to a list that lets locksmiths exchange secrets. In these public mailing lists, a letter sent to the list goes to the entire group. You can use the same technology in a private list to reach your customers or prospects interested in new product announcements.

This is a remarkably powerful technique. For example, if 100,000 Net users send you e-mail because they liked your last movie, you could instantly send a letter to each and every one of them to announce your next film. The mail will get there in moments, and it will cost you nothing. This combination of breadth and focus has never before been achieved in any sort of marketing.

The Two Burning Questions About E-Mail

First, how do you get someone's e-mail address? You can't send e-mail to someone until you know her address, but the Net has no central address directory or phone book. There are a handful of search services, such as WHOIS, but none of these are comprehensive or guaranteed to provide the information you want in a logical format.

There are two solutions. For limited audiences, the best way to get someone's address is to phone her and ask for it — silly as this sounds. Companies who want to contact existing customers online should make sure all employees dealing with customers routinely ask for e-mail addresses.

This approach obviously isn't practical if you want to build a prospect list. In that case, the only solution is to give people a reason to write to you. If you offer a benefit and publicize your e-mail address, you can expect to receive a lot of mail.

TV Guide sponsored a sweepstakes and gave an e-mail address that readers could use to register. It received more than 250,000 responses in two weeks. While many were duplicates, the magazine now owns at least 200,000 unduplicated e-mail addresses of *TV Guide* readers.

Joe Boxer sells men's boxer shorts in fanciful prints. The company publicized its e-mail address (joeboxer@jboxer.com) via billboards and magazine ads. Since then, it has received about 300 letters a day through the Internet. Eighty percent of those messages are requests for catalogs and product information.

The second question is more challenging: Once you get someone's e-mail address, what can you do with it? Many marketers would like to use e-mail just like traditional mail — to send unsolicited junk mail to as many locations as possible. After all, they reason, e-mail is so much cheaper than real mail that even if a promotion has a low response rate, they won't waste much money.

CAREFUL! This approach will cause you untold trouble. As we mentioned earlier, a self-policing culture has grown up around the Net. The 22 million people online will not sit idly by while a marketer uses the Net to distribute junk mail.

Net users will always respond to unsolicited junk mail — by "flaming" the sender (a flame is an angry, offensive, or derisive message designed to provoke the recipient). Really angry users will spend many, many hours making a junk mail distributor's life miserable.

A small publisher of books decided to promote a new geography book by sending unsolicited letters via the Internet. As a test, he sent 2,000 letters. Each letter was a definite soft sell, offering a free sample as well as some interesting trivia from the book.

Within eight hours, the publisher had received 30 flames criticizing the mailing. A warning went out on the geography discussion groups, urging people to boycott the book. A group of users threatened to contact bookstores around the country to urge them to join the boycott.

Clearly, junk mail is not a concept whose time has come to the Internet. It may never be acceptable. That's why marketers need to start looking now for smarter and more efficient ways to get attention for their products.

The secret of selling via e-mail on the Net is to send only solicited junk mail. By providing users with information or entertainment, you can begin a relationship with them. Once you've created a dialogue, you can describe your products and services in great detail.

MICHAEL STRANGELOVE ON INTERNET ADVERTISING AS A PARADIGM SHIFT

From the essay, "The Theory of Internet Advertising," which originally appeared in the book How to Advertise on the Internet. *Written by Michael Strangelove (mstrange@fonorola.net), publisher of* The Internet Business Journal.

The advertising industry is on the verge of being shattered into a thousand fragments due to the knowledge explosion and the proliferation of new technologies. There are no more grand theories that hold sway over the entire industry. There are no more central premises, techniques, or laws that can be relied upon for commercial success. All the familiar categories of Madison Avenue have been shattered by the postmodern marketplace.

Into the midst of this chaos the Internet has arisen with 30 million members in almost one hundred countries. Doubling in size every year, the Internet has dropped out of the sky like a bomb and exploded onto the scene of popular culture. The mass media has not shown such a prolonged and intense fascination with a new technology since the introduction of the personal computer over a decade ago.

The first thing the business community desperately needs to know about the Net is not how to use it, but how to comprehend it. What, indeed, is the Internet? Any effective advertising and marketing will be built on the basis of a correct understanding of the Net.

The Internet is a technology, a culture, and a tool. The Internet is a distributed and open systems technology. Distributed means that it has no central location and open refers to the fact that the operating codes are not proprietary or secret. Everyone can contribute to the design and development of the overall system.

Now there is a very precise relationship between the Internet's core technology and its core cultural characteristics. As global technology that is distributed and open the Net is not subject to central control or monopolistic ownership. This is the first technology of its kind to achieve global scope in human history. This is significant because culture interiorizes the technologies of society and any radically new technology, such as the Internet, will have an equally radical effect on culture.

It is one of the great historical ironies that the Internet arose out of a Dr. Strangelovean plan to create a communications system that could survive a nuclear holocaust. What was to have been a communications system for the surviving elite of a military-industrial complex has mutated into a subversive neo-democratic (more precisely, anarchistic) cyberculture. The unique technological character of the Internet has endowed it with a fundamentally subversive nature. It is not subject to privatization, centralization, or control and therefore stands in direct opposition to the historical dynamics of capitalism and commercialization.

So we see that the character of Internet technology is the source of its primary cultural dynamics. This open and distributed system has spawned a consensual community with no central forms of government or bureaucracy. Businesses that want to advertise through this technology and culture will have to be prepared to adapt to the unique character of cyberspace. In many cases, business and government will also have to be prepared to be affected by this culture.

Companies that integrate Internet-based communication into their structure run the risk, for better or worse, of being influenced by the dynamics of nonhierarchical communication. Networked electronic communication has in many cases had a dramatic effect on the power structures and communication patterns within organizations. Depending on the willingness of an organization to accept these changes such effects can be less than welcome.

The technological structure of the Internet serves as the genetic code for its cultural character. This open and distributed technology has created, quite by accident, an entirely new form of human behavior — mass participation in bidirectional, uncensored mass communication. Mass communication, while itself a relatively new phenomenon, has always involved controlled broadcasts to passive audiences. The mass audience has never had any significant input or control over the content of mass communication.

With the Internet these characteristics of mass communication have forever changed. On the Net we find massive numbers of people broadcasting information to massive numbers of people. Whereas the introduction of the Gutenberg Press made mass communication possible for the very, very few who would ever own a printing press, the Internet has turned every owner of a $1000 computer, a modem, and a telephone line into a publisher, a radio station, and soon enough, a TV studio. This is the second Gutenberg revolution. This is the new economy of information.

The main social and economic process we are witnessing in cyberspace is the democratization of mass communication. To adapt and survive the Information Age, the business community must recognize this paradigm shift and the nature of the new form of human behavior it generates. Not only is it bi-directional, with audience and content provider (broadcaster) acting as one, but it is uncensored.

On the Net you have the freedom to say anything you want, within the very large confines of libel laws, self-censorship, and quite liberal community norms. The only insurmountable restriction on freedom of speech in cyberspace is that conversation must remain within the prescribed topic of any given online conference. You can say anything you want, but you must say it in the designated forum for your subject. These mitigating forces do not lessen the significance of the Internet as the first forum for uncensored mass communication, and its role as the final preserve of freedom of speech.

Throughout history, mass communication has always been tightly controlled by members of the ruling elite. In antiquity, crowds were always perceived as a threat by the ruling elite, and quickly (and usually violently) disbanded. In modernity, all forms of mass communication have been subject to either direct government ownership; indirect control, manipulation, and censorship through regulatory bodies such as the CRTC and the FCC; and further indirect control as the result of the mass media's corporate sponsorship. Even shortly after the invention of the Gutenberg press, the Tudor kings began to institutionalize censorship and control over early mass printing.

On the Internet today you can legally access information that is banned in many countries including Canada and the US. Whether it is the Terrorist Handbook, information subject to court-ordered publication bans, censored articles, or details on growing or making illegal drugs, you will find it on the Net. And no one can stop you from accessing it, retrieving, and reading it.

On the Internet today you can retrieve information that is daily impounded by your country's official censors and border guards. With less than $1,000 in hardware and software you can start an Internet-based radio station that would not be subjected to the regulations of the FCC. Because the new paradigm of cyberspace shatters all the old categories of our antiquated and decaying institutions, the Internet defies traditional bureaucratic structures and hierarchical power relationships.

Power, advertising, and the Internet are all inescapably related. Traditional advertising is not merely a matter of paying to disseminate a message. There is an often overlooked matter of what messages advertising serves to exclude from media. Advertising is a multi-billion-dollar industry that underwrites all major forms of mass communication. This endows advertising with substantial power in society. Without question, the financial dependency created by the relationship between advertising and mass media has had the function of controlling the overall content of the media it has supported.

The ad industry continues to deny that it influences content, and most editors and publishers naturally deny editorial interference from sponsors. Listening to the industry constantly deny this incestuous relationship is reminiscent of listening to tobacco industry executives repeatedly trying to convince a congressional hearing that cigarettes are not harmful. Yet the past 30 years of communication studies have produced a small mountain of evidence which demonstrates that the mass media is constantly subject to the influence and bias of its primary commercial sponsors. The myth of the lack of bias and influence has been necessary to gain trust and maintain the appearance of legitimacy.

It is here that we see how the nature of the Internet and the nature of advertising (as it is traditionally practiced) are at odds with each other. The Internet liberates the audience from the control of corporate and state content providers. In cyberspace, the most basic relationship between programming, content, and advertising is absent. Thus far, the Internet is the first form of mass communication to arise without the sponsorship of advertisers. In cyberspace content is uncontrolled and reigns supreme. The challenge facing the business community is to adapt to this new medium and the emerging paradigm.

Advertising will continue to exist in cyberspace, but it will lack the ability to exercise control over content which it has grown accustomed to in other environments. Most of the present difficulties being faced by advertisers on the Internet can be attributed to the industries' painfully slow realization that it is the virtual community, and not the business world or the state, that has the final say over content in a bi-directional, uncensored environment.

But the news is not all bad for traditional businesses. As a tool, the Internet does present unparalleled opportunities for effective advertising.

The Internet provides the delivery of an audience for vertical marketing of highly customized products to microcommunities in a cost-efficient manner not previously available to the manufacturer, retailer, or service provider. One of the effects of the integration of the Internet into the business community will be the rapid growth of low-volume products efficiently marketed to small global consumer groups.

Take the narrow casting feature of the magazine industry which is characterized by its ability to deliver an affinity group, and fragment it to the point of infinity, and you have a metaphor for the future of the Internet: the cost-effective delivery of niche markets to the business community.

The Internet is the single most significant new tool for business, particularly for small to medium enterprises. What makes the Internet such a powerful tool for the world of the entrepreneur and small business is that it provides the entrepreneur with the ability to communicate with a global audience that already numbers in the tens of millions.

Prior to the integration of the Internet into the cosmology of the collective consciousness, most small businesses only had access to local markets. Advertising costs of mass media functioned to clearly delimit the possible growth of most local businesses. Now on the Internet every business, no matter how small, is a multi-national business in a global marketplace.

The Internet's historically unique ability to facilitate inexpensive global communication is destined to have a widespread impact on the shape of international markets, national and international economies. Take the elitist nature of the past thirty years of multinational corporate economics and extend it to every small business, and you have the democratization of the global marketplace through cyberspace. This is the meaning of Internet as an advertising medium.

No company has yet mastered the Internet as an advertising and marketing tool. Expect this to change as today's paradigm begins to shift into the digital, wired Information Age.

Using Interactivity: E-Mail

O S/2 is an operating system that competes with Windows. It has spawned a wide range of add-on products, as well as a host of technical questions. A small mail-order company in Georgia decided to specialize in OS/2 products. Rather than spending a nickel on advertising, the head of marketing for the company decided to spend most of his time on the Internet.

He offers free advice to people online. He suggests solutions and alternatives to frustrated users. Guess who gets their business? This low-key approach has given the fledgling company double-digit sales increases every year.

Joe Boxer is another example. The company is compiling a humorous book about boxer shorts, and has invited people to send in funny stories by e-mail. By making underwear fun, the company has attracted exactly the audience that will also be interested in buying its quirky products.

The Boston Globe is also trying to use the Net effectively to build its business. It publicizes its Net addresses in many of the paper's columns and features.

To anyone who sent the paper an e-mail note in the last few months, the paper recently sent the following message, also by e-mail:

Date: Wed, Jul 27, 1994 5:53 PM EST
From: adhoc@globe.com
Subj: Message from The Boston Globe
To: JAMES@BIG.COM

Posted on: America Online (using the Internet)

Hi.
I'm Dave Kagan, and I work in electronic publishing for The Boston Globe (I'm one of the guys trying to figure out how to get The Boston Globe on the information highway...)Because you're on America Online, and you sent The Globe e-mail at some point over the past few months, I wanted to let you know that we've taken another step toward getting online: The Globe's archive is now searchable on America Online, using the keyword "newspaper library." Using this archive you can search back issues of the Globe (1980–1994) for information on the Boston area, people, places, companies or whatever else you might be interested in. The

fee for the service, in addition to AOL's normal fees, is 10 cents a minute ($6/hr.) weekends and weekday nights (6p.m. to 6a.m., EST), and 80 cents a minute ($48/hr.) weekdays (6a.m. to 6p.m.).

To use the service, call up keyword "newspaper library," enter the library, then select Boston Globe. You'll be prompted first for the year or years you wish to search, then for a word or words.

I hope this is something you will find useful.... it's an experiment for us, so let us know what you think. I can be reached days at (617) 929-2735.

Take care.

Sincerely, Dave Kagan

Electronic Publishing

The Boston Globe

d_kagan@globe.com

P.S. In light of recent controversy over advertising on the Internet, we debated whether to send out this message. In the end we felt the service was so useful that Globe readers would want to know about it. If you'd rather not receive such notices (very) occasionally from The Globe in the future, please let us know. Thanks.

Note the steps the writer took to avoid being flamed. First, he only sent messages to people who had already used e-mail to contact the *Globe* (and he reminded them of that relationship early on). Second, the letter is far more informative than hard-sell. Third, he provides a direct phone number, hoping to nip flames before they get out of hand. Last, and most important, he gives recipients a chance to get off the *Globe*'s list. It's pretty hard to criticize this letter to other Net citizens.

A car dealer in Silicon Valley gives his e-mail address to car shoppers. A potential customer can send him an e-mail message, and he'll send her price estimates, lists of options and in-stock models, a dealer's rebate coupon, and other information to convince her to buy from him. This low-cost service shows prospects that the dealer is committed to offering good service in innovative ways.

A sports memorabilia dealer acquires an autographed Mickey Mantle bat. He could contact his 100 best customers via e-mail and offer them a chance to bid on the bat. By conducting an auction electronically, he can dramatically increase the number of people involved and guarantee that he'll receive the best price.

INTERVIEW WITH MARY J. CRONIN

Mary J. Cronin, Ph.D., is a professor of management at Boston College and author of Doing Business on the Internet: How the Electronic Highway Is Transforming American Companies *(Van Nostrand Reinhold, 1994).*

Q: What advantages will the Internet give small businesses?

A: The Internet offers small business an unprecedented opportunity to compete at the same level as much larger companies. Connecting to the Internet immediately provides a small business owner with access to information resources, software and navigational tools, technical expertise, and business contacts. Because the Internet is a global network with connections in over 100 countries, it opens up an international market for every company — customers in Japan and Great Britain, Brazil and Singapore can find out about what a small business in the United States has to offer them. So companies don't have to be limited by geographic location or lack of branch offices — they can have a presence online that reaches millions of people around the world, even if their "headquarters" is a home office with one workstation.

Closer to home, small businesses can also benefit from using the Internet to access their own vendors and suppliers online. Most companies find they get faster response time and better service when they use e-mail to contact customer support desks. Substituting e-mail over the Internet for more costly phone and fax communication will save money and project the image of a well-connected, technically advanced company. And the more the Internet grows, the more valuable all these advantages become.

One of the greatest attractions of the Internet for small business is that despite its global dimension and dynamic growth, it is truly an environment where knowhow, creativity, and innovation can count just as much as capital investment and size. Entrepreneurs with ideas for network-based new business have found the Internet offers real opportunity for success.

Q: How can businesses use the Internet more effectively?

A: Using the Internet effectively requires two things: familiarity with the network's capabilities and liabilities and a strategic business plan for adding value to a particular company. Some businesses make the effort to investigate the Internet and its resources, but they underestimate the importance of matching network capabilities to their company's needs and competitive opportunities. Start with the business plan — an in-depth assessment that spells out your company's most important objectives and identifies just how the Internet connection can expand market share or provide a new distribution channel or other capability for your company. Then you will have a framework for implementing the Internet applications that are going to move your business toward those objectives.

Companies can also increase their effectiveness by finding out what services are available from Internet access providers, from Internet service bureaus, trainers, and consultants. Internet support services are a burgeoning and very competitive sector, and small businesses don't have to reinvent the wheel in designing an application. Often it's worth the investment in professional assistance up front to get off on the right foot with your connections and your online image.

Finally, businesses have to make sure that their Internet message is reaching the right people. While it's true that products and interest groups as diverse as antique collectors and beer drinkers, wool-spinners and zoologists are all connected to the Internet, it won't help your business to send them all the same message — especially if it doesn't relate to any of them directly. Remember that the Internet is actually thousands of separate markets and user groups; get to know its culture, norms of communications, and many different segments before you attempt to design a network-based marketing plan.

Q: How will the commercial Internet change the way consumers are reached by industry?

A: Because the Internet allows users to interact with each other and with companies in a global "electronic village," the norms for reaching consumers are definitely changing. Customers online expect to give direct feedback and have their suggestions taken seriously. They want a response, and they want to see some evidence that their ideas matter. This is a lot more powerful than the traditional relationship of consumers to broadcast or print advertising, but it requires business to respond at a much higher level. Companies that can make this adjustment are the ones that will be successful in the networked environment. There is no substitute for the convenience of browsing, ordering, and getting support for products right at your workstation. Once a consumer adapts to this mode of doing business, they want to get more information and buying opportunities online.

Q: What are the most effective ways that businesses can work to overcome the anti-commercial attitude of the Internet?

Businesses should avoid using the Internet to broadcast limited-content advertising — it will generate an adverse reaction and defeat their purpose for participating in the network. The key is to think about being a participant in a dialogue, not "using" the Internet but gaining and adding value through joining a global community, finding out more about the electronic marketplace and what customers really want. That may sound idealistic, but in fact it reflects proven principles of marketing and selling — and it works!

Companies should continuously look for ways to add value to their products and their interactions with Internet users. One way is to design Internet servers that do encourage customer interaction and offer useful content beyond simple sales information.

Q: How do you think the Internet itself will change as the result of increased commercial usage?

A: The Internet has been extremely adaptable to a tremendous diversity of applications over the years, and I believe this will continue. There is room for education and research, community information, hobbies, literature, chat, entertainment, and just plain fun on the Internet, along with commercial applications. I do think that the new tools developed to support business and marketing will continue to open up the network to more nontechnical users; these new users will need support as well as low-cost navigational tools. I see a lot of new business opportunities developing around serving the information and support needs of the expanded Internet community.

Q: **What advice would you give to a small business owner investigating the possibility of using the Net for marketing and sales?**

A: Most of what I have already mentioned. First, analyze your market — existing and potential — to determine if the Internet is a good match for your product and your customers. Make a realistic business plan. Then explore what other companies, especially those with comparable products or services, are already doing on the Internet. Take advantage of the expertise available over the network — check discussion groups and FAQs (Frequently Asked Questions) in relevant areas for a description of the resources and the issues around creating an in-house information server directly connected to the Internet vs. renting space in an existing "Internet storefront"; decide if you have the resources to do it yourself or if it will be better to at least start with a service bureau to handle all the details. Include in your planning time to talk to providers of direct Internet connections and "Internet storefronts" to find out specifically how they would serve your business needs. Compare the costs and the level of services provided — get references from existing customers, and check on the transaction level that the connection they offer can handle effectively. For sales, find out if encryption and privacy services are available — for example, how effectively can the provider support taking credit cards or purchase orders online?

This may sound like a lot of work up front, but it will help ensure that your relationship with the Internet gets off to a good start and continues to be positive and profitable for everyone.

e

Using Interactivity: Mosaic

M ost nonstudent Net users are only able to use e-mail. More sophisticated interaction with other computers requires phone lines and modems that aren't widely available.

As public use of the Net increases, though, far more sophisticated connections will become available, and more Net users will be able to use applications such as Mosaic to find their way around the Net.

Currently used by about 250,000 people, Mosaic provides a graphic interface not unlike the screen presented by a Macintosh or CD-ROM application. It combines graphics, photos, and text into a multimedia magazine format.

Mosaic will allow the user to jump from article to article at will by following a trail of relationships between documents. The people who make the information available in the first place — universities, libraries, and other information providers — will create the trails to facilitate access.

Mosaic supports hypertext, a system which lets people use a word in one article to find another article on a totally different, but related, topic. Users can access the related information by simply selecting (clicking or highlighting) the item on their screen. These hypertext links will provide a whole new way of accessing information, giving the reader far more power. Users will be able to make links to documents or files on almost any of the computers offering information through the World Wide Web (we'll talk more about this later).

While it's too early for most companies to use Mosaic as a marketing mechanism, a firm can use it to establish itself on the cutting edge.

The Country Fare restaurant in Palo Alto, California, uses Mosaic to keep in touch with its high-tech clientele. It has a Mosaic site that lets users look at its menu and find out about weekly specials. The site provides information about the restaurant's cookbook and lets users browse through some of the recipes. It even provides a picture of the restaurant and a road map. Overkill for a restaurant? Sure. But the site has increased business, and taught the management valuable skills that will pay off once the entire Silicon Valley is wired with high-speed Internet access.

O'Reilly and Associates, one of the leading publishers of Internet books, has put its money where its mouth is by creating a monthly Mosaic-based electronic magazine called the *Global Network Navigator*. Available free to anyone who subscribes, it offers articles about the Net and free updates to existing O'Reilly books. The magazine is designed to be supported by advertising — each page of the *Global Network Navigator* includes a small ad. The reader can get more information about the ad by clicking on it.

Building a Mosaic application from scratch is neither simple nor easy. You should probably contact one of the organizations offering turnkey systems or Mosaic advertising.

Using Interactivity: Gopher

F inding information on the Net used to be nearly impossible until a simple-to-use application called Gopher came along. A Gopher server is an organized database of the information contained on a given machine. For example, the first level of a Gopher server for information about government agencies might have choices like this:

- *CIA*

- *FBI*

- *NASA*

- *LIBRARY OF CONGRESS*

The user selects CIA and then sees this:

- *COUNTRY ANALYSIS*

- *PRESS RELEASES*

- *SATELLITE IMAGES*

After he chooses SATELLITE IMAGES, the choices are:

- *ALASKA*

- *NEPAL*

- *PERU*

    etc.

If he selects PERU, for instance, the user will see a message saying that there is an image available, which he can download to his computer.

It's fairly easy to create a Gopher server to organize all of the documents and files that your company makes available to the public.

Almost all EDU computers support Gopher applications. So do many

MIL and GOV sites. As a result, millions of users have access to your Gopher menus. Now that America Online supports Gopher, an additional one million users have fast and easy Gopher access.

As just one example of the potential for marketing with Gopher, a leading New York publisher intends to make excerpts of its 3,000 backlist titles available via a Gopher server. The user will be able to choose the topic or the author she's interested in, find relevant titles, then easily read or download descriptions of the book and the author and an excerpt from the book.

Gopher is an ideal tool for organizing large amounts of product information. If your company intends to offer more than a few dozen technical documents, catalog descriptions, or graphics files, you can give your prospects easy access with Gopher.

Using Interactivity: WAIS

While a Gopher server allows users to search by the indexes you create, a WAIS (Wide Area Information Server) permits users to do searches on all the text in a document as well.

For example, suppose Nabisco wanted to make a number of technical documents available. It could put a special report titled "Oreos" in a Gopher server. But if a researcher was looking for information on creme filling, and didn't realize that Oreos are creme-filled cookies, he wouldn't think to check that listing. A WAIS server, on the other hand, creates speedy indexes to every word in the document, making searches a snap. It would alert the researcher that the text of the report on Oreos contains the words "creme filling."

WAIS is in far less general use than Gopher, but experts expect that to change as the technology evolves.

Using Interactivity: FTP/Telnet

Telnet is a fancy way to describe the access of one computer by users at another. You can allow users to log onto your computer, access your files, and run real-time programs.

For example, a roofing shingle company could offer a program that would compute the number of shingles a contractor needs to cover a given size roof. Using Telnet, the contractor could log on to the Net, then go into the roofing company computer and run the program. He would see the results as they're computed.

Telnet is tricky to describe. The commands can be arcane and time-consuming to learn if you aren't going to use it regularly. It is most useful to people who need access to information or services on a regular basis — for example, your salespeople could access your mainframe while they are on sales calls to run price estimating programs for their clients.

Users who simply want to retrieve a file from you can use FTP (file transfer protocol) to download a file from your computer to theirs. This protocol lets you make graphics, software, and large text files available to anyone, while giving you more control over what users do on your computer than you have if they're using Telnet. However, FTP requires some technical knowledge, so Gopher is probably a better way to make your information available.

Using Interactivity: World Wide Web

T he discussion of Mosaic above touched on the World Wide Web, or WWW. Mosaic is one way of viewing the series of documents and links that are part of the World Wide Web. The Web evolved as a result of hypertext, the technology that lets users select a word or graphic and jump to another document that relates to the original word or graphic.

One of the first businesses to use the Web technology was Grant's Florist. For a small fee, this Michigan florist had a company create a WWW site for his information. He features information about his services and prices of the flowers. A user can even click on the name of an arrangement to see a picture of it before ordering. Another click on the words "Press here to order" calls up an order form. Anyone in the world with access to the Internet can place an order with this system from his own computer, without ever leaving his desk.

A graduate student at MIT, Henry Houh, maintains a WWW page that lists the companies providing services on the Web. By clicking on the name of the company, users are automatically linked to that commercial site so that they browse through its online information. Thousands of people access this Web equivalent of the Yellow Pages every day. At the moment, more than 200 companies are listed there.

Using the Web is similar to using Gopher, except that the Web is much more flexible and graphical. The Web also provides access to many other features, such as Telnet, FTP, and newsgroups (see glossary). More hypertext documents have been created and added to the Web as the system has become more popular.

Mosaic is one of the more popular ways to access information that is linked together on the Web, but there are many others. Contact a service provider for more specific details on accessing the Web from your computer.

Getting Internet Access

I f you're new to the Net, try starting with America Online (AOL). It's inexpensive, easy to use, and comes with unlimited technical support. My book *Point and Click Internet* (Peachpit, 1994) contains a diskette and step-by-step instructions on how to use the Net.

Once you've explored via AOL, you'll probably want to expand your company's access. A number of service providers offer access to the Net, for users ranging from individuals to major corporations. The Resources section at the end of this chapter lists a few of the many Internet service providers. More extensive listings are available in books such as *The Internet White Pages* (IDG, 1994). To get a complete listing, send e-mail to info-deli-server@netcom.com or to info@internic.net.

The number of small consulting companies that help businesses use the Internet is growing. Some of these firms are listed in the Resources section, but many are local. You can track them down in the Yellow Pages, or by talking to staff at your local computer store.

52 Ways to Use the Internet

1. *Send updated price and product information to your current customers*

   A software company can post not only price lists and product specifications, but huge documents such as technical manuals. It can even post updated versions of software.

2. *Create a newsgroup*

   Start your own newsgroup where fans of your company's products can exchange information.

3. *Offer free technical support via e-mail*

   Not only software companies can take advantage of this opportunity to offer technical support. Any company that makes a complex product —

stereos, videocameras, cars, geiger counters — can increase customer satisfaction this way.

4. *Provide additional information automatically*

Kellogg's could save time and money via offering diet or exercise tips by
auto-response e-mail. A magazine could send supplementary information
on articles in the current issue to subscribers.

5. *Send reminders to regular customers*

A florist could e-mail reminders three weeks before holidays, birthdays,
and anniversaries. Car companies could remind their customers to bring
their cars in for servicing. A veterinarian could warn customers that it's
time for their cats to get their annual rabies shots.

6. *Create a newsletter*

Share stories about your company and its employees with your customers.
Show how you created a new product. Talk about the company's customer service philosophy. Write an article about one of your researchers
who recently won an industry award. Strengthen your relationship with
your customers by making them feel part of the family.

7. *Generate fan mail and testimonials*

Offer customers a chance for fame (if not fortune) by giving them a
chance to tell you what they like about your products. This action will
generate positive feelings and word-of-mouth recommendations.

8. *Offer an electronic suggestion box*

Print your e-mail address on every product you ship. Include it on your
letterhead and business cards. Let customers know where to find you and
that you're ready to listen to their praise...and complaints.

9. *Manage by walking around*

De-isolate the executives in your company. Publish their e-mail addresses
far and wide. The vice president of a car manufacturer who drives one of
the company's top-of-the-line luxury sedans will suddenly find out, in
vivid detail, what it's like to jump-start one of the company's subcompacts
on a January night.

10. *Announce new products*

Many customers are delighted to hear of the latest products. Give those
on your e-mail list first shot at the new stuff. This tactic is especially useful for record companies, publishers, and other firms whose customers
pride themselves on being on top of the latest trends.

11. *Offer technical information*

Using an auto-replay mailbox (or a series of them), you can provide
enhanced information. For example, your catalog may carry one para-

graph on the new spark plugs you're introducing. But if you mention the address (spark@note.com or whatever) where people could write for more information, you can give really keen prospects enough detail to cement a sale.

12. *Customer surveys*

You can reach more customers than you ever dreamed possible when you had to pay postage to mail out every survey. If you make a hugely popular mass-market product — Coca-Cola, say, or Nike shoes — you can get feedback almost instantly from thousands of users. Using this information, you'll be able to develop new products and improve your advertising more quickly.

13. *Offer your service directly*

Law firms spend a huge amount of time deciphering client requests, reentering data, and processing paper. e-mail can make it easy for the client to do most of this work. Many customers will be glad to do so if they know it will save them money they would otherwise pay in lawyers' fees.

14. *Distribute news releases*

If you've read a mass-market magazine or big city paper lately, you already know that the media love the Net. You can distribute news releases and publicity materials more quickly and inexpensively by e-mail than by regular mail. And many journalists prefer to receive information this way.

15. *Target your best prospects*

It's difficult to reach many executives by traditional means. e-mail can sometimes cut through the clutter of letters, memos, and reports on an executive's desk and get you a meeting or a chance to make a presentation. Just be sure that your e-mail is short, personal, and to the point.

16. *Send financial information to stockholders*

Create a mailing list that automatically sends financial information to stockholders. Investors who get frequent updates on your company's status are more likely to feel confident in their investment.

17. *Alert customers to recalls or upgrades*

Car companies spend thousands of dollars to inform their customers about product recalls. Not only do they have to mail printed notices, they usually send out news releases to make sure customers who have moved since buying the car still hear about the recall. A mailing list can give the company further assurance that all its customers know about the safety problem.

18. *Start a fan club*

Do you promote an author, rock band, or actor? Start a fan club for your client to let fans trade information and ideas. You can post notices of the client's upcoming book, album, or movie, complete with interesting bits of trivia fans can't find anywhere else.

19. *Do market research for a book*

If you're contemplating writing about Jane Austen, you could subscribe to the Austen-L mailing list at McGill University and ask other subscribers if such a book would interest them, or if they think the market is already overcrowded with good biographies.

20. *Let customers share information*

A company that makes videocameras could start a newsgroup where its customers could share tips on shooting in dark or rainy conditions, capturing children and pets on video, or making batteries last longer.

21. *Create an automail server to send your annual report to anyone who requests it*

Stockholders aren't the only people who are interested in your annual report, although they're often the only ones who receive it. Journalists can use it for background information. Job applicants will want to read up on your company's history before their job interview.

22. *Create a Gopher server to allow users to download pictures of your resort*

In effect, you can distribute a full-color brochure to thousands of potential guests for next to nothing. For the price of a tiny classified ad in an upscale travel magazine, you can attract well-heeled travelers and give them a vivid picture of your resort.

23. *Create an automail server to answer frequently asked questions about your company's services*

How many times a day does your receptionist answer questions about your company's hours, fees, and policies? Save her time and your prospects' time by making this sort of information available on the Net.

24. *Offer free real estate information*

A realtor can offer free information on schools, landmarks, businesses, and property values in various neighborhoods using Mosaic. Users can point and click to find out detailed information on the items that interest them most.

25. *Offer travel advice*

Travel agents can offer advice in the travel newsgroups about how to get the lowest ticket prices and hotel rates. By positioning themselves as experts on bargains, they'll attract new cost-conscious customers.

26. *Contribute to newsgroups for pet lovers*

Pet store suppliers can visit the appropriate newsgroups and become useful contributors to the discussion. If asked, they could supply prices and descriptions of available products.

27. *Offer sneak previews of upcoming movie scripts by Gopher server*

Pique movie fans' interest in upcoming films by making excerpts from particularly dramatic scenes available by Gopher server. Like a movie trailer does, you'll create a desire to see more.

28. *Post all your product brochures in a Gopher server menu*

A sporting goods manufacturer can build on the loyalty of his existing clients by posting all his product brochures in a Gopher server menu. The manufacturer may not know that one of the best customers of its fishing gear catalog is also an avid skier. By giving customers easy access to all your brochures, you'll increase your share of each customer's discretionary spending.

29. *Provide car rental information*

Provide a complete rate structure, descriptions of cars, and availability information for your rental car agency. You can even let users with a credit card reserve a vehicle.

30. *Supply banking and financial information*

Make information on your bank's services, hours, locations, interest rates, mortgage products, and investment services available through a Gopher server or WWW link.

31. *Answer bicycling questions*

Bicycle store owners can participate in the bicycling groups online and answer questions about new products and equipment. A tour company that organizes bicycle trips can give advice about packing for a long tour. Clothing manufacturers can discuss which types of shorts are best for marathons.

32. *Offer safety and security information*

A security company could provide an online Gopher menu with information about safety and security issues, broken down into subject areas such as "Burglarproofing Your Home," "Preventing Car Theft," and "Safety Tips for Female Travelers."

33. *Maintain a Telnet site for salespeople*

Hospital suppliers can maintain a Telnet site so that salespeople can call in and run inventory programs to assist clients with purchasing decisions.

34. *Promote a university*

Schools can maintain a Mosaic site that features pictures of the campus, information on tuition fees, articles from the campus newspaper, profiles of famous graduates, information on available dormitory space, and detailed course catalogs.

35. *Provide basic insurance information*

Insurance companies could create a Gopher or WWW site which discusses insurance terms and policies to help the consumer make decisions about the type of coverage she needs.

36. *Keep in touch with preferred investors*

An investment company can contact its preferred investors via e-mail about up-and-coming investment opportunities and free seminars.

37. *Keep up students' language skills*

Foreign language schools use the Internet to correspond with former students so that they can maintain their foreign language skills. Such a service could help a school stand out from the competition. A school BBS could also help former students keep in touch with each other, fostering good feelings about the institution. There are even bilingual newsgroups.

38. *Provide information on seminars*

Seminar bureaus could provide detailed information about conferences they have done, and excerpts from speeches made by people they have booked. They could also upload photos and biographies of all their featured speakers.

39. *Offer home-repair advice*

Hardware stores can become regular participants in home-repair groups and offer information and advice about home maintenance tasks and tools.

40. *Make the Internet an extension of your newspaper*

Newspapers can make additional information on high-profile stories available through a Mosaic site. The paper can also upload ad rates, deadline schedules, and more information about advertisers.

41. *Provide home health care information*

Home health care services can create a Gopher menu that gives users access to the latest research about Alzheimer's or cerebral palsy, tips for caring for the patient at home, and information on programs that provide respite for caregivers.

42. *Offer painting tips*

Retail house painting firms can offer FTP or Telnet sites that provide homeowners with tips on painting and information on the types of products available. They can also include a program that will help customers calculate how much paint they will need for a particular job.

43. Post menus

A group of restaurants offering home delivery could create a Gopher menu with information about each restaurant: menus, price lists, photos of popular dishes, and the phone number to call for delivery.

44. Critique résumés

A résumé-writing service could offer a one-time free critique of a user's electronic résumé via e-mail. Later, it could contact the user to provide advice about its full range of services.

45. Provide information about your church

Churches could maintain Telnet sites that would allow current and prospective members to download texts of sermons, get schedules of services and Sunday School classes, and learn more about the church's charity work.

46. Keep in touch with fitness club members

A recreation facility could contact members by e-mail to notify them of changes in the center's hours, to promote new classes, or to remind them to renew their memberships. The center could even set up a BBS where members could exchange health and fitness tips.

47. Provide antique information

A large antique shop could establish a Mosaic site that gives customers tips on restoring old furniture and evaluating jewelry, information on upcoming antique shows, and information about items the store has recently acquired.

48. Offer moving advice

Storage and moving companies could offer a program via Telnet that would allow users to calculate how much space, how many boxes, and how much packing material they will need for an upcoming move.

49. Prepare tax returns

A tax-preparation center could allow clients to retrieve a form via Gopher and e-mail it back, along with their financial information. The company could then prepare the return for filing.

50. Keep in touch with alumni

A large university could keep in touch with graduates all over the world via e-mail. It could even set up a newsgroup where alumni could exchange news, gossip, and family photos.

51. Publish pet care information

Veterinary offices can make general health and feeding information available through a Gopher menu. Users could choose specific information on

any type of pet, even somewhat exotic creatures such as ferrets and taran-
tulas. They'll appreciate the access to hard-to-find information.

52. Let users select groceries

Grocery stores can let shoppers Telnet in from home to access a program
that lets them select items to be delivered or prepared for pickup.

Internet Resources

Service Providers

Alternet

3110 Fairview Park Drive, Suite 570
Falls Church VA 22041
(800) 488-6383
sales@alter.net

Alternet provides a full range of network connections and services. It
has also published a guide called *How to Select an Internet Service
Provider* that outlines the questions you need to ask to decide what level
of service you need and to select a service provider.

ANS

2901 Hubbard Road
Ann Arbor MI 48105
(800) 456-8267

ANS is a nonprofit organization that provides a wide range of network connections to the Internet. It also provides some hardware, such
as routers and connection programs.

Sprintlink

13221 Woodland Park Road
Herndon VA 22071
(703) 904-2167

Sprintlink provides network connection services and dial-up accounts
to businesses and individuals. It serves both American and international
markets. Sprintlink can provide both ISDN and T1 lines to customers in
areas where the regional phone service supports one or both.

Consultants

Internet Consulting Corporation
(212) 741-3227
407 W. 14th St., #4
New York, NY 10014
info@icons.com

Through seminars and consulting, Internet Consulting Corporation shows companies how to use the Internet to market its products. It can provide an introduction to the Internet, business strategies, and case studies of businesses that are already online. Full-time consulting and management services are also available.

Modern Media
J. Walter Thompson
500 Woodward Avenue
Detroit MI 48226-3428
(313) 964-2923

This advertising and marketing firm has an online division, Modern Media, that helps clients use online services for marketing, advertising, and information distribution. Many of their clients work closely with bulletin board services provided by commercial online services such as America Online and Prodigy.

Publications

Internet Business Journal
208 Somerset Street East, Suite A
Ottawa, Ontario
Canada K1N 6V2

This monthly newsletter follows the development of commercial interests on the Net. *IBJ* frequently addresses such issues as advertising and marketing on the Internet. In every issue, it profiles businesses operating on the Internet and provides information accessing their services.

Administration

Internic

Internic Information Services
General Atomics
P.O. Box 85608
San Diego CA 92186-9784
(619) 455-4640
info@internic.net

The Internic is the central resource on the Internet for administrative matters. Internic provides a wide range of services ranging from domain name assignment to directory services and technical support.

Commercial Online Services

America Online

8619 Westwood Center Drive
Vienna VA 22182-2285
(800) 827-6364
info@aol.com

America Online provides access to some features of the Internet and an extensive online service of bulletin boards and other features.

CompuServe

5000 Arlington Center Boulevard
P.O. Box 20212
Columbus OH 43220
postmaster@csi.compuserve.com

CompuServe offers extensive features and bulletin boards as well as access to e-mail. Its marketing brochure outlines the company's rates and services for businesses, and provides complete demographics about the system's users.

Internet Glossary

Electronic mail (e-mail): a system of sending messages between any two computers that are linked through a network or bulletin board. E-mail is similar to regular mail, only instant and free.

Encryption: a method of encoding messages so that only the intended recipient can read them. On the Internet, encryption is used to keep e-mail messages private. Businesses that sell products on the Internet use encryption to protect customers' credit card numbers when customers order products online. A fairly good encryption system for credit card numbers has recently been invented, but better ones are in development.

Flaming: verbal warfare on the Net used to enforce netiquette (see below) and ensure that breaches of netiquette don't happen again.

Gopher: a menu-driven way to make files available to users on the Internet. Gopher lets you create multiple layers of directories to organize your information logically, making it easier for your customers to find the information they seek. You can design your own Gopher menu to reflect the services your company offers.

Internet: a worldwide network of computers, used by universities, the military, business, and consumers. You access the Internet, and all the services described in this chapter, through a service provider.

Mailing list: a group of people who send and receive mail to each other on a particular topic. Mailing lists are a cross between e-mail and newsgroups. To join a mailing list, you usually send a message to someone asking to subscribe. These subscriptions are free.

Modem: a device inside or outside your computer that converts data transmitted over telephone lines into files your computer can read. It allows computers and other electronic devices to talk to each other.

Mosaic: a graphical interface for World Wide Web (see below). It allows users to look at documents created with hypertext and select items in them (words or pictures) that have more information linked to them.

Netiquette: the generally accepted rules of behavior on the Internet. Violations of netiquette (such as sending bulk unsolicited e-mail) are dealt with by harsh methods such as flaming (see above).

Network: a group of computers and/or electronic devices that are connected to each other so that they can communicate and exchange information. A PC cabled to a printer is a small network. The Internet is the biggest network in the world.

Newsgroups: public places on the Internet where people can post messages and reply to messages about a particular topic. They are similar to bulletin boards. Newsgroups may be very specific, such as rec.pets.dogs.golden.retrievers, or very broad, such as soc.politics.

Service provider: the person or organization that provides you with a hookup to the Internet and a means to access it. Service providers can be universities, small independent businesses, or online services, such as America Online or CompuServe.

UNIX: an operating system that is widely used by many of the groups that make up the Internet. Difficult enough that it should be avoided by the layperson.

World Wide Web (WWW): a service that organizes information on the Net by linking words, phrases, and pictures from one document to related files using a format called hypertext. WWW is one of the newest services to develop on the Internet. It is similar to Gopher in many ways, but it is more flexible and can be better organized.

MONEY-SAVING OFFERS

1 Month Free World Wide Web Service

Receive one month of free service with the purchase of three months from *The Internet Consulting Corporation*, (212) 741-3227.

20% Off a Seminar on the Internet

Get 20% off the seminar registration fee for any full-day workshop that is part of the series of Internet-oriented seminars offered by *The Internet Consulting Corporation*, (212) 741-3227.

$100 Savings on Fax Services

Take $100 off your first invoice (no commitments, no strings) for broadcast fax and fax on demand from *Touch Tone Services*, (206) 271-7200. For a demonstration of fax on demand, call (800) 791-1082 and ask for document #101.

Free Multimedia Demo Disk

Techno Marketing, Inc. produces custom designed interactive multimedia programs. If your company is seriously considering using interactive multimedia to meet your marketing or training needs, call *Techno Marketing* at (612) 830-1984 and request a free twin platform interactive multimedia demo disk (PC and Macintosh compatible).

Three Free Months of *The Internet Business Journal*

Receive three free months with your annual subscription to *The Internet Business Journal*, (613) 565-0982. Also inquire about a $20 discount on the book *How to Advertise on the Internet*.

Save $20 From *Adweek*

Adweek is the publisher of the first *Directory of Interactive Marketing*— covering interactive developers, suppliers and services. Order the *Directory* and pay only $139 — that's $20 off the cover price. To order, call (800) 468-2395.

Free E•News Demo Disk

Call for a free demonstration disk of the software that automatically formats electronic newsletters and supports fax on demand. *Ion Development,* (314) 937-9094.

Valuable Savings From *Marketing 1:1*

Receive $1,000 off any keynote speech or workshop, or $3,000 off any consulting engagement of two days or more with *Marketing 1:1, inc.* Call (203) 221-7534.

Infomercial Marketing Report

The *Infomercial Marketing Report* is the bible of the television direct-response industry. Call for a sample issue and take $50 off a yearly subscription. (310) 472-5253.

Infomercial Conference Savings

If you have an innovative or interesting product that has the potential to explode through television exposure, take $100 off the semi-annual Home Shopping Network Product Conference. The Conference is the one place in which top buyers from the home shopping networks and the infomercial companies will meet with you one on one. Call (310) 472-5253.

Free Fax Technology Marketing Advice

The Kauffman Group is an enhanced facsimile services consulting firm, focused on the sales, marketing, and communications benefits of fax technology. As a special service to *eMarketing* readers, Mr. Kauffman will offer complimentary advice to those who request it. Fax your business card and any one question pertaining to enhanced fax services to him at (609) 482-8940.

Note: All offers are subject to change. Call each company directly and mention this book to receive your discount or offer.